Praise for In Search of Beethoven

'This book has had a profound effect on me. Suchet has brought Beethoven to life. Anyone and everyone will gain something from it – musician, music-lover, historian, even gossip-lover. I read it in one sitting. I want to fly off to Vienna immediately.'
Carol Barratt Hon RCM GRSM ARCM, Pianist and Composer

'John Suchet's unusual combination of biography and autobiography is full of fascinating details about Beethoven's life, conveyed with enthusiasm and imagination, but cleverly dovetailed with personal reminiscences.'
Professor Barry Cooper, University of Manchester, Author of *Beethoven: An Extraordinary Life*

'John Suchet lives with Beethoven, learning something every day. This is a wonderful tale of self-realisation, of what we can gain from turning to genius in life's many crises.'
Norman Lebrecht, Author of *Why Beethoven*

'John Suchet weaves into the narrative his own experiences as a foreign correspondent and news anchor to create a compelling and moving account of events which are inextricably linked with Beethoven's struggle with destiny and the ensuing path to victory and emancipation that almost always bring many of his works to a triumphant close. This is an indispensable book for every Beethoven enthusiast as well as for every performing musician.'
Dr Marios Papadopoulos MBE, Music Director, Oxford Philharmonic Orchestra

'John Suchet's account of his own difficult times, and those challenges which the composer faced, are brought to life by the author's incredible skill, drawing on his years as a frontline journalist with an acute eye and ear for detail . . . A gift for any Beethoven fan!'
Sandra Parr, Artistic Planning Director, Royal Liverpool Philharmonic

'As always, John Suchet's diligent and persuasive detective work throws new and fascinating light on seminal moments and aspects of Beethoven's life . . . an excellent and eye-opening read.'
Howard Shelley OBE, Pianist and Conductor

'You can't help but be swept away by John Suchet's infectious enthusiasm, as well as being mightily impressed by his almost unquenchable thirst for knowledge about his musical hero. This is a comprehensive yet accessible history of Beethoven wrapped up in an inviting, immersive tale of adventure and discovery, delivered in an inviting, engaging and endearing way typical of this master storyteller.'
Debbie Wiseman OBE, Composer and Conductor

ALSO BY JOHN SUCHET

*For my darling Nula
whose idea this book was.*

Contents

Preface

In July 2022 my wife Nula and I were in Vienna, for no other reason than it is a city we both love. Nula honeymooned there with her late husband James. I visited it several times with my late wife Bonnie, researching my earlier Beethoven books.

A planned Danube music cruise I had been due to host fell victim to the global Covid lockdown of 2020, and the hotel in Vienna I had booked for a few days' stay at the end of the trip kindly held my deposit for two more years until we could finally make it.

Nula's James, a TV documentary writer and director, was passionate about Mozart. He had written a six-part TV series called *The Family Mozart*, which was due to go into production when he was diagnosed with dementia in 2004.

My Bonnie succumbed to the same appalling disease, diagnosed in 2006. Both James and Bonnie were in the same care home, in adjacent rooms, which is how Nula and I met. A friendship developed and, nearly two years after losing our spouses, we married. Nula found that she had exchanged a husband with a passion for Mozart for a husband with an equal passion for Beethoven.

James had taken her round all the Mozart sites in Vienna, relating the story of the composer's life. In Vienna with me on that July visit, she asked me to show her the Beethoven sites. The most important of these is the small cottage in the village of Heiligenstadt in the foothills of the Vienna Woods where, at the age of thirty-one, realising his deafness would inexorably worsen, Beethoven wrote his Will. Now in a suburb of Vienna and easily reached on the U-Bahn, the cottage has been tastefully restored. We walked round it, then sat on a bench in the garden. Trees and plants were in full summer bloom. I talked – on and on and on.

'You must write all this down,' she said.

'I have already, several times,' I said, laughing.

'No, do it differently. Make it personal,' she urged. 'Listen to the passion in your voice. Walk in his footsteps. Eat and drink with him. This will be your Beethoven journey.'

1

At 5 p.m. on 26 March 1778, a stocky, powerfully built man walks out in front of a small audience in the Sternengasse in Cologne. He is dressed smartly but uncomfortably. He might have borrowed the frockcoat and breeches: they do not fit properly and look out of place on him. His abundant dark hair is scraped back and a thin pigtail falls across his collar. There are pockmarks on his face.

But it is his eyes, open wide and blazing, that command attention. His jaw is set. Intensity and determination emanate from him, accentuated by the clenched fists at his side. The leonine head is thrust forward as he opens his mouth to speak.

'I am Beethoven,' he says, 'and it is my honour to present my student, Mademoiselle Averdonck, contralto singer at the princely court in Bonn. She will sing several beautiful arias. She will be accompanied at the piano, after which there will be several pieces played on piano alone. These will be performed by my son, who is greatly accomplished even at the age of six.'

Mademoiselle Averdonck, smiling, ushers the small boy out in front of her. Ludwig van Beethoven, aged seven not six, is about to give his first public performance.

Precisely forty-nine years later, to the day and the hour, as a storm breaks over Vienna, the most celebrated composer and musician in the world is about to draw his last breath.

2

I was sitting high up in the gods at the Vienna State Opera for a perform-ance of Beethoven's opera *Fidelio*. Those punchy opening chords of the overture hit me like a wall of sound. The curtain rose; the singing began. The next thing I heard was a very different wall of sound – thunderous applause and cries of 'Bravo!' The curtain had fallen. It was 1961 and I was seventeen. I had slept through the whole thing.

Twenty-three years later, at midnight on Thursday, 8 March 1984, I stood at the railing of a passenger ferry as it pulled away from the dock at Limassol in Cyprus and turned east for the overnight journey to Beirut, capital city of a country in the grip of civil war.

I was one of only two passengers on board. The other was a Danish businessman. Beyond initial salutations we did not speak again. We knew that what we were doing was madness. Any sane person would be heading in the opposite direction.

The air was crisp and fresh, the saltwater spray invigorating. I imagined the sweet exotic scent of the Middle East, although we were still some way out from Beirut. Four hours later, in the twilight of dawn, I could see a dis-tant red glow. My stomach churned with a mixture of fear and excitement. I was an ITN reporter, en route to join my camera team, who were already in the city. I was on one of the biggest stories in the world.

I reached into my anorak pocket and pulled out my battered Walkman. In the other pocket was a single cassette tape, the only one I had with me. Beethoven's Symphony No. 3, the *Eroica*, played by the Berlin Philharmonic conducted by Herbert von Karajan. I blew the sound into my ears. When it finished, with that gloriously affirmative upward rush to the final chords, I played it again. And again.

What had happened in that intervening quarter-century, between a *Fidelio* that had floated past my unhearing teenage ears, and the *Eroica* on that night-time sea voyage, an *Eroica* that lifted me up and filled me with confidence and determination in the face of fear and uncertainty?

The *Fidelio* I slept through was the culmination of a trip to Vienna and Salzburg organised by the Anglo-Austrian Friendship Society. I cannot recall how I found out about it but I do remember pestering my dad relentlessly to let me join, even though the cost was £25. I also remember being chosen, as the most proficient German speaker in the group (recently awarded a prize at school for my prowess in the language, the only academic accolade of my entire school career), to deliver a short speech of thanks to the Mayor of Vienna in the ornate Gothic Town Hall on our final morning.

'Don't worry,' said Mr Black, our team leader, the night before. 'It's only four or five sentences long and I've written it for you. All you have to do is read it.' I stood by my bed till well after midnight learning the words. I was determined to deliver it from memory.

The next morning, with the piece of paper reassuringly in my pocket and a cold trickle of sweat running down my spine, I managed to deliver it without a stumble to a mayor who was rather impressed (as was Mr Black). Unfortunately for a permanently crowded brain, I can still remember it, word for word, more than sixty years later.

At the age of seventeen I was in my 'Tchaikovsky phase'. What had turned me into a teenage Tchaikovsky obsessive? One school summer holiday, not long after the Vienna trip, I got a job selling records at the flagship HMV store in Oxford Street in London. The manageress, a Miss Forrest, asked me which department I wanted to work in. 'Classical music, please.' She put me in rock and pop.

In a lunch hour I went upstairs to the classical music department and leafed through the letter T, Tchaikovsky being the only composer whose tunes I could whistle. I bought an LP of Tchaikovsky's Symphony No. 4, played by the Royal Philharmonic Orchestra conducted by Sir Thomas Beecham, primarily because I liked the cover. It showed a Russian couple in traditional rustic costume, and I had just begun to learn Russian at school. The music captivated me from the first time I played it.

I wore the record out on my box gramophone. That opening call on French horns and bassoons!

I followed it with an LP of Tchaikovsky's Violin Concerto, Alfredo Campoli the soloist. It had a similar effect on me. At Chappell's music store in Bond Street I found a score of the solo part of the Violin Concerto, and also a book of Tchaikovsky's favourite melodies arranged for Grade Three piano.

Back at school I proudly presented the piano book to my piano teacher. 'Why Tchaikovsky?' he asked. 'You'll grow out of it.' I was shocked. Could he be right? I wavered, metaphorically losing my musical balance, unsure which way to fall. The *coup de grâce* was delivered by my violin teacher, who found the solo part of the Violin Concerto in my music case. 'That's a bit ambitious, isn't it?' she said, thereby killing my enthusiasm for the violin in a single sentence. I sought solace by teaching myself the more forgiving trombone and indulging a different kind of musical passion, trad jazz.

The demotion of Tchaikovsky from the number one spot in my classical music affections created a vacancy. I tried Bach – too much the perfection-ist. I explored Mozart – sublime, but where was the passion? Mendelssohn – pretty. Sibelius – dark. Simplistic, I know, but I was a teenager.

It would be so nice, so neat, to be able to say there was a single revelatory moment, the musical equivalent of a blinding flash of light, when I heard Beethoven and it changed my life. The fact is, Beethoven crept up on me. What I certainly do remember is a period in my life in the early 1980s when I was going through a difficult time. My marriage was unravelling, and my professional life wasn't going too well either. The two were clearly connected, though I struggled to see it at the time.

I had a newfangled cassette tape player that you could carry in your pocket and listen to the music through tiny earbuds. No more 12-inch LPs that warp and scratch and styluses that go blunt. I bought a single cas-sette tape. I cannot remember where I bought it or why I chose Beethoven's *Eroica* Symphony. But it was about to become the soundtrack to my life. I was at my lowest ebb. Here was music with sorrow, defiance, triumph. And passion. It lifted me up; it inspired me. I would come through all this, and ultimately I would triumph. This was the kind of emotional journey that other people continue to recount, more than forty years later, when they talk to me about Beethoven.

Who was this man who had created something that could have such an effect? I knew only one fact about Beethoven the man, the single fact that anyone who knows anything about classical music knows. He is the one who went deaf. But if a composer loses his hearing, how can he compose? Even more incomprehensible, if Beethoven went deaf, how could he write music of such intensity and emotion – and passion – that it could transform lives?

In the summer of 1983 I took Bonnie to a Beethoven concert in the Kennedy Center in Washington, where I was based as ITN's US correspondent. I forget who the performers were; I remember only that the conductor and solo pianist were father and daughter. The *Egmont* Overture opened the concert, followed by Piano Concerto No. 3 and, after the interval, Symphony No. 7. That swirling final movement, faster and faster, a headlong charge to the end, brought the audience to its feet amid shouts of 'Bravo!' We left the concert hall flushed and breathless.

A short taxi ride to Georgetown for a late supper, and we passed a bookshop, open even at this late hour. Browsing in the music section, I saw a thick paperback book, blue spine, the cover entirely taken up by a photograph of a monumental statue of a seated Beethoven. It was Thayer's *Life of Beethoven*, edited by Elliot Forbes. Rather sheepishly, I said I'd like to read it. 'Why don't you?' Bonnie encouraged me. I bought it.

My worries of a daunting read were soon confirmed: it was over a thousand pages long. The first forty pages were about the prince-elector's court at Bonn. Not a single mention of Beethoven. I struggled through two or three hundred pages, then gave up. Inside the back cover I made a few pencil notes. That paperback book is sitting in front of me now. The spine has long since collapsed. The whole thing is held together by brown parcel tape. The pencil notes have faded to illegibility. I have devoured every page more times than I can say.

In 1992 my mum died after a long illness. It was a deeply painful time. Beethoven's *Eroica* Symphony helped me through that, as it had done with my personal crisis a decade earlier. By now I had quite a collection of Beethoven cassette tapes. Music had been an essential part of my life since my teenage years, but this passion for Beethoven's music, which had begun slowly, had overwhelmed me. It was no craze. I knew, deep down, not only that it would never go away, but that it would intensify.

I had been casually reading up on Beethoven's life throughout the 1980s. Now I needed to know more. That is how I came to be in Bonn, visiting the house where Beethoven was born, in 1993. A year later I started writing my own account of his life. Thirty years on from that, and eight books later, I am still writing about his life and music.

3

The story begins with a young man in search of love, though exactly what led Johann van Beethoven to conduct that search some fifty-five miles or so upriver from his home town of Bonn in the small commune of Ehrenbreitstein on the opposite bank of the Rhine, we do not know. Most likely he had sung with his choir there, and spotted a charming girl whose name, he discovered, was Maria Magdalena.

An added motive for seeking a bride away from Bonn was undoubtedly to escape from the overbearing influence of his father, Ludwig van Beethoven. It is not easy for a son who follows in his father's profession to realise that he will never come up to his father's exacting standards. It is all the more difficult when the father also realises this and frequently berates the son for his mediocrity.

'There are in reality three Johanns standing together like in a clover leaf,' a neighbour heard Ludwig van Beethoven say in front of his son. 'The apprentice lad is Johann the muncher, always gobbling away; the lad in the house is Johann the chatterbox, and then there is this third Johann,' – and these are cruel words for a father to use to his son – 'Johann the runner. Keep running, keep running, one day you might even reach your destination.'[1]

Lodewijk van Beethoven (who would become grandfather to the composer), also called himself by the classier French equivalent of 'Louis', had reason to be proud of his achievements. Born in Mechelen[2] in the Netherlands, around twenty miles north of Brussels, he saw his own father work as a baker day and night but still fail to stave off bankruptcy. He himself was blessed with a fine voice, and found employment as a bass singer at the Cathedral in Liège. There, as a young man, he was heard by the Prince-Elector of Cologne, who offered him employment as a court musician in Bonn.

Lodewijk left Mechelen and moved to Bonn on the banks of the Rhine, where the prince-elector had his palace. There he soon married a young woman by the name of Maria Josepha Poll, adopted the German form of his own name, and as Ludwig van Beethoven forged a successful career as court musician.

So successful in fact, showing organisational skills as well as musical prowess, that in 1761, aged forty-nine, he was appointed to the highest musical position at court, Kapellmeister, in charge of all musical activity – most unusual for a musician who was neither composer nor instrumentalist.

Of the three children born to the Beethovens, only one survived into adulthood, a son who was christened Johann. In time Johann developed a fine tenor voice, and his father secured him a position at court as a member of the prince-elector's choir. Johann also gave singing and piano lessons on the side, which supplemented his income.

Kapellmeister Ludwig van Beethoven had a rather different secondary source of income. He dabbled in the wine trade. In fact he did more than dabble; he was a rather prosperous wine merchant. He rented two wine cellars, and through his friendship with the court cellar clerk, Johann Baum, learned where the best wine-producing vines grew, and the techniques of grape-pressing and fermentation. The wine he produced he shipped back to the Netherlands, where it was highly rated by connoisseurs. He also sold locally to Bonn residents.

A comfortable family set-up, then, with father and son in well-paid jobs, both earning extra income on the side. It was common gossip in musical circles that the son would be front runner to succeed the father as Kapellmeister in the fullness of time. But ominous clouds were gathering over the heads of the Beethoven family.

The culprit was the demon drink. Inevitably, as the wine business prospered, there was plenty of wine on the Beethoven table too. This was to have a devastating effect on the family. Maria Josepha, wife of the Kapellmeister, became an alcoholic. Husband and son were either unable, or unwilling, to look after her at home. She was put into an institution in Cologne, where she remained for the rest of her life. Of more importance to our story, their son Johann would increasingly turn to drink, which ultimately ruined his career, blighted his family and led to his death just one month after his fifty-second birthday.

History, and Beethoven scholarship, have broadly been kind to Ludwig van Beethoven, Kapellmeister. Neighbours and friends remembered him as good-hearted and respectable. But they also described how his vitality and strength could easily transmute into stubbornness, forcefulness, even violent temper – qualities that later manifested themselves in abundance in his famous grandson.

Maria Magdalena, in the Kapellmeister's eyes, was thoroughly unsuited to be his son's bride. At the age of nineteen she was already a widow and the mother of a child who had died in infancy. A mother and a widow – hardly an exemplar of bridal purity. Added to this she was an outsider from a small town somewhere south of Bonn. For a man who undoubtedly had a degree of snobbishness about him, Maria Magdalena was simply not of a high enough class to marry into the Beethoven family. His own inquiries established that she had once been a chambermaid. 'This I would never have believed of you, that you would have sunk so low,' he remonstrated with his son.[3]

In fact the Kapellmeister's informant was mistaken. Maria Magdalena had never been a chambermaid. Her maiden name was Keverich, and she belonged to an important and well-respected family in Ehrenbreitstein. Her father oversaw the kitchens at the prince-elector's court, and her mother's family included several high-ranking local officials.

Nevertheless, the Kapellmeister had made up his mind. He wanted nothing to do with his son's marriage. The antagonism of the Kapellmeister to the Keverich family was reciprocated. No Keverich relatives made the short journey to Bonn to attend the wedding. Thus, when on 12 November 1767 Johann van Beethoven married Maria Magdalena Leym née Keverich in St Remigius parish church in Bonn, neither family was represented.

The ceremony was hurriedly arranged and kept as short as possible. In later life Maria Magdalena would say she could have had a good wedding were it not for her father-in-law's opposition to the match and refusal to attend the ceremony. For that reason too, the wedding was never mentioned in the Kapellmeister's presence.

The day after the wedding the newly married couple travelled by coach south along the Rhine to Koblenz, and across the river to Ehrenbreitstein to show the bride's family and friends she was married and to introduce her husband to them. The couple remained there for three days before returning to Bonn for further celebrations.

Seventeen months later Maria Magdalena gave birth to a son, Ludwig Maria, who lived for less than a week. One year and eight months after that, on 16 December 1770, she gave birth to her second son. It was a bitterly cold December day, and for that reason the baby was born in the kitchen of the small house in which the Beethovens rented first-floor rooms.

The infant was baptised the next day in the Remigiuskirche, the same church of St Remigius where his parents had married, and was given the Latin form of his grandfather's name, Ludovicus.

4

The church of St Remigius stands tall today on the Brüdergasse in the heart of old Bonn. To walk in Beethoven's footsteps and those of his family, it is imperative, I felt, to walk up the aisle of the church where his parents married, where he was baptised and where he would play organ at Sunday morning Mass at the age of just twelve.

'It's simple,' I said to Nula, map unfolded. 'Here is Remigiusplatz. It'll be on the square, obviously.' Heroically we set off for Remigiusplatz, a small, tightly packed square of shops and cafés. But where was the church? On our third circuit of the square, having checked it wasn't hidden behind one of the façades, Nula suggested that maybe there was no church here at all.

'But look!' she said. 'There's a spire. That must be it.'

There was indeed the welcome sight of a spire rising above buildings some distance away.

'Too far,' I said. 'Why would St Remigius Church be so far from St Remigius Square?'

'Because names change over the centuries,' Nula replied reasonably.

We walked and walked. Tired by now and somewhat frustrated, we were relieved to find ourselves at the entrance of a large Gothic church that proclaimed itself to be St Remigiuskirche. The interior was vast, with a high vaulted ceiling. It seemed rather more modern and in better repair than I had expected. No service was being held, and there was just one other person inside, an elderly man sitting alone in the back pew.

My enthusiasm got the better of me. 'It's amazingly grand, isn't it? I wasn't expecting anything so huge. Incredible to think Ludwig's parents, and then Ludwig himself – try to imagine him as a small boy at the organ, he must have been dwarfed by . . .'

To my horror the elderly man turned, his face grim. His eyes locked with mine. He raised himself slowly from the pew, held onto the side for a moment to steady himself, then began – purposefully – to walk towards us. Already in my head I was framing my apologies in German for disturbing him.

As he reached us, his stern expression melted and a smile lit up his face. He spoke in heavily accented Rhineland German. '*Grüss Gott!* Have you come here because of Beethoven?'

I nodded vigorously.

'Hah! Then you know you have come to the wrong church.'

I played back his words in my head. Had I misunderstood? Had I heard a *falsch* when there was none? He repeated it, shaking his head.

'Where are you from?' he asked, smiling.

Swiftly I explained, willing him to get back to the subject. 'I am English. My wife is Irish. I am researching for a new book I am writing on Beethoven.'

'Then let me explain,' he continued. 'Come with me.' He took us to the side wall of the church, where there were screens containing old black-and-white photographs of a bomb-damaged church.

'This is the church we are standing in. It was hit by bombing in 1944. Look at this church now. They have renovated it beautifully, don't you think?'

'Yes, they have,' I said, mentally wondering if there was anything left of the original, 'and to think, before the dreadful bombing, this is where Beethoven was baptised, and his parents . . .'

'Ah no,' he said. 'As I told you, this is not where baby Ludwig was baptised.'

It took a moment for this to sink in. It was the second time he had said it, and this time there was a definite *nicht*.

He saw my confusion and smiled. He was rather enjoying himself. 'You see, in 1800, I think it was, the original church of St Remigius – in Remigiusplatz – where Beethoven was baptised, was hit by bolts of lightning in a storm. It caught fire and was destroyed. They decided not to rebuild it. Instead they gave the name of the church, St Remigius, to this newer church, in memory of the old one.'

This meant that the church we had been looking for in Remigius Square, which had witnessed a Beethoven wedding and a baptism, no longer existed. It had not existed since around 1800. The church we were now standing in therefore had nothing to do with the Beethoven family. It bore the name alone of the original church.

A wave of disappointment washed over me. It was all a waste of time. Well, maybe not entirely. If we had not met him, I would confidently have asserted that Nula and I had walked in the footsteps of the Beethoven family in the church of St Remigius. So I had learned something important, even if it was entirely negative.

But our old man was not finished. He sensed my disappointment and a smile crept over his face as he prepared to deliver his punchline, raising his hands for effect and building in a slight pause, like the finest raconteur. I braced myself, concentrating on every word delivered in that quick-fire Rhineland accent.

'The font that Beethoven was baptised in, the actual font, is over there in the corner.' He turned and pointed behind him.

Taufbecken – I had never heard the word. It had to mean 'font', surely? Or had I misheard him? Well, there was a simple way to find out.

Our friend was pointing vigorously to the far corner of the church. Nula and I walked across. As we came closer, I felt my chest constrict and my heart quicken. There, on a slightly raised floor, a small stained-glass window gazing down, a tall candle to the side, was an ornate heavy-lidded font. The lid was attached to a pulley so that it could be raised.

'That's what fonts were like in the old Catholic Church,' Nula said. A sign to the side stated that this was indeed the font in which the baby Ludovicus was baptised on 17 December 1770 in the church of St Remigius. When the old church burned down, they had had the presence of mind to save the historic font.

I gazed in wonder. We had failed to find the old church because it had not existed for more than two centuries. We were now in the wrong church, but looking at the font around which had stood Beethoven's parents, his grandfather the Kapellmeister who was godfather, and a next-door neighbour, Gertrud Baum, who was godmother. And which, prior to this day, I had not known existed.

It was all thanks to our old man who, he told us, was eighty-seven years old. He had lost his wife twenty-five years before and liked to come and sit in this church and reflect. Nula hugged him like an uncle and he held her close. He extended his hand to me for the warmest of handshakes. We looked at each other with tears in our eyes.

5

The town of Bonn was built on slightly raised ground a safe distance from the Rhine, which was prone to burst its banks in winter. Several streets led down to the river, their residents collectively celebrating each spring if they had survived the winter unflooded.

Johann van Beethoven rented rooms on the first floor at the back of a tall house at Bonngasse 515, owned by a lacemaker named Clasen. It was situated in the centre of town a short – but safe – distance from the river. After his wife was sent to Cologne to be looked after, the Kapellmeister lived alone, directly across the narrow street. The windows of the rooms housing the Beethoven family looked out over a small dark courtyard.

The house still stands today, with a different number – Bonngasse 20. That is not all that has changed. The house remained in private hands for most of the nineteenth century, the ground floor opening as an inn in 1873, with the name 'Beethoven's Geburtshaus' (Beethoven's birthplace). A decade and a half later a beer hall where music was played was built in the courtyard at the back. A merchant took over the house in 1888 but put it up for sale the following year.

Although it was clearly well known as Beethoven's birthplace, the city of Bonn was not interested in buying the house. So the Verein Beethoven-Haus (Beethoven-House Society) was founded, with the aim of purchasing the house and turning it into a permanent memorial to Bonn's most famous son. Once the house was acquired, extensive renovations were carried out, inside as well as out. Rooms were enlarged to accommodate display cases and memorabilia, as well as a library. Space was allocated for the society's office, as well as an apartment for the caretaker. A second staircase was added to the rear of the building. The beer hall was demolished, the courtyard was paved and a small garden created. Today a bust of Beethoven on a plinth stands at the back of the garden, his stern gaze directed downwards to the ground.

Beethoven's birthplace was officially opened on 10 May 1893, but that is far from the end of the story. In 1907 the house next door, where his godmother Gertrud Baum and later his boyhood friend Franz Wegeler had lived, was acquired to house the Beethoven-Archiv, which is today the most important research centre into Beethoven's life and music in the world. Among original letters and autograph manuscripts, it contains the ultimate treasure of treasures: a life mask of Beethoven made by Franz Klein in 1812.

Minor damage suffered during two world wars was repaired at the beginning of the 1950s. Twenty years later there was more extensive restoration work, and again in the 1990s.

It is easy to say that today the house bears little resemblance to the one in which Beethoven was born, that it is impossible to imagine the warm, steamy kitchen where Maria Magdalena, flushed and breathless, gave birth to her third child on that cold December day. The house is one of the few in Bonn that date back to the eighteenth century, and stepping inside you get an unmistakable sense of a time long gone. Stand in the small garden where once a beer hall stood and look up at the first-floor windows – the rooms Johann rented – and you realise the smallness of their living quarters. If they were at the windows gazing down at you they would not see a pretty grassed garden but a dark, dank, narrow courtyard.

We should marvel that the house has survived in any form at all, after nearly a century in private hands and then two world wars. For each of my previous three visits – the earliest in 1993 – a room on the first floor has been designated as the room in which Ludwig van Beethoven was born. The third time a marble bust stood on a pedestal and the room was roped off. The fourth time, in October 2022, the day before our St Remigiuskirche encounter, the room had a large video installation that stretched across the window showing musical manuscripts. You could enter the room but not see out to the garden. This seemed strange for a room previously held in such esteem.

I mentioned this to one of the guides, who said, 'We now believe Beethoven was born in the kitchen here on the ground floor. It was mid-December and in Bonn it is very cold in December. The kitchen was the warmest room.'

'Where was the kitchen?' I asked.

She pointed behind us and smiled. The room contained display cases and pictures. There was nothing to say it was the birth room, because after all the renovations and restoration it really is impossible to know.

I have been told by a Beethoven musicologist with close ties to the Beethoven-Haus that in fact it has never been possible to say in which room Beethoven was born, given the extensive renovation work. But over the years so many visitors asked to know in which room the great composer was born that the society decided to designate that first-floor room, which on an earlier visit I had found roped off.

When I first visited in 1993, the 'gift shop' in the birthplace was a table under the back staircase. On offer was a small collection of cassette tapes and some leaflets on various aspects of Beethoven's life. On my next visit, just a few years later, a dedicated shop had been opened in the building next door. It was not large, but there was a good selection of books and CDs. One of the CDs was of my favourite piano sonata, the middle of the final set of three, No. 31 in A flat, Op. 110. The saleswoman told me it was recorded in 1967 on the Graf piano that was in Beethoven's Vienna apartment when he died, and that now stands in the birth house, its keyboard protected by a perspex cover. 'That was the last time Beethoven's voice was heard,' she said.

Now there is a huge souvenir shop directly across the Bonngasse from the birth house, with a vast array of books, CDs, DVDs, pens, paperweights, umbrellas, socks, and much else. When Nula and I visited in July 2022 I was delighted to see the special 250th anniversary edition of my book *Beethoven – The Man Revealed* on the shelf. Nula took a picture of me pointing at it and grinning like a Cheshire Cat. When I came to buy two entry tickets to the birth house opposite, the saleswoman refused to take my money.

The birth house itself is one of the most visited sites in Germany, which is not the case for a much more important location, just a short distance down the gently sloping hill towards the Rhine.

The Beethoven brood was growing. Ludwig had survived infancy and Maria Magdalena had since given birth to another son. It was clear the family needed larger accommodation. But before we accompany them to the house where Ludwig was to spend the formative years of his youth, I have to recount an event that shook the Beethoven family to its roots – an event that Ludwig would carry with him for the rest of his life.

6

On Christmas Eve 1773 Kapellmeister Beethoven, having suffered a stroke earlier in the year, died at the age of sixty-one. To an extent his family had time to prepare, but it still came as an enormous shock. Johann van Beethoven suddenly found himself head of the family, with all the responsibilities that brought. But with those new responsibilities came one or two unwelcome discoveries.

His father, it appears, had not been quite as efficient at running his wine business as he had been at organising his own and others' musical lives. When Johann examined the books, he discovered wine producers to whom his father had loaned money and who had not repaid it, and others who had been paid in advance for their wine but had not delivered it.

When Johann confronted the vintners, they demanded written proof. Johann was forced to concede that his father was such an honest man that he had relied on promises and handshakes alone. He also knew that vintners had often paid his father in kind – a good fresh slab of butter and a fine mature cheese, for instance, instead of cash. What Johann had most certainly not expected to inherit from his father was considerable debt.

But his demise also meant there was one propitious development in the offing, and it mitigated Johann's grief considerably. He was the natural successor to his father in the highest musical post in Bonn – Kapellmeister – an appointment that would bring with it not just prestige but a greatly enhanced salary. He considered it his birthright. In order to be seen to be doing the right thing, Johann wrote a letter to the prince-elector putting himself forward for the post, using the most florid language to state that he was not just the best but the sole musician at court worthy of such a prestigious appointment.

Unfortunately, he was the only one who thought so. Johann's unsavoury habits had not gone unnoticed. It was difficult to sing adequately or perform properly as a music teacher after a heavy drinking session the night before. He would have to continue to feed a growing family on a relatively meagre salary, supplemented by fees for teaching, with no prospects of advancement. Maria Magdalena was five months pregnant when her father-in-law died. Her second son was born on 8 April 1774 and christened Caspar Carl.

Just as history has been unstintingly kind to Ludwig van Beethoven the Kapellmeister, with universal praise for his musical prowess and blameless life, so it has been equally harsh in its condemnation of his son Johann for his dissolute and profligate ways. In the case of both individuals the truth is more subtle. Besides his carelessness with money, the Kapellmeister, as we have seen, had an arrogance about him, dominating and constantly criticising his son.

As for Johann, he might have been profligate but he was certainly not mean. Nor was Maria Magdalena inclined to censor her husband's drinking habits. Gottfried Fischer, who grew up in the same house as Ludwig, described how at the end of the month, when Johann van Beethoven brought home his earnings, he would shake the money into his wife's lap and say, 'Now, wife, keep house with that.'

She would give him some back so he could buy a bottle of wine, saying, 'You can't let men go away empty-handed. Who'd have the heart to do that?'

'Quite right,' he would respond, 'so empty-handed.'

She'd then say, 'Yes, so empty-handed, but I know you'd rather have a full glass than an empty one.'

Johann would end the exchange with 'The wife is right, she is always right, and what's more she will always be right.'[1]

The marriage was not always so harmonious, as we shall see later. For the moment, though, we rejoin the Beethoven family in their small apartment in the Bonngasse, the infant Carl and his devastated elder brother. Yes, devastated. For no one in the family was hit harder by the Kapellmeister's death than Ludwig.

We have, obviously, little information from Beethoven himself about his grandfather, since he was just three years and eight days old when the old man died. We do know, though, that Beethoven grew up with a portrait of the Kapellmeister showing him dressed in the finery of his office – a fur hat and purple cape over a tassled, fur-trimmed jacket – and holding a manuscript and pen. His father would later pawn the painting, but when Beethoven moved as an adult to Vienna, he wrote to an old friend back in Bonn, asking him to retrieve the portrait from the pawnbroker and forward it to him. It then hung on the wall of every apartment that Beethoven lived in, including the one in which he died.

We know from the same friend[2] that the young Beethoven 'retained the most vivid early impression of him' and would often talk about his grandfather with his childhood friends.[3]

In 1776, when Ludwig was five and his brother Carl two, the family moved into a rather fine house just a stone's throw from the Bonngasse in the Rheingasse, which, as its name implies, leads down to the mighty river – then, as it still does today.

Johann rented a spacious second-floor apartment consisting of no fewer than six rooms. Two large rooms faced the street, with a connecting door that could be opened to create a space for musical recitals. Four rooms faced the courtyard behind. With interruptions, the Beethoven family would live here for nine years.

The house was owned by master baker Fischer, and it was his son Gottfried who, with the help of his elder sister Cäcilie, would later write his memoir of growing up in the same house as the great composer.

There was a piano in one of the front rooms. Here Johann gave keyboard and singing lessons. And it was here that the boy Ludwig first began to play music – not just the piano but the violin too.

That was not all he did to amuse himself, and his other pleasures had nothing to do with music.

7

There is no river in Europe, or in the world, so steeped in legend as the Rhine. The Loreley, the rock to which a siren maiden lures sailors to their death; the Mäuseturm (Mouse Tower) in the middle of the river, in which a hapless bishop took sanctuary from rampaging mice, only to be devoured by them; treasures thrown into the river and hidden below the river bed.

And, most important for our story, the Drachenfels (Dragon Rock), which stands on the opposite bank about eight miles upriver from Bonn. The Drachenfels is the largest of the Siebengebirge (Seven Mountains) that stretch away from the opposite bank, and which every Bonner knows were created by giants digging out lakes and throwing shovelfuls of earth over their shoulders.

Every Bonner would also know the legend of the Drachenfels, one of the most powerful of all Rhine legends, and how the dragon who lived in a cave halfway up the rock was denied his annual feast of a virgin by the timely arrival of the Teutonic hero Siegfried, who slew the beast with his invincible sword.[1]

Every Bonner includes the youthful Ludwig van Beethoven. Gottfried Fischer tells us in his memoir that the Beethoven family loved the Rhine. He also tells us that in the attic of their house were two telescopes, one large and one small. The Fischer house was one of the tallest in Bonn and so afforded a beautiful view across and up the Rhine. Ludwig, if no one could find him, was certain to be in the attic, gazing up the Rhine through one of the telescopes.

The ruined castle that stands jagged on the peak of the Drachenfels had already been part of the Rhine landscape for several hundred years by the time Ludwig brought it into focus through the telescope. The sight of it from Bonn, reaching up like a broken hand from the summit of the Drachenfels, is today just as it was when Ludwig gazed at it, though he would no doubt marvel at the sight of the rack-and-pinion railway that since 1883 has taken visitors from Königswinter, the small town that lies at the foot of the Drachenfels, to the viewing platform high up on the rock.

The dragon, said superstitious tongues, exacted its revenge when, in 1958, the train derailed and seventeen people lost their lives. I knew nothing of that tragedy when I eschewed the train and climbed the rock by foot back in 1993 in the early days of my Beethoven research. Surely Ludwig, as a boy, must have made the climb. We know he spent days away from home, walking and climbing in the Siebengebirge, content in his own company – as he would walk in nature all his life. For my part, I remember having lunch in a wood-panelled restaurant in Königswinter, and making the climb well fortified by a half-litre of local white wine.

We can imagine Ludwig playing out the legend of the Drachenfels in his head, as he stared at it through the telescope. On one occasion Cäcilie Fischer recounted how she asked him, 'What are you looking at, Ludwig?' He gave no answer. Later she asked him why he had not answered her, pointing out that was rather impolite.

'No answer is an answer too,' Ludwig replied. 'I was just occupied with such a lovely deep thought, that I could not bear to be disturbed.'[2]

Ludwig might have wished for more time with the telescopes, but for his father there was another path to pursue. How Johann first noticed his son's musical talent we do not know. Most likely Ludwig doodled on the piano keys in ever more impressive ways. The keyboard was too high for him so he would stand on a low bench to play. Johann began to teach him to read music. Soon the child was playing pieces of considerable technical difficulty in a way that astounded the father.

It was time for Johann to start making money from his son's prowess – just as Leopold Mozart had capitalised on the extraordinary talent of young Wolfgang Amadeus. He arranged a recital at a concert room in Cologne. He announced one of his singing pupils would perform, accompanied at the piano by his young son, aged six, who would then play solo pieces.

Ludwig was seven on 26 March 1778, not six, and this discrepancy has led to much speculation. Why would Johann reduce his son's age by a year? Simple answer: to exaggerate his extraordinary talent, and thereby encourage more comparisons with Mozart. This is backed up by the fact that Ludwig's birth certificate has not survived. Why? Because Johann destroyed it, so he could continue to falsify Ludwig's age without fear of contradiction. The continued fiction had a lasting effect. Until middle age Beethoven believed himself to be at least one year younger than he was, possibly two years younger.

The choice of Cologne for his son's debut was a strange one. It was away from Bonn, true, so if it all went wrong it would stay safely away from musical colleagues at court, at least for a time. On the other hand, Cologne was a large important city with a thriving cultural scene. It would be a more difficult nut to crack than small provincial Bonn.

There are no contemporary accounts of the recital, but it must have gone well, because Johann decided his son's musical talent needed more careful nurturing. By coincidence a room in their apartment that the Beethovens were subletting was occupied by a musician – a pianist, oboist, flautist and actor by the name of Tobias Friedrich Pfeiffer, who was in Bonn as a member of a theatrical touring company.

Johann van Beethoven hired Pfeiffer to give his son music lessons. It was both a good and a not so good decision. To take the not so good first. Pfeiffer was a drinker. When he fell ill, the maid of the house reported that late at night, after the others had gone to bed, he would order her to bring him wine, beer and brandy, which he would then drink one after the other.

Johann van Beethoven soon found in Pfeiffer a convivial drinking companion, with whom he would stay out till midnight drinking. And thereby has arisen an imperishable legend.

Watch any film or documentary on the life of Beethoven, and you will see the drunken father pulling the sleeping boy from his bed in the middle of the night, dragging him to the piano and forcing him to play, rapping his knuckles as tears fall down his cheeks.

This did not happen. The legend is based on a single sentence in a memoir by an obscure court cellist by the name of Bernhard Joseph Mäurer, in which he wrote that often, when Johann van Beethoven and Pfeiffer had been out drinking till eleven or twelve at night, they would return home, Johann would shake Ludwig awake, and Ludwig, crying, would go to the piano, where Pfeiffer, seeing how talented he was, would teach him till dawn.

Not the sort of thing most loving fathers would do, it is true, but there was no suggestion of violence and no dragging him to the piano against his will. And Pfeiffer continued to teach him through the small hours because he recognised the boy's talent.

Furthermore, it is Gottfried Fischer who tells us in his memoir about Pfeiffer's prodigious drinking habits, but he makes no mention of Johann drunkenly dragging his son from bed to piano. Living in the same house as the Beethovens, he would surely have known about this at first hand if it had happened. Mäurer can have heard about it only second or third hand. Johann van Beethoven may well not have been a perfect father, but he was far from the monster he is so conveniently depicted as.

There is, though, some evidence of stress in Ludwig's young life. Fischer writes that Ludwig was afflicted with a 'childhood defect' for longer than was considered normal. In fact it went on for so long that his mother asked Frau Fischer for advice on how to stop it. As it happened, Frau Fischer had herself once been given good advice about the subject, but – 'God be thanked!' – had never needed to use it. She passed on the advice to Maria Magdalena, who apparently put it to good use, and it was very helpful to Ludwig. That is all we know – no details about the affliction or the cure, which must have been somewhat drastic given the exclamation 'God be thanked!' The likely problem was bed-wetting, suggesting that Ludwig might have been affected by strains in his parents' marriage or the pressure his father put him under to show results from his musical tuition. From what we do know, we can assume it continued until Ludwig was at least eight or nine years of age, perhaps even longer.

Pfeiffer is one of those characters who would be lost to history had he not come into contact with greatness. As well as musical talent he had dubious eccentricities. His habit of stamping around his room in heavy boots directly above the bedroom where the master baker was trying to sleep caused Herr Fischer to ask him to remove his boots. Pfeiffer's response was to remove one boot and continue stamping with the other. The family barber, paying a visit, somehow upset Pfeiffer, who threw the barber bodily down the stairs, causing the poor man several broken bones.

Yet it was also Pfeiffer, during his year-long stay in the Beethovens' apartment, who first nourished Ludwig's musical talent. At first he played flute – an instrument he professed to detest – accompanied by Ludwig on the piano. They were then joined by a young man named Franz Georg Rovantini, a relative of Frau van Beethoven from Ehrenbreitstein, who was also staying in the Fischer house. Rovantini was an excellent violinist. It was said that the music the trio produced was so beautiful that people would stop in the street outside to listen.

This is the first we hear of Ludwig van Beethoven performing with other musicians, both of whom were a decade and a half older than him, and receiving praise for it. Word spread fast. The people of Bonn began to talk of the extraordinary talent of the boy who lived in the Fischer house in the Rheingasse.

Word was about to spread further afield, to another country, in fact – the country of his ancestors.

8

Franz Rovantini died suddenly. He had begun to give the ten-year-old Ludwig van Beethoven instruction in both violin and viola, and the boy felt his tutor's death keenly. Rovantini's sister, who lived in Rotterdam, later came to Bonn to visit her brother's grave and invited Ludwig's parents to bring him to Rotterdam, where she could introduce him to wealthy and powerful patrons, whom she knew from her work as governess.

In November 1783, a month before Ludwig turned thirteen, mother and son boarded a sailing boat to travel down the Rhine, Johann being unable to accompany them because of court commitments. It was bitterly cold – a much colder winter than usual, which was to have devastating effects.

It was an uncomfortable journey. There were no cabins or inside quarters, which meant they had to sit on deck. So cold was it that Maria Magdalena cradled Ludwig's feet in her lap to prevent frostbite.

Once they arrived in Rotterdam Ludwig was kept busy. He performed in several of the great houses, astonishing audiences with his skills at the keyboard. And in an extraordinary development – we do not know how this came about – he made the short trip with his mother to The Hague. There, on 23 November, he performed with full orchestra at the Royal Court of Prince Willem V of Orange-Nassau. It is possible he performed his own Piano Concerto in E flat.[1]

Sadly, the concert was not open to the public, so no record of the programme exists, nor any account of how the concert went. Of crucial importance in the life story of the future great composer, Ludwig van Beethoven had given his first performance with orchestra at the age of just twelve.

The journey home several weeks later must have been even more uncomfortable, the boat now ploughing south against the strong currents of the

Rhine. The air was colder. That was not the only difficulty. Expecting his son and wife to return with bagfuls of money, Johann was devastated to find plenty of gifts, but very little money – leading his son to say later in life, 'The Dutch are penny-pinchers who love money too much.'[2]

Maria Magdalena and Ludwig returned to find the city of Bonn in the grip of a colder, icier winter than anyone living could remember.

∽

There had been further joy, mixed with pain, for the Beethoven family over the previous couple of years. A third son, Nikolaus Johann, had been born in 1776. Three further babies all died in infancy. In fine weather, the three Beethoven boys – Ludwig, Caspar Carl and Nikolaus Johann – would be taken by the Fischers' maid-of-all-work to walk in the palace gardens or play in the sandy area with other children. Closer and less formal was Father Rhine, just a few steps down the hill, where the mossy banks and shallow waters provided endless, if messy, fun.

As autumn turned to winter in 1783 and the Beethovens were planning the Rotterdam trip, wise local heads were warning of a difficult winter to come. Cloud formation was not normal, winds coming from unexpected directions. Some shrugged their shoulders, dismissing old wives' tales. Who could tell what the river would do tomorrow, let alone across the winter months?

The wise heads nodded, then smiled grimly when their predictions came true – truer than even they had expected. In late December and again in January there were two freezing cold spells. Snow fell relentlessly throughout December, January and February. The Rhine froze over, something that had not been seen in Bonn or the Rhine valley in living memory.

The Bonners heard from friends and relatives across central Europe that the Moldau, Elbe, Danube, Oder and Vltava had all frozen over, which again was unheard of. So severe were conditions that the winter of 1783–84 would come to be known as the Little Ice Age.

Then, suddenly, a warm southerly wind swept across Europe, to be followed by torrential rain. The ice floes began to break up, then melt, causing river levels to rise dramatically. The Rhine, cascading through Bonn, burst its banks.

The atmosphere in the Fischer house was febrile. They could see the waters of the Rhine overflowing and beginning to climb the hill. There was one house below them, then it was just a few paces to the river. That bottom house was in imminent peril.

Master baker Fischer gathered up as many belongings as he could and stored them in the attic. Johann van Beethoven did the same. Maria Magdalena was surprisingly pragmatic. 'Why the fuss? You are just not used to it. I grew up with this. In Ehrenbreitstein we often have high water, but we don't make a fuss of it.'[3]

She would soon change her tune. The bottom house in the Rheingasse was flooded out, and the water was rising to the second floor of the Fischer house, containing the Beethoven apartment. Maria Magdalena confessed herself surprised, and then took control.

She set about evacuating her children, but the staircase was now flooded. Fischer, outside in the courtyard behind, set a ladder against the wall and a plank of wood across the courtyard. One by one Frau van Beethoven carried her children down the ladder to safety.

Eventually the waters began to recede, but the house was uninhabitable. The Beethovens, with their three boys aged thirteen, nine and seven, took up temporary lodgings at the house of a musical colleague. The master baker was left to bemoan his fate. The cellars below and the bakehouse on the ground floor were full of mud and sludge. His baking oven was covered with four feet of wet mud. He had it removed, spread dry, rough sand over the oven, and fired it up for two twenty-four-hour periods with heavy bundles of wood, hoping to produce rye bread. But the result was useless and he fed the bread to the pigs. He cleaned the oven out again, fired it up, and it was a success. He could begin to bake bread again.

There was just a single loss of life. The Fischers had a canary that whistled a lovely little song. Fischer was struggling to get out of the flooded room, but the water was already too high for him to reach across for the canary's cage. 'I had to get myself out of the room or I would have drowned. I had no time. The water was so high. I've never seen anything like it before.'[4]

When the waters receded and he returned to the house, he found the cage was still hanging, its lifeless occupant inside.

9

When the Beethoven family moved back into the Fischer house, Gottfried Fischer recalled that all the boys could talk about was the perishingly cold winter and the ensuing devastating flood. That winter literally left its mark on the youngest Beethoven. The bitter cold caused a festering sore to erupt on seven-year-old Nikolaus's head. This was to affect his features, damage that could clearly be seen for the rest of his life. Just a single portrait of Nikolaus was done in middle age. The hair is combed forward to hide any scarring but the lid of his right eye is almost closed – a lasting reminder of that dreadful winter.

The tall house in the Rheingasse stood until 1860, home to successive master bakers of the Fischer family. None of the buildings survives today, but the Rheingasse still runs down to the Rhine. When I visited Bonn in the late 1990s, the end of the row of houses was occupied by a hotel, appropriately named Hotel Beethoven. I went in, to see if there were any memorabilia or old photographs. The receptionist uninterestedly answered, 'No.' I asked him if he knew why the hotel was named for the composer. He shrugged and shook his head. Next time I was in Bonn, fifteen or so years later, the hotel was gone and the plot was a building site, with diggers and cement mixers.

On my most recent visit, with Nula, in October 2022, there stood at the bottom of the Rheingasse a large seven-storey block of flats. Across the road immediately beyond it the Rhine flowed sedately by. I gazed up at the top floor, so much taller than the Fischer house, and smiled at the thought of how much Ludwig would have loved to keep his telescopes up there. I tried to imagine the Fischer house, and the house immediately below it, with the river almost up against the walls. There was a road there now, obviously constructed on reclaimed land, running along the banks of the Rhine, busy with traffic.

We walked down to the river and round to the other side of the block. On the back of the building were balconies. In my head I tried to picture master baker Fischer putting up a ladder for Maria Magdalena to evacuate her three boys. My imagination could not stretch to it.

On a ground-floor balcony a woman was enjoying a morning coffee in unseasonably warm sunshine. Nula said, 'We must look suspicious, prowling around, gazing up at the windows. I'm going to talk to her.' She smiled at the woman and explained we were doing Beethoven research for a new book I was writing.

To my amazement the woman got up and began speaking animatedly, gesticulating further up the Rheingasse. Nula had spoken to her in English. She had understood fully and was replying in German. I begged her to repeat what she had said, and then again.

The smile and the enthusiasm never left her face. She was telling us that the house the Beethoven family had lived in was not where this block of flats stood, but the next house up, and that there was a small plaque on the wall commemorating the fact. We thanked her profusely and walked back out onto Rheingasse.

The first house up from the block of flats stood at the end of a row of houses probably dating back to the 1950s or 1960s. It was, like its immediate neighbour to the right, two storeys high, with dormer windows in the roof. With my imagination now in overdrive, it was easy to imagine the Fischer house in exactly the same spot.

A plaque on the wall explained, in German and English, that here once stood the house of master baker Gottfried Fischer, where the Beethoven family lived, off and on, for around a decade, and where Ludwig's brother Nikolaus Johann was born. There is no mention of the flood.

Suddenly everything dropped into place. Two hundred years ago the Rhine was a much wider river. Where the modern block of flats stood today was water. The river came much higher up the Rheingasse to the row of houses I was staring at. And, as I stared, I saw something I had hitherto missed that caused me to gasp out loud.

One house up from the Fischer house was . . . a bakery. A bakery with all kinds of bread, chocolate cakes and patisseries in the window. In the corner of the window, staring out at me, a half-smile on his face, hands casually in his pockets, in an altogether relaxed pose that he never assumed in real life, was a four-foot-high gilded chocolate statue of Beethoven.

Behind the counter, in a starched white baker's jacket, stood the master baker. Brimming with confidence, I asked, 'Is this where master baker Fischer baked?'

'No,' he said smiling, pointing to his right. 'Next door.'

'He baked in the house?' I asked incredulously.

'Yes,' he said. 'The bakery was in his house.'

Of course it was! Fischer said as much in his memoir – the oven covered in sludge from the flooded river. Something else that had suddenly dropped into place.

We sat at a table and the waitress politely asked us to move, since this table was reserved. Several more were reserved too.

'People reserve for morning coffee?' I asked.

'Yes,' she replied.

This, I learned, was one of the finest, and most popular, bakery-cafés in Bonn. Fitting, given the history.

As we enjoyed a peerless coffee and sensational chocolate cake, Nula said, 'Do you realise, if I hadn't spoken to the woman on the balcony, we wouldn't know anything about this, the house and the bakery?'

'And I would confidently have placed the Fischer house where the block of flats now is,' I added faintly.

Do you sense a touch of déjà vu? First the wrong St Remigius church and the old man who put us right. Now the woman on the balcony who said it wasn't here and pointed us to the next house up the Rheingasse.

Nula looked up from her coffee. 'I'm beginning to think Ludwig is looking after you.'

10

It was a different Beethoven family that returned to the Fischer house after the flood. Maybe it was the temporary change of scenery, the disruption to daily life – or maybe it was none of this and would have happened anyway. Johann van Beethoven was beginning to lose his bearings.

His behaviour became erratic, his attendance at court unreliable. Pupils began to drift away, which affected his income. Instinctively he relied more and more on his eldest son. He arranged recitals in the apartment, even small concerts, charging for entry. Ludwig thrived on these performances, but his relationship with his father was becoming difficult.

Ludwig now devoted most of every day to music. His great pleasure was sitting at the piano and improvising. He improvised too on the violin and viola, both of which Rovantini had taught him to a high standard during his stay in the Fischer house. But improvisation was not to his father's liking.

'Why are you scraping around stupidly like that all over the place?' Johann complained angrily when he caught Ludwig improvising on the violin. 'You know I can't stand it. Scrape from the music or don't scrape at all.' And when he found Ludwig at the keyboard, 'What, are you tinkling around again? Go away or I'll clip your ear.'[1] Not the first, or last, father to complain his son was not practising enough, and to a degree we can forgive Johann for not fully realising in these early years the sheer genius he had bred. But if he was trying to encourage Ludwig, he was certainly going about it the wrong way.

When he had to sing in the court chapel, Johann would begin his day by sucking a raw egg or eating two plums, but this singer's recipe was slowly losing out to the effects of alcohol. It would elicit less criticism if he failed to turn up than if he sang and was found to be below par. If there was a storm, Johann would sit behind the entrance window of the Fischer house and call across to Klein the fishmonger who lived directly opposite. Amicable insults would fly across the Rheingasse. We do not know what Johann called Klein, but we know Klein would habitually call out, 'What do you want, you note cruncher?' As soon as the downpour abated, the two men would go out drinking together.

Johann's behaviour at home veered between boorish and farcical. Cäcilie, named for the patron saint of music, was now a pretty teenager. Her brother Gottfried recalls an incident when Johann said to her, 'Cäcilie, you are our patroness of music, and I am very fond of you. You must give me a kiss.'

She refused, saying, 'I am not your kissing girl. You've got a wife. Kiss her, not me.'

'You're a naughty little witch,' Johann retorted. 'You know how to answer back, but I'll still have my fun with you.'

Johann lunged drunkenly at Cäcilie. She nipped nimbly out of the way. Johann fell against the stove, which was alight. The stove, with its pipe, fell off the wall, still alight, and burned on the floor. Cäcilie clapped her hands gleefully as Johann struggled to put out the flames.[2]

Ludwig, despite his father's discouragements, was beginning to compose as well as play. Word of this boy's talent – he was still only in his early teens – spread fast, and beyond Bonn. Wealthy music lovers began to turn up at the house on the Rheingasse and offer money to hear Ludwig play. This his father gladly accepted.

But there was a problem. The inevitable day came when master baker Fischer summoned Johann van Beethoven and told him things could not continue the way they were. 'I am a baker. I wouldn't mind strangers turning up to hear your boy play if I wasn't a baker. But because I am a baker, I have to get up at one in the morning and bake, so during the day I have to sleep in the afternoon and evening. With all the disturbances I can't sleep at all. If I go on like this, I'll become ill. Herr van Beethoven, I'm sorry to have to say this to you, but you must look around for other lodgings.'[3]

And so the Beethovens' tenancy in the Fischer house in the Rheingasse came to an end. It was in that house that Ludwig van Beethoven found his calling, in that house that he first performed alone, and then for audiences. He had embarked on his life's work.

❧

There was a middle-aged man in Bonn by the name of Stumpf who, it was well known, had been a musician and composer at court, and who had lost his wits. Habitually he would walk through the town with a conductor's baton in his right hand and a roll of manuscript paper in his left. Down the Rheingasse he would walk and enter, uninvited, into the house of master baker Fischer. In the entrance hall he would beat with his baton on the roll of music, then point up towards the Beethovens' apartment, as if to indicate that there were fellow musicians there. Then he would leave without speaking.

Ludwig van Beethoven would often laugh at this and say, 'You can see what happens to musicians, can't you? Music has driven this one mad. That could happen to us too.'[4]

11

The year 1784 was a fateful one for the Beethoven family, and not just because of the floods. With the water receding and the town struggling to get back on its feet, a different sort of disarray occurred. The prince-elector, employer of Johann van Beethoven, died.

It was said in Bonn that every table was nourished by the electoral court – in other words, practically everybody in Bonn was salaried by the court in one role or another. A change of elector was bound to have an impact. No one liked a new broom.

And this new broom was determined to sweep clean. Maximilian Franz was of fine aristocratic pedigree. He was the youngest son of Empress Maria Theresia, brother of the emperor, and brother of Maria Antonia, who would become known to history as Marie Antoinette. Beyond that he did not have much to recommend him. A fall from his horse had put an early end to a military career, which left only one occupation open to a member of the imperial royal family: the church. The fall had left him with a permanent limp, and his difficulty in moving had led him to put on a vast amount of weight. He swiftly became the butt of cruel humour among Bonners.

The tables turned, though, when the new broom got down to work. Max Franz ordered reports into every aspect of local government – who was employed, in what role, and on what salary. And, most important, did they provide value for money?

This, as everybody – except the one individual himself – knew, would sound the death knell for Johann van Beethoven's career. The report described him as having 'a very stale voice'. It would be a little while before the axe fell, but the first cut had been made. It could be that the reason he was not immediately dismissed was that his son, Ludwig, received a glowing report. It is worth quoting in full:

> Ludwig van Beethoven, aged thirteen, born in Bonn, has served two years, no salary. He is the son of the Betthoven [*sic*] sub. No. 8, has no salary, but during the absence of the Kapellmeister he played the organ, is of good capability, still young, of good and quiet deportment, and is poor.[1]

How had it come about that Ludwig van Beethoven was serving as musician at court at the age of just thirteen, and had been thus employed for two years? The answer lies in a decision Johann van Beethoven took, after the departure of Tobias Pfeiffer, to hire a new teacher for his son. Why he chose an outsider from the distant town of Chemnitz in Saxony, and a Protestant at that, is not known, but it proved to be an inspired decision.

Christian Gottlob Neefe first came to Bonn, as Pfeiffer had, with the Grossmann–Hellmuth theatrical company but, unlike Pfeiffer, had stayed. When, in 1782, the elderly court organist died, Neefe – who had already demonstrated his skills as organist, in addition to being known as a composer – succeeded to the post.

He was already teaching young Ludwig, for we hear now of the boy standing in for him at Mass in St Remigius church, when Neefe was away on tour. Neefe was quick to recognise Ludwig's extraordinary talent, and in 1783 he wrote an article for a music magazine about musical life in Bonn. He devoted a generous paragraph to praising the musical skills of his pupil, ending with the words:

> This young genius deserves support so that he can travel. He would surely become a second Wolfgang Amadeus Mozart, if he were to continue as he has begun.[2]

This is remarkably prescient. Neefe is the first to call Ludwig a genius, and the first to link his name with the great composer from Salzburg.

Neefe did more than use words. When Ludwig began to write music, Neefe, a composer himself, encouraged him. A less sympathetic teacher might have admonished him, telling him to learn to walk before he tried to run. In 1782, when Ludwig was just eleven years of age, he wrote a set of nine variations on a march by the German composer Ernst Christoph Dressler. Each variation becomes more complex than the one preceding it, and the final variation tests the most accomplished pianist.

Neefe was so impressed he arranged to have the piece published. And so Ludwig published his first piece of music at the age of eleven. Only a year later he was composing again, and this time it was on an entirely different scale.

Three full piano sonatas, each three movements long, of a complexity that is astounding for a twelve-year-old. It is highly probable Neefe assisted him – what teacher wouldn't? – but he certainly did not attempt to quell the free spirit. In all three sonatas there is clear evidence of the future genius.[3]

Neefe certainly did influence what action Ludwig took with the sonatas. He dedicated them to the prince-elector, with wording clearly dictated, or at least strongly influenced, by Neefe. Only one sentence rings rather less than true. Ludwig writes that he was 'almost too shy' to compose, but his Muse insisted. Not the natural words of a twelve-year-old, and certainly not of this particular twelve-year-old. But the fact remains that before he was thirteen Ludwig van Beethoven was a published composer, with a set of variations and three piano sonatas to his name. He therefore now had compositions of his own to perform in the salons of the nobility, of a difficulty even the most accomplished amateur pianist could only struggle with. His career as composer and performer was firmly under way.

Something else was happening to the boy as well, and again it was entirely due to his teacher. The Protestant Neefe was living and working in a Catholic town. This in itself is extraordinary, and it says a lot about the rather relaxed atmosphere in this outpost of the Habsburg Empire. Vienna, capital of empire, seat of the Holy Roman Emperor, might have been a mere 550 miles away to the south-east but, with its formality, protocol and strict adherence to convention, it might have been on another planet. It is to the credit of the prince-elector's court at Bonn that Neefe was appointed court organist purely on merit.

But Neefe was more than simply an adherent of the 'wrong' religion. This was a time of utter turmoil in Europe. In France there was already talk of revolution. The cataclysmic events that would culminate in the Great Terror and the execution of a king and his queen were only a handful of years away. Enlightenment ideals were beginning to sweep Europe. The divine right of kings was being questioned. The power of the clergy was being challenged.

In the intimacy of a small piano room, is it not inevitable that a teacher, sitting alongside his pupil, might fill his young head with ideas, musical and non-musical? And what twelve-year-old could fail to be impressed? I believe that it was in the confines of a piano room that the boy Ludwig van Beethoven not only set out on his musical path but also formed the revolutionary ideas that would stay with him for life.

The turbulent year of 1784, which had begun with that freezing winter, followed by devastating floods, and then the death of the prince-elector, would end well for Ludwig. Under the new prince-elector, Neefe secured for him the permanent post of assistant court organist, on a salary. It was the first, and last, salaried position of his life.

Sadly for both pupil and teacher, Ludwig's salary was partly carved out of Neefe's, in order to save costs. Neefe had a wife and young family to support, and he decided to leave Bonn and move on. Later, Ludwig would write to Neefe to thank him for all he had done for him. 'Should I ever become a great man, much of the credit will be yours,' he wrote.

Ludwig might have lost Neefe, but he was about to acquire something very valuable: in effect, a second family.

12

Ludwig van Beethoven stands today eight feet tall at the top of the Münsterplatz in the centre of Bonn, a look of determination and defiance on his face. He is cloaked in a gown held by his folded left arm, the left hand holding a notebook, his right arm slightly extended, a pen between his fingers, his little finger delicately crooked, one foot slightly in front of the other. He cuts a larger than life figure, this bronze statue set on a plinth, capturing the character of the man, maybe, but according him a superhuman, almost godlike, appearance – as does practically every statue and bust of Beethoven ever created – that in real life he most certainly did not have.

If the statue were able to turn its head slightly to the left, it would see a faceless row of shops with offices above. What Ludwig saw as a young lad of thirteen or fourteen was very different. I imagine him standing in the same spot where one day the statue would be raised to his memory, in the company of a boyhood friend – Franz Gerhard Wegeler, five years older than him – and staring nervously at an imposing two-storey house, no fewer than four windows each side of the front door, nine on the first floor, and ornamental dormer windows set into the roof, with an elaborate gated front garden.

I imagine Wegeler having to encourage and cajole him, trying to convince Ludwig that the lady he was about to meet was charming and delightful, and might even have some rather good news for him.

The lady in question was Helene von Breuning, widow of a court councillor who had lost his life endeavouring to save important documents from a devastating fire at the electoral palace a few years earlier. At the time of his death, his wife was pregnant with their fourth child. The family was well liked and respected by the people of Bonn, who honoured the memory of the man who had given his life in such a heroic fashion.

Wegeler came to know the family through a friendship with the children. When Helene von Breuning had told him that two of her children were showing signs of some talent at the piano, and she wondered whether Wegeler knew of somebody suitable who could give them lessons, well, of course he did. But he knew it would take some convincing to persuade Helene that a boy in his earliest teenage years, whose appearance at the best of times was unkempt and whose manner when addressing his elders would sometimes border on the disrespectful, was the right person.

How did Wegeler persuade Ludwig to walk through the front door of that imposing house? By telling him, certainly, that if Helene von Breuning took him on, he would earn some much-needed cash. He might also have added that the eldest of the two children requiring lessons was a lovely young girl by the name of Eleonore. The clincher might well have been the fact that in the drawing room stood a fine piano, to which he would have unlimited access.

Wegeler, in the memoir he would later co-author about his childhood friend, gives us no detail of how that first meeting went, other than to say Helene did indeed take Ludwig on to teach Eleonore and her youngest brother Lorenz. He does, though, give us some wonderful details about the Breuning household, and the degree to which young Ludwig relished being a part of it.

Johann van Beethoven had taken his eldest son out of school early, probably at around the age of ten or eleven, so that he could concentrate on musical studies, with the explicit aim – in Johann's eyes – of earning money through his talent. The result of this was that Ludwig left school with no more than a smattering of arithmetic and Latin, appalling spelling and handwriting that would remain untidy and bordering on the illegible for the rest of his life. To say that the Beethoven household was chaotic and, apart from the diminishing frequency of musical recitals, lacking in culture is to state the obvious. The Breuning household was entirely different.

Helene von Breuning not only employed Ludwig to teach two of her children; she also took him under her wing in other respects. She set about smoothing the rough edges and teaching him a little etiquette, so that when he taught or performed in other salons, he would conform a little more closely to the behaviour that was expected of him. She also took it on herself to educate him academically. She taught him classical history, Homer and Plutarch, and introduced him to the works of two emerging giants of German literature, Schiller and Goethe.

For the next few years, Wegeler tells us, Ludwig spent more time in the Breuning house than in his own family home. He would spend whole days there, and even many nights. Helene von Breuning became, in effect, a surrogate mother to him. He would later say of her, with a certain touch of arrogance, 'she knew how to keep the insects off the flowers'. She it was who, when he was due to cross the square to the imposing house at the top to give lessons to Count von Fürstenburg, made sure he was on time and properly attired. She would watch him set off, and more often than not, stop, turn and return to the house, saying he was in no mood to teach today. 'Ludwig has his raptus again,' she would sigh.

Ludwig was closer to the Breuning children than he was to his own brothers. With the third child Stephan, known as Steffen, he developed a close friendship that would last – with interruptions – for the rest of his life. Steffen will reappear in this story many more times.

Not so with his other pupil. It was a different kind of close friendship that Ludwig developed with Eleonore, known as Lorchen. We know from two letters he would later write that Lorchen was Ludwig van Beethoven's first love. But something went wrong. When bidding her farewell on the eve of his second, and final, trip to Vienna in November 1792, he did something to upset her. He offended her to such an extent that he wrote to her from Vienna, pleading for forgiveness and begging her to send him something made with her own hand. She sent him a knitted scarf. But the friendship was not rekindled, and he never saw her again. The upset, in my view, had been caused by a costly and clumsy attempt at a kiss.

As if to put a seal on the break, who should Eleonore go on to marry but Ludwig's old teenage friend, Franz Wegeler? Much later, in the final year of Beethoven's life, Wegeler and Eleonore would write him a long joint letter, pleading with him to return one last time to Bonn, to see the Rhine again, to talk of the early days before he achieved everlasting fame. They told him they sat frequently long into the evening with Helene von Breuning, now in her late seventies, reminiscing of those days when he spent hours in the Breuning house. Helene would smile at the memory, but they were not sure how much she could recall.

Beethoven dictated a letter to his old friends promising to return, but he never did.

❧

The monumental bronze statue that today stands in the Münsterplatz owes its existence largely to the efforts of Franz Liszt, who was instrumental in raising – and contributing – the funds necessary to mark the seventy-fifth anniversary of Beethoven's birth in 1845.

For the unveiling, a balcony was built onto the front of Count von Fürstenburg's house to accommodate the royal guests who had been invited. And what a distinguished collection of personages they were! Queen Victoria of Britain was there with her German consort Prince Albert, King Friedrich Wilhelm and Queen Elizabeth of Prussia, and Archduke Friedrich of Austria.

There were speeches and much ceremony, as the dignitaries and officials of Bonn, led by the mayor, stood in line to the side of the statue, which was covered in a large tarpaulin. Almost hidden in the crowd were master baker Gottfried Fischer, now sixty-five years of age, and his sister Cäcilie, eighty-three, who had known the six-year-old Ludwig. How they must have smiled wistfully at the memory of the boy taken to the piano to play through the night, or gazing at the Rhine through the attic telescope, now immortalised in a monument of bronze.

The moment for the unveiling came. To the beating of drums, the firing of cannon, the ringing of bells, the cover was removed – to reveal Beethoven showing his back to the royal guests seated on the balcony. The mayor could hardly speak for embarrassment. Beethoven would have loved it.

In January 2022 the statue, badly corroded, was removed for renovation, which took six months. It stands today – its back to the post office headquarters, which is what the count's house now is – glistening and spotless, as it was on that day in August 1845.

13

Beethoven met Mozart. There's a sentence – just three words – to stop you in your tracks. The facts are well known. As a sixteen-year-old boy, Ludwig was given leave of absence by the prince-elector to go to Vienna to study with Mozart. In the event he was there for no more than two weeks, before having to leave for home because he heard from his father that his mother was dangerously ill and they feared for her life.

Those are the facts? Well, they have been for nigh on a hundred years – ninety-six to be precise, as I write this. It's all thanks to a German musicologist by the name of Eduard Panzerbieter, who, in 1927 – the centenary of Beethoven's death – published this account with irrefutable evidence. He had uncovered two entries in the weekly newspaper *Münchner Zeitung* for 1 and 25 April 1787, showing that a certain Herr Peethofen (*sic*), musician from Bonn, had stayed in the *Schwarzen Adler* ('Black Eagle') hotel in Munich. It is therefore certain, Panzerbieter writes, that Beethoven stayed in Munich on his way to Vienna, then again on his way back a little over three weeks later. Why such a short stay in the capital? He must have heard from his father about his mother's failing health.

It is a compelling account, and has remained accepted and unchallenged until just a few years ago, when a German musicologist by the name of Dieter Haberl, doubtful about Panzerbieter's estimates of travelling time, decided to dig a little deeper.[1]

Haberl found an entry in the *Regensburgische Diarium* that an organist from Bonn by the name of Bertenhoven (*sic*) checked into the *Goldenen Spiegel* ('Golden Mirror') hotel in Regensburg on 5 January 1787, en route from Bonn to Vienna. He remained in the capital until late March. His return journey was via Munich, where he checked into the *Schwarzen Adler* on 1 April. Ludwig then decided to break his journey with a second visit to Regensburg, around eighty miles north of Munich, where the local newspaper had a Herr Bethhoffen (*sic*) arriving once again. (German newspapers clearly had trouble with Dutch names.) He left Regensburg on 24 April, checking in the following day to the *Schwarzen Adler* in Munich. From there he travelled via Augsburg back home to Bonn, receiving word at every stop on the way from his father about his mother's worsening condition.

This new research suggests that Panzerbieter's account is therefore accurate – Ludwig did indeed check into the *Schwarzen Adler* on the dates he says – but it is his conclusions that are wrong. The two stops in Munich were not made going to and returning from Vienna. They were both made on the return journey. Also, Ludwig could not have received word from his father about his mother's dire condition while in Vienna, or he would never have broken the return journey with the unplanned detour to Regensburg.

So, we know Ludwig van Beethoven was in Vienna from early January until late March. Unfortunately we have no further details – where he stayed, how he paid his way, and most importantly, any contact he might have had with Mozart.

Mozart was in Prague from 8 January to 12 February, supervising and conducting performances of *The Marriage of Figaro*. That gives a window of approximately six weeks during which the thirty-one-year-old Mozart and sixteen-year-old Beethoven were both in Vienna and could have met. But did they?

The earliest published account saying that an encounter did take place came in the first full-length biography of Beethoven, written after the composer's death by his secretary, Anton Schindler. Schindler came to know Beethoven only in the last few years of his life. This means that anything he knew about the teenage Beethoven meeting Mozart must have come verbally from Beethoven himself more than thirty years after the event.

Schindler's account of the single meeting between these two iconic musical figures – one already famous, the other soon to be – is riveting, albeit brief. Mozart asked Ludwig to play something. Ludwig did. Mozart dismissed it as a piece the boy had obviously prepared.

'Play something of your own.'

Ludwig asked Mozart to give him a tune, any tune, and he would improvise on it. This he did, and so impressively that Mozart turned to others in the room and said, 'This boy will certainly give the world something to talk about.'[2]

And that is it. There is no suggestion of any further meeting, which has for the last hundred years lent credence to Panzerbieter's (false) conclusion that Ludwig had to leave Vienna suddenly and in a hurry. We have to bear in mind that this account must have been given to Schindler by Beethoven decades after it happened. Beethoven might well have embellished, or even imagined a version of the encounter that, over the years, had taken hold in his mind. The quotation might well have been said to him in his youth, but how can we know it was Mozart who said it? Also, if Ludwig had six weeks in which he could have taken lessons with Mozart, why is there no account of any further meeting? Besides, Schindler's biography, in many other respects, is notoriously unreliable.

Are there, then, any contemporary accounts of this, or more, meetings? In a word, no. No one who witnessed it wrote about it. A future pupil of Beethoven in Vienna, Carl Czerny, would – many years after Beethoven's death – write that Beethoven had seen Mozart play, and described his playing as 'delicate but choppy'.[3]

The one person we might expect to give an account of Ludwig's trip to Vienna to meet Mozart, and whose testimony is reliable, is Franz Wegeler, who was more than five years older than Ludwig, and knew him well at this time. Yet, in his memoir, not a word.

The only other person who actually knew Beethoven in Bonn at the time of the trip to Vienna, and wrote about it, was Ferdinand Ries. But Ries was a two-year-old toddler in 1787. He soon showed real skill at the keyboard, and Ludwig taught him as a boy, but he was still only eight years old when Ludwig finally left Bonn for Vienna. It is more than likely that Ludwig will have told him about the trip, but how much would a child remember? In the memoir he co-wrote with Wegeler, Ries tantalisingly says only that Mozart gave Beethoven some lessons, but sadly Mozart did not play the piano for him. 'Some lessons'? Why no further detail of something that would have intrigued Ries, who was himself a professional musician? And a teacher who does not himself play? Is that really likely?

If, indeed, this one encounter did take place, but there were no more to follow, we can perhaps put it down to Mozart's circumstances. He was under considerable pressure at the time. His health was not good. Only recently he had been taken ill at a performance of one of his operas, 'sweating through all his clothes', and he had not yet fully recovered. He had received news from Salzburg that his father was seriously ill – Leopold would in fact die before the year was out. He was in the process of moving his family out of the large apartment in the shadow of St Stephen's Cathedral to cheaper premises further out of the city, and he was fully immersed in composing his new opera, *Don Giovanni*. The last thing Mozart needed right now was a visit from a teenage boy from somewhere in the north-west of Germany, dressed in ill-fitting clothes and with a Rhineland accent that sounded rough and harsh to sophisticated ears.

The apartment where the supposed encounter took place is now the only one of several apartments occupied by the Mozarts that is still standing. It bears no resemblance to the original. The entrance today is from the Domgasse itself, which was the rear entrance when the Mozarts lived there. The original front entrance was walled up many years ago. Interior rooms contain exhibits relating to Mozart's life.

There is no mention anywhere that I could see of the visit to Mozart by sixteen-year-old Ludwig van Beethoven in March 1787.

Frustratingly, then, although we now know the dates and itinerary of Beethoven's first journey to Vienna, we know very little, possibly nothing, about his stay there. The paucity of information has caused one German musicologist to suggest that in terms of actual results, the trip might as well not have happened at all.

Beethoven scholarship does not stand still. Only in the last few years has that crucial new evidence about dates and itinerary been uncovered. Dieter Haberl himself states, in the concluding sentence of his research, that now we know Beethoven was absent from Bonn for at least four months, rather than just two weeks, more information about his activity during that period is bound to emerge.

That means, inevitably, that any biography of a great life is at risk of becoming outdated in its detail at any moment. I readily confess I had this chapter written some months ago, and then I discovered Dieter Haberl's research. For the last twenty years or more I have travelled around the UK giving talks about Beethoven. Always I tell the story of his journey to Vienna to meet Mozart, his sudden departure after just two weeks and a single encounter, based on Panzerbieter's research. That will now have to change.

The sheer excitement of learning new facts easily outweighs any frustration at having to go back, rewrite and rethink. Learning about Beethoven is a joyful journey without end.

14

Ludwig must have been relieved to arrive back in Bonn to find his mother bedbound but still breathing, yet devastated to see how greatly her condition had deteriorated. Maria Magdalena had consumption – tuberculosis, as it is known today. This is a disease that does not come on suddenly or overwhelm its victim in a short space of time. Although there is no mention in contemporary documents, she would have been seriously ill when Ludwig had left for Vienna four months previously.

Maria Magdalena van Beethoven died on 17 July 1787 at the age of forty. It is difficult to form a clear understanding of her character, or her qualities as a mother. Cäcilie Fischer, in her brother's memoir, recalls that she never once saw Frau van Beethoven smile, and that she was always very serious. She also suggests that her maternal instincts might not have been very strong. Maria Magdalena allowed the maid of the house to look after the three boys, taking them down to the river or to the court gardens. When Cäcilie told Maria Magdalena that she felt the maid was not supervising the boys carefully enough, particularly given the massive dangers of the fast-flowing Rhine so close to the house, Maria Magdalena said she would talk to the maid, but did nothing about it.

Could this lack of attention account for the fact that a school classmate of Ludwig's, who went on to become a councillor at court, described many years later how Ludwig would turn up at school in such a scruffy state, with clothes in such disrepair, that he and other pupils teased Ludwig that his mother must be dead, otherwise she would never let him attend school looking like that? It seems hard to square this with the mother who warmed her child's feet on that boat trip to Rotterdam.

Two months after Maria Magdalena's death, Ludwig wrote in a letter, 'She was to me so good a mother, so deserving of love, my best friend. O, who was happier than I when I could still utter the sweet name of mother, and it was heard. And to whom can I say it now?'[1] Those words, *meine beste Freundin*, Beethoven would later have engraved on his mother's tombstone.

I want to pause for a moment to look more closely at Maria Magdalena; it is perhaps not so surprising that we know relatively little about her, given her early death.

Ehrenbreitstein, where her family had lived for generations, was a small town with an importance beyond its diminutive size. High on the hill above it was a medieval fortress that guarded the middle Rhine, at the confluence of the Rhine and Moselle. Sacked by the French in the nineteenth century, it was rebuilt, and is today a tourist attraction reached by cable car. Ehrenbreitstein was the seat of the prince-elector of Trier, and it was in his palace that Maria Magdalena's father worked as overseer of the kitchens.

At the tender age of just sixteen Maria Magdalena married a thirty-year-old widower who was a valet at court. In the first two years of marriage she saw both his children by a previous marriage die. She gave birth to their son, Johann Peter Anton, only to lose him at the age of just one month. Eleven months later her husband died.

At eighteen years of age Maria Magdalena had witnessed enough death for a lifetime. Two years later she married Johann van Beethoven, against the opposition of both families, and once again there was ineffable sadness when a son, christened Ludwig Maria, died at just six days old.

One can only imagine the joy and hope, mingled with fear and apprehension, when their next child was born. They gave him just the single name of Ludwig. Did they fear it might be tempting fate to give him more? The baby survived into childhood, followed by two more sons, but unquestionably there was something different about Ludwig, an apartness that Maria Magdalena could not penetrate.

Three more pregnancies followed, with the infant dying in each case before reaching its second birthday. Including her first marriage, Maria Magdalena had given birth eight times, with only three children surviving. As well as struggling to bring up the family on her husband's meagre – and diminishing – salary, she could only watch as he slowly doomed his career with alcohol.

Did she suffer in silence? It has been suggested that the youngest surviving son, Nikolaus Johann, with that extraordinarily square jaw and aquiline nose, bears so little resemblance to his elder brother Ludwig, that they could not possibly have the same father. Could Nikolaus Johann be the illegitimate child of Maria Magdalena and an unknown lover?

Then there is the question of whether Beethoven was black. A youthful portrait shows distinctly dark skin, and a bust done from a life mask does not show a fair-skinned northern European. His dark skin earned him the nickname 'The Spaniard' at school. It has been speculated that his paternal grandmother came from a Spanish family with roots in Moorish eastern Spain. Did she introduce Moorish blood into the family? An article in the Spanish newspaper *El País* entitled 'Beethoven's Spanish grandmother' states categorically that Beethoven's grandmother was either born south of the Pyrenees, or else was descended from a Spanish family who undertook the journey north during the War of the Spanish Succession.[2] As recently as 2021 the German musicologist Theo Molberg reported that the baptismal certificate of Beethoven's paternal grandmother had been discovered, showing that she was baptised on 13 February 1713 in Châtelet near Charleroi (then in the Netherlands, now in Belgium).[3]

Cäcilie Fischer describes Maria Magdalena as much loved and respected, but states that she had serious eyes, and Cäcilie had no recollection of her ever laughing. No wonder Maria Magdalena advised the young girl to stay single if she wanted a peaceful, beautiful and joyful life. What was marriage, Cäcilie recalled Maria Magdalena saying, but a little joy then afterwards a chain of sorrows?

Beethoven's friend from his youthful years in Bonn, Ferdinand Ries, says that in later life Beethoven always spoke of his mother with great love and affection. He rarely spoke of his father; when he did it was with harsh words.

Maria Magdalena is buried today in the main cemetery in Bonn, her headstone against a perimeter wall. On it are those words, *meine beste Freundin*. It is not known where Beethoven's father is buried.

Ehrenbreitstein is today designated as a suburb of Koblenz. It still has a natural beauty, nestled at the foot of a hill on the banks of the Rhine, gazed down on by the historic fortress.

The half-timbered house in which Maria Magdalena Keverich was born has been restored, and was opened as the 'Mutter Beethoven Haus' in 2001. There is information on the Keverich family, as well as Beethoven's circle of friends in Bonn, along with details of his life in Vienna. We learn little more about Maria Magdalena than we already knew.

The death of his mother was a blow to Ludwig in more ways than the obvious. His father Johann had lost the steadying hand of his wife. Who was there now to curb his drinking, or to berate him for returning home late at night and drunk, putting his job and income at risk?

The answer is that the onus would fall largely on the eldest son, and this would soon place an almost unbearable burden on Ludwig.

But, for the moment, as 1787 gave way to a new year, there was to be an extraordinary development in the life of Ludwig van Beethoven – one that would change the course of his life, and change it immeasurably for the better.

15

Waldstein. There is a name etched in musical history. Go to your recording of the complete Beethoven piano sonatas and you will find it a little past the halfway mark, Piano Sonata No. 21 in C, Op. 53 (*Waldstein*). What's in a name? In this case, plenty.

Count Ferdinand Ernst Joseph Gabriel Waldstein und Wartenberg von Dux. A name that, despite its grandeur, would be entirely lost to history had its owner not come into contact with a teenage boy in Bonn who was rapidly making his mark as pianist and composer.

Count Waldstein was a member of one of the most aristocratic families in Vienna, whose father had the ear of the emperor, no less. But his misfortune was to be the youngest son, and as such he struggled to find a role in the imperial capital. Taking a path well worn by those in a similar situation, he joined the Teutonic Order, a largely ceremonial body dating back to the Middle Ages.

No doubt to his, and his family's, surprise, he was summoned to Bonn to assist the prince-elector, Maximilian Franz, in his duties as Grand Master of the Teutonic Order. He arrived in this outpost of the Habsburg Empire in 1788 and felt immediately at home. Waldstein was passionate about the arts, particularly music, and was a dilettante pianist and composer himself. He was overjoyed to find that the prince-elector maintained an orchestra and chorus, and that there were regular performances. Naturally, it was not long before he heard about this amazing teenager who, it was said, was the best musician in Bonn.

Waldstein met Ludwig, now seventeen years of age, heard him play, heard him improvise, heard him perform his own compositions – and found his goal in life. He could see the difficult circumstances the Beethoven family were living under. They rented an apartment in the Wenzelgasse, further into

---

the town and away from the river than the Rheingasse. Maria Magdalena was newly interred in the cemetery on the outskirts of Bonn. The father employed a maid but could barely afford to pay her. His three sons were now aged seventeen, fourteen and twelve. Living conditions were somewhat chaotic. The eldest son Ludwig spent most of his time at the Breunings'; the younger two more or less looked after themselves, and Johann van Beethoven drank himself into oblivion most days.

Waldstein secretly gave the family money. Exactly how he did it we do not know. He probably disguised it as payments from the court channelled through Ludwig. One way or another Johann had achieved his ambition of using Ludwig's musical skills to enhance the family's income, though hardly in the way he had imagined. Franz Wegeler, in his memoir, describes Waldstein as 'Beethoven's first, and in every respect, most important, Maecenas'. It is probably not an exaggeration. Ludwig van Beethoven had found his first true patron.

It was at about this time that matters came to a head within the Beethoven family. Johann van Beethoven's behaviour was becoming ever more erratic. One evening he was so drunk he could no longer walk straight and was deemed a menace to others – 'drunk and disorderly' in today's parlance. The police had no alternative but to arrest him and take him into custody. At the police station they put him behind bars and notified his eldest son. Ludwig had to go the police station where, apparently, he entered into a furious row with the police, before obtaining his father's release.

Something had to be done. With Waldstein's help and support, Ludwig took the drastic step of petitioning the prince-elector to dismiss his father from court service and pay half his salary over to Ludwig himself. The prince-elector, no doubt having discussed the issue with Waldstein, went further. He not only agreed to Ludwig's request but ordered Johann to leave Bonn and live in a village in the country. In the event the banishment was not enforced. Johann remained confined to the house until his death.

In one sense this episode, which Ludwig would remember for the rest of his life, was a liberation. No more did he have to make excuses for his father. It was all out in the open. He could now concentrate on the one and only pursuit that mattered to him, his music.

Soon after coming to Bonn, Waldstein was made a Knight of the Teutonic Order by the prince-elector. He made plans to celebrate this in the most exotic, and traditional, way, with a procession through the town of knights and members, dressed in traditional German costume, followed by a musical performance accompanied by ballet scenes from German history.

Events, however, intervened. In Vienna on 20 February 1790, Emperor Joseph died at the age of just forty-nine. The Habsburg Empire went into mourning. This sad and unexpected news provided Ludwig with the most important musical opportunity of his young life. It was decided in Bonn that a local composer would be commissioned to compose two cantatas, one marking the death of the emperor, the other marking the accession of his successor.

There were several candidates, musicians in the court orchestra who had proved their worth as composers – all considerably older and more experienced than Ludwig. But his 'Maecenas' intervened once again. Using his influence at court, Waldstein secured the commission for nineteen-year-old Ludwig van Beethoven, who proceeded to produce his first compositions for full orchestra.

Unsurprisingly, the awarding of the prestigious commission to this young man, however talented he might be, caused a certain amount of resentment among more senior musicians. They bided their time, and then exacted revenge in the cruellest way. Members of the court orchestra – wind players in particular – declared the cantatas unplayable. The composer simply does not understand our instruments, they argued. Let him gain more experience before he attempts to write for full orchestra.

The orchestra won the day. The two cantatas were not only not performed as intended – on the day of the funeral and then on the day of the coronation. They were not performed in Beethoven's lifetime. He never heard his first orchestral compositions.

His next orchestral composition he most certainly did hear, and it is one of the most delightful – and rather bizarre – pieces of music he would ever compose.

With the period of mourning over, Waldstein resurrected his plan to celebrate his elevation to Knight of the Teutonic Order by combining it with a pageant to mark the beginning of the annual Carnival on Easter Sunday 1791. The procession would take place as planned. Then, at La Redoute palace on the outskirts of town, a 'ballet' would take place – in effect, members of the Teutonic Order, in medieval German dress, taking up characteristic poses illustrating the activities of their forebears – activities such as marching, hunting, drinking, romancing and giving battle.

Waldstein needed someone to write the music. There was no choice, obviously. But here is a remarkable thing; something that strikes us today as unthinkable but at the time was not that uncommon. Waldstein asked Ludwig if he would allow him to publish the music under his own name, in other words '*Ritterballet* ["Ballet of the Knights"] by Count Waldstein'. Ludwig, undoubtedly remunerated for his efforts, agreed.[1]

So here we have Ludwig van Beethoven, nineteen years of age, composer of two huge cantatas, a delightful small 'ballet', three piano sonatas, a piano concerto begun but not completed, several chamber works, and an unchallenged reputation as the most talented musician in Bonn – though not without the tensions and jealousies these achievements had caused.

Music was now Ludwig's life, and a necessary escape from living with a father who was killing himself through drink, and two younger brothers with whom he had nothing in common. And music was about to provide him with a physical escape too, a boat journey that would broaden his horizons both figuratively and literally.

∽

It is unlikely you will have the two Emperor cantatas in your Beethoven collection. You really should have though, not just because they are the first orchestral compositions by Beethoven – full chorus and soloists too – but because of how they point the way to the later Beethoven.

Listen to the *Cantata on the Death of the Emperor* and you will hear the seeds of the *Eroica* Symphony to come. In another passage the oboe soars above the orchestra exactly as it will in the dungeon scene in *Fidelio* many years later. No composer wastes a good idea, and Beethoven is no exception.

You definitely will not have the *Ritterballet* in your collection. It is a curiosity. There is a main melody, simple, short and sweet, that punctuates the scenes, clearly written to allow the knights to take up positions for each section. I find an overall sense of humour in the piece, imagining the young composer to be smiling as he writes it. Nothing serious, nothing heavy. This is music to accompany a spectacle, and Beethoven rises to it with energy and wit.

What of the man who commissioned it, his 'Maecenas', who did so much to advance Ludwig's career – and who, in eighteen months' time – would achieve for him the unthinkable, earning Beethoven's undying gratitude in the form of a dedication?

The bare facts of his life are known to history, and make sad and rather eccentric reading. He later left Bonn, and the Teutonic Order, and married a countess twenty-three years younger than himself in Vienna. He left her to join the British Army. Obsessed with the aim of defeating the French, he set about raising his own regiment in England, appointing himself colonel-in-chief. But he ran out of funds, was unable to pay his soldiers, and to avoid a mutiny the regiment was disbanded. Waldstein died in poverty, aged sixty-one.

Around thirty years ago, I was researching Beethoven's life in the Beethoven-Archiv, the building immediately adjacent to the birthplace in the Bonngasse, once occupied by Anna Gertrud Baum, Ludwig's godmother.

I found an obscure article, published in Austria in the nineteenth century, on the life of Count Waldstein. It was written in Gothic script and in opaque German, and with much thumbing of the dictionary I translated it – and gasped out loud at what I learned.

Waldstein's young wife was a wealthy woman. Waldstein used her money to raise his army. Then, when that project failed, he continued to work his way through her fortune until it was all spent. The distress this caused brought about his wife's early death at the age of thirty-three. To raise funds, Waldstein sold off his wife's family estates in Bohemia, but continued to live above his means, squandering whatever money he was able to raise.

He ended his days penniless in a home outside Vienna for aristocrats who had fallen on hard times. On the day of his death, a letter arrived for him from the family lawyer, advising him of his elder brother's death, and that he now inherited the full Waldstein title and the family's wealth.

In my impetuous and youthful excitement I failed to make a note of the source material for this additional information, and have been unable to find it since.

Of more importance to our story is that in or around 1804 Count Waldstein was reported to be in Vienna, in disguise to avoid his creditors. Word reached Beethoven, now living in Vienna, that Waldstein was in the city. He was at the time working on a new piano sonata, which he brought to fruition later that year. Hearing of the plight of the man who had done so much to forward his early career in Bonn, Beethoven decided to dedicate the sonata to Waldstein.

And so Count Waldstein, who led an ultimately tragic life and whose name would otherwise be forgotten to history, lives on, his name immortalised by the composer for whom he did so much.

At this point in our story, the greatest achievement he would accomplish for the young Beethoven still lies ahead. But, first, to that boat journey.

16

In late August 1791 a sizeable group of musicians gathered on the quayside in Bonn, ready to board two yachts – twenty-one members of the court orchestra plus seven singers from the choir. Near the bottom of the list was the name Beethoven. He would fulfil several musical roles – as viola player, organist, and also providing keyboard continuo.

The mood on the quayside was jovial. Maximilian Franz, prince-elector, in his capacity as Grand Master of the Teutonic Order, needed to make the journey south-east to Mergentheim, where he was due to preside over a meeting of fellow Knights. For his own, and his associates', enjoyment, he decided to take the court musicians with him. He and his retinue would make the journey by carriage, the musicians following at a more leisurely pace, by boat up the Rhein and Main, finally descending on the smaller River Tauber to Mergentheim. Sailing against the current on the mighty Rhine, their yachts would be drawn by horses.

The first task for the musicians was to elect a Great King of the Journey. This honour was accorded to the bass singer and actor, the highly popular Joseph Lux, who shared the viola desk with Ludwig. It then fell to King Lux to assign duties to various members of the group.

We owe one of the least-known facts about the man who would become (I believe) the greatest of all composers to his friend Franz Wegeler, who recounts it in his memoir. Ludwig van Beethoven, being at twenty years of age the youngest member of the group, was given the lowliest of duties, that of kitchen scullion. He must have performed rather well. The musicians had to leave the yachts at Rüdesheim to allow the boats to negotiate the narrow rapids at Bingen, where the river turns sharply east. They gathered in the thickly wooded hill, the Rüdesheim Heights, above the bend in the river.

There, with appropriate ceremony, King Lux announced that Ludwig van Beethoven, in recognition of his devotion to duty, was to be promoted through the kitchen ranks to a more senior position.[1] He was ceremoniously presented with a diploma, attached to which were several threads cut from the yacht's rigging, at the other end of which a large seal was attached to the lid of a small box, into which the document and its threads folded neatly. For years after, Beethoven treasured the memento and displayed it proudly in his Vienna lodgings.

The Rhine leg of the journey will have held particular fascination for Ludwig. You will remember Ludwig, as a child, gazing through the telescope in the attic of the Fischer house at the Drachenfels, a mere eight miles upriver. Now, for the first time, he was passing directly by it. Did he stand on deck, hands gripping the railing, eyes scanning the surface of the rock for the dark opening to the dragon's cave?

Soon after, they passed another giant rock steeped in legend, the Loreley. Did King Lux command silence so they could listen out for the irresistible siren song of the beautiful maiden who, spurned in love by a sailor, threw herself from the top of the rock into the Rhine, and now lures sailors to their deaths on the lethal rocks lying just below the surface, known as the *Sieben Jungfrauen* ('Seven Virgins')?

From the Rhine the party moved on to the less turbulent and not so legendary River Main. A stopover at Aschaffenburg led to a significant musical encounter for Ludwig. Several musical colleagues took Ludwig to the palace to meet the prince's house musician, a renowned piano virtuoso by the name of Abbé Sterkel.

The older man, well established in musical circles, was rather piqued to be introduced to a youth who, he was told, was unlike any pianist before him. For one thing Ludwig, short of stature, untidy and unkempt, looked nothing like a musician. It was therefore natural that Sterkel would accede to a request to show off his skills. He sat at the piano with a dismissive air, as if to say, 'I'll show you what playing the piano means.'

Ludwig's friends were surprised to see that the young composer leaned forward, watching every movement of Sterkel's hands, studying his style of playing, concentrating intensely. That style was totally unlike Ludwig's own method of playing. It was, in the words of one of those present, almost ladylike, very light and highly pleasing. Ludwig knew, they all knew, that his own style was very different – virtuosic, yes, but 'rough and hard' in Wegeler's words, lacking in finesse and revealing nothing of the finer nuances of the instrument.

Polite applause greeted Sterkel's performance, as he stood and offered the seat at the keyboard to Ludwig, who shook his head. Sterkel encouraged him, rather patronisingly. Ludwig still declined. Then Sterkel made a mistake. It was a mistake that finer pianists in Vienna would soon make, and they would learn the lesson Sterkel was about to learn. Ludwig had recently published a set of piano variations, which had reached Sterkel and astounded him with the virtuosity they demanded. He suggested Ludwig play them now. 'I have the music. I will find it for you.'

Sterkel looked through several piles of music on the piano, more on a table nearby, but could not find the variations. He apologised profusely to Ludwig, and then came the mistake. 'Perhaps the young man is a better composer than pianist, and even he cannot play the variations all the way through.'

It was a feature not only of Beethoven's youth, but of his entire career, that he would deflect criticism of his appearance: unshaven, hair a mess, ill-fitting and inappropriate clothes, his ill manners and rough language. But challenge his musical prowess and it was like red rag to a bull. Indeed, once his fame was firmly established in later years, it was not unknown for his talent at the keyboard to be mocked with the express aim of forcing a virtuoso performance from him.

And that was precisely what Abbé Sterkel now got. Ludwig pushed him out of the way, sat at the piano and played the variations entirely from memory. For good measure he added more variations, created on the spot, which were no less difficult. What struck his friends most, and no doubt riled Sterkel, was that Ludwig played exactly in the style of Sterkel, imitating his more delicate action. They assumed he was mocking Sterkel. There might well have been an element of that but, more importantly, Ludwig was absorbing what was to him a new style of playing. He was, in the process of demolishing Sterkel, becoming a better pianist himself.

When they reached Mergentheim, Ludwig was more relaxed and at peace with himself than at any time in his life. We know this from a certain individual by the name of Karl Ludwig Junker, who happened to come into a room where Ludwig was improvising on the piano. Far from stopping or ordering the man out, as he might have done in Bonn or later in Vienna, Ludwig not only continued to play but invited Junker to give him a theme to improvise on.

'I heard one of the greatest of pianists, the dear good Bethofen (*sic*) . . . he is exceedingly modest and free from all pretension . . . the members of this remarkable orchestra are, without exception, his admirers,' wrote Junker.[2] One can only gasp, and wonder if Junker was describing the same Beethoven as the one the world has come to know, or indeed the admiring orchestral players who had refused to play his Emperor cantatas!

A very different description of Beethoven – one we might more readily recognise – may also owe its origin to this trip. One of the singers was a soprano by the name of Magdalena Willmann, who was one year younger than Beethoven. Her father and sister, violinist and pianist in the court orchestra, were also part of the group. A few short years later, in Vienna, Beethoven would accompany Magdalena at recitals she gave in aristocratic salons in the city. He had clearly fallen in love with her, dating back to the Mergentheim trip, because he proposed marriage.

Thayer interviewed Magdalena's niece for his magisterial biography. He asked her why her aunt had turned down Beethoven's proposal of marriage. 'Because he was so ugly and half crazy,' she replied with a laugh. Ah now, that's the Beethoven the world knows.

All good things have to end, and Ludwig knew he was returning to a difficult family situation. Also musically he was becoming frustrated. What was there left for him to achieve in the small provincial backwater of Bonn? He had outgrown his home town, and the musical life within it. He needed broader horizons.

He could not know it, but salvation – in the most unexpected form – was at hand.

At the time the court musicians arrived in Mergentheim, it was a small provincial town sitting on the banks of the Tauber, notable only for its plain-walled palace, which served as the headquarters of the Teutonic Order.

Some thirty-five years later a shepherd stumbled by accident on underground springs that had bubbled up to the surface. The early nineteenth century was a time of rapid expansion of natural spas across central Europe, none more beneficial to the health than those of central and southern Germany.

On later analysis the waters of Mergentheim were found to contain the highest concentration in Europe of sodium sulphate, renowned for its curative effects on digestive disorders. In 1926 the town acquired the prefix 'Bad' (Bath) in recognition of this.

Bad Mergentheim remains best known for its natural spa waters. That does not mean it is oblivious to the visit in 1791 of an aspiring young musician who would go on to achieve everlasting fame. The town holds an annual Beethoven Festival and conducts musical walking tours through its streets. The headquarters of the Teutonic Order, where the Bonn musicians played, is today a museum to the Order, though it is fair to say – judging by the day Nula and I visited – that the natural spring waters are a greater draw than the museum.

17

In July 1792 Europe's most renowned composer arrived in Bonn on his way home to Vienna. Franz Joseph Haydn was exhilarated but tired, and there was a sadness about him that he was finding difficult to shake.

The exhilaration came from the knowledge that the tour of London he had just undertaken had been more than a success; it had been a triumph. He had performed with an orchestra two or three times a week at the Hanover Square Rooms, several times premiering new symphonies he had composed specially for the occasion. His works had been cheered and encored. He was the darling of the cultured English nobility. If he was not performing, he was likely to be guest of honour at a formal dinner. He was also earning serious money.

Haydn was now sixty years of age, hence the fatigue, which was exacerbated by the long journey. The sadness came from the fact that, while he was in London, word reached him that his musical colleague and great friend, Wolfgang Amadeus Mozart, had died. They had last met on the eve of Haydn's departure from Vienna. Given the arduous journey ahead, involving a sea crossing, the younger man had urged 'Papa' Haydn, as he called him, to take care and look after himself, intimating that it would be a tragedy if they were not to meet again. The tragedy had come about, but who could have suspected it would be the much younger of the two whose life would end?

Arriving in Bonn, Haydn was naturally feted by the court musicians and the prince-elector himself, who organised a performance of one of Haydn's oratorios in his honour. An elaborate dinner followed. Haydn had in fact ordered a quiet dinner in his hotel, which he had to apologise for missing. All he had really wanted was an early night.

At some point before he left Bonn for Vienna, Haydn met the twenty-one-year-old Ludwig van Beethoven, who had with him the score of his *Cantata on the Death of the Emperor*. Haydn, a kind and tolerant man, perhaps remembered the young friend whom he would not see again, and whose genius he recognised in every note. He had heard word of this young Beethoven, so agreed to look at the manuscript.

Haydn was stunned by what he saw. What he then said, to whom he said it, or how he said it, we do not know. But somehow or other he made a firm commitment: if Beethoven could make his way to Vienna, he would take the young composer on as a pupil.

If Count Waldstein was not actually in the room when Haydn made that commitment, he certainly heard about it very soon afterwards, possibly from Beethoven himself, corroborated by other musicians. He then made it his responsibility to ensure that somehow he would persuade the prince-elector to send Ludwig to Vienna to study with Haydn.

Events played into his hands. In October 1792 the French Revolutionary Army invaded German territory and marched towards the Rhine. On the 22nd they took Mainz and headed north. The towns and cities of the Lower Rhine were at their mercy. People in Bonn began to load their belongings onto carts and leave. It was decided that the prince-elector and his family should leave too and go into exile.

Waldstein seized the moment. Amid the chaos of evacuation, there were more pressing things on the prince-elector's mind than whether one of his musicians should be given leave of absence to go to Vienna and study with Haydn. We do not know what words passed between Waldstein and Max Franz. Probably the prince-elector dismissed Waldstein with a wave of the hand and a nod of the head. All we do know is Waldstein gave Ludwig the news he could scarcely have believed possible. He was going to Vienna.

At six o'clock on the morning of Friday, 2 November, Ludwig boarded a coach for the first leg of the journey to Vienna. He had a bag full of musical scores, some finished, some unfinished. He also had an autograph book signed by friends and colleagues wishing him good luck. There were not many; none from his father or brothers.

Count Waldstein had written, 'Dear Beethowen! [*sic*] You journey now to Vienna in fulfilment of your long-frustrated wishes. The genius of Mozart is still in mourning and she weeps for the death of her pupil. With the inexhaustible Haydn she has found refuge but no occupation. Through him she now wishes to be united with someone else. With persistent hard work you shall receive <u>Mozart's Spirit through Haydn's hands</u>.'[1]

It was the second time Beethoven's name had been mentioned alongside that of Mozart – first by Neefe, now by Waldstein. His words would reverberate down history, making Beethoven's dedication of the piano sonata to him all the more deserved.

The prince-elector had agreed to a leave of absence for Ludwig of six months, possibly a year. The carriage crossed the Rhine at Koblenz and passed through Ehrenbreitstein, where his mother was born. The carriage did not stop as he passed the waters he had grown up alongside, certain he would return not many months hence. He could not know it, but he would never see the Rhine, or Bonn, again.

Ludwig van Beethoven, composer, had come of age.

18

When I first visited Bonn more than thirty years ago, it was almost unthinkable that this was where Beethoven was born.

There was the birthplace, the house in the Bonngasse, with the Beethoven-Archiv next door, where the souvenir shop was a sparsely laden table under the staircase. There was the monumental statue in the Münsterplatz – but beyond that? Not much else.

Maybe it is understandable given that in 1949, to universal surprise, Bonn became the capital of West Germany, and stayed the capital until the fall of the Berlin Wall and the collapse of the Soviet Union. For more than four decades, Bonn had other things on its mind.

To say the city has now embraced its most famous son is an understatement. Road signs with directions to the main railway station, university, parking and so on, have at the top of the sign *Beethovenstadt Bonn* ('Beethoven City Bonn'). There are digital pillars, with interactive buttons, at points on the recommended *Beethovengang* ('Beethoven Walk'). Statues of Beethoven stand in shop windows – bakeries, hairdressers' salons, clothes shops, bookshops, cafés and more – ranging in size from two feet tall to life size. The tourist office has a larger-than-life-size papier-mâché statue of Beethoven enveloped in a bright blue cloak of musical notes. The hotel where Nula and I stayed in 2022, opened just the year before, has a permanent exhibition of Beethoven artefacts, facsimiles and a bust in the main lobby. The old town of Bonn is mainly a pedestrian area, with a cluster of street signs on practically every corner directing you to the Beethoven-Haus and other relevant locations.

Beethoven is, at last, everywhere in his home town.

19

Wien, du Stadt meiner Träume ('Vienna, City of My Dreams'). The title of the city's best-known song, its anthem, captures Vienna in a single sentence. Gaiety and laughter, the waltz and champagne. If only it were true. Actually, in many respects, it is the exact opposite of the truth.

Vienna was the first place I ever went abroad without my parents. Yes, in 1961, the time I fell asleep at the opera. Why I pestered my dad to let me go on that trip, I cannot remember. I knew only one thing about Vienna: it was the home of Johann Strauss II and the waltz. Not a particularly sound reason to obsess about a city. But an obsessed seventeen-year-old I was, and my dad probably decided it was easier to let me go than endure any more haranguing. I went, I fell in love with Vienna and I remain so to this day.

The sheer thrill of being there filled every pore of my body, even though there was a greyness about the city, alleviated occasionally by flashing neon signs, a testament to capitalist consumerism. The Cold War was at its height. Vienna was a frontier town. Gaze east, and not many miles away was Hungary: barbed wire, sentry boxes and grim-faced border guards with machine guns. An iron curtain had fallen across Europe and any predictions, including my own, that it would soon be lifted had proved unfounded.

As I walked the streets, shops seemed drab, people unsmiling, and yet all I could hear in my head was *The Blue Danube, Tales from the Vienna Woods, Vienna Blood*. Vienna to me was the Vienna of Strauss. I knew precious little about its history, and nothing about the dark currents underneath the unforgettable melodies. I was unaware of Austria's numerous defeats on the battlefield throughout the nineteenth century; the murder-suicide of the heir to the Habsburg throne at Mayerling; the death of his mother, Empress Sisi, at the hands of an anarchist on the banks of Lake Geneva; or the assassination of Archduke Ferdinand in Sarajevo, which led directly to the First World War and the end of the Habsburg monarchy. I did not know that the Viennese were waltzing to Strauss and drinking champagne as they headed towards the First World War and oblivion.

I grew up in the shadow of the Second World War. The books and comics I read at school all centred on this recent dreadful conflict. Germans were blockheads, *Dummkopfs* and Huns. We fought Germany. I was unaware of any Austrian participation. I actually went through school believing Hitler was German. It seems I was not alone. A German friend told me some years ago that Germans have a joke about Austrians: 'They're very clever. They've managed to convince the world that Hitler was German and Beethoven was Austrian.'

Vienna was the first place abroad that Beethoven, too, went without his parents, and it was a frontier town even then. In the Middle Ages the Ottoman Empire had twice sent an army across the Hungarian plain to besiege the city of Vienna. Although Habsburg forces had finally defeated the Turks and annexed Hungary, peace never truly reigned. To the people of eighteenth-century Vienna, the sight of Turkish troops kicking up dust as they neared the city was an ever-present image.

The experience left its mark on the Viennese, as they themselves wryly acknowledge. An old Viennese motto says, 'Matters are desperate, but not serious.' And a citizen of Vienna will tell you it is very difficult to read what a Viennese is thinking, because 'one half of the face is smiling, while the other half is serious'.

Life in a frontier town, whichever century you are living in, has its challenges. There will be spies, from both sides of the border. You do not cross certain barriers, literally or figuratively. Above all, words are dangerous. And when words are dangerous, what is safe? Music. That is why Vienna, from Mozart's time onwards, was the capital city of music, and has remained that way. But how did that come about?

The answer is war: the Thirty Years War, the Seven Years War, the War of the Spanish Succession, the War of the Austrian Succession. Seemingly endless conflict on the continent of Europe. War creates refugees. Vienna sits roughly at the crossroads of continental Europe. It was as if all roads led

to Vienna. Here is what a traveller wrote about Vienna just six years before
Beethoven arrived there for the second, and definitive, time:

> [The streets of Vienna teem with] Hungarians in their close-fitting
> trousers, Poles with their flowing sleeves, Armenians and Moldavians
> with their half-Oriental costumes, Serbians with their twisted mous-
> taches, Greeks smoking their long-stemmed pipes in the coffee-houses,
> bearded Muslims with broad knives in their belts, Polish Jews with
> their faces bearded and their hair twisted in knots, Bohemian peas-
> ants in their long coats, Hungarian and Transylvanian waggoners with
> sheepskin greatcoats, Croats with black tubs balanced on their heads.

With them they brought their music – and they played it, because music was
safe. And so, the same traveller wrote,

> One cannot enter any fashionable house without hearing a duet, or
> trio, or finale from one of the Italian operas currently the rage being
> sung and played at the keyboard. Even shopkeepers and cellar-hands
> whistle the popular arias . . . No place of refreshment, from the high-
> est to the lowest, is without music. Bassoonists and clarinettists are as
> plentiful as blackberries, and in the suburbs at every turn one alights
> upon fresh carousing, fresh fiddling, fresh illuminations.[1]

In other words, from the highest echelons of society – even members of the
emperor's own family were accomplished musicians – to the humblest, music
was in the air. Little has changed in two centuries. Any visitor to Vienna
today will be familiar with young men and women – music students, mostly
– dressed in wigs and costumes, handing out flyers for that night's concerts.
Dinner in a *heuriger* tavern is likely to be accompanied by Schrammel music,[2]
strictly speaking with violins and double-necked guitar, but more often than
not with accordion and Austria's national instrument, the zither.

The Vienna where Ludwig van Beethoven, aged twenty-one years and
eleven months, arrived in November 1792 was thus a city full of music, but
it was also a city over which there hung a fog of fear, where you dared not
express political views openly – not in a café, nor on a street corner, and most

definitely not in the back seat of a horse-drawn fiacre, where drivers had their ears permanently cocked, and where anything seditious that might pass your lips would be on the desk of the interior minister the next morning.[3]

Why such an atmosphere of fear? Why were words so dangerous? Because three years previously on the continent of Europe an event so seismic, so cataclysmic, had occurred that it would change the course of history. In Paris the Bastille was stormed and the French Revolution had begun. In the same month that Beethoven arrived in Vienna, Louis XVI was arrested and in January he mounted the steps of the guillotine. Nine months later his Queen, Marie Antoinette, despised by the French as the 'Austrian whore', christened Maria Antonia, youngest daughter of the mother of the Austrian nation, Empress Maria Theresia, followed her husband to the scaffold.

The unthinkable had happened. Which was now the longest-ruling royal dynasty in continental Europe? The Habsburgs, and their seat of power was in the Hofburg Palace in Vienna. Would the ideals of the French Revolution spread? If so, the obvious next target was the House of Habsburg.

In France the reign of the Bourbons was about to be replaced by the Reign of Terror. Thousands were sent to the guillotine in an attempt to obliterate an entire class – the ruling class, the aristocracy, the nobility. No other capital on the European continent had an aristocratic class comparable to that of Vienna, where there was an abundance of princes and dukes, and where it seemed practically everybody but the poorest was a count or countess.

Another revolution was also under way in Europe: a revolution of ideas. History would call it the Enlightenment. If a monarch could be deposed, what did that say about the divine right of kings? If a king could be dispensed with, it meant he was nothing more than a mere mortal. And if there was no divine right invested in a monarch, what did that say for the authority of the Church? For the first time the rule of the monarch and the authority of the Church were being challenged.

All this fed easily into the mind of a young man who had formed his political ideals in the intimacy of a music room with a teacher who as well as being a fine musician was also a radical thinker. Vienna, capital city of music, centre of new ideas, the city in and around which Beethoven would now spend his entire adult life, was ideally suited for him to develop his genius.

20

Beethoven would recognise today's Vienna. If he were suddenly to materialise in the Kärntnerstrasse or Graben or Kohlmarkt, he would know exactly where he was and which turning to take to get to his destination, which might be the *Alten Blumenstock* or the *Schwarzen Kameel* or the *Schwan* inn. He'd be able to eat and drink in the first two, but would be rather surprised to find that the *Schwan* inn in the Neuer Markt is now a bookshop.

In the Neuer Markt itself, though, I imagine him patting the naked rump of the bronze bearded figure forming part of the central fountain, which the sculptor positioned precisely so that the man's bottom was amply displayed in front of the window of a patron who had reneged on his promises.[1] A few steps from the fountain – and the patron's home – is where a concert venue once stood, where both Mozart and Beethoven performed. They knew it by the name that defined its historical use, the *Mehlgrube* ('Flour Pit'). I will allow Beethoven a shake of the head and perhaps a grimace to see that it is today a five-star luxury hotel called the Ambassador.

I have on my wall a map of Vienna published in 1827, the year of Beethoven's death. Just as Beethoven would be able to find his way around today's Vienna, so we too can easily navigate this 200-year-old map. The inner city of Vienna has changed less over the centuries, I would hazard, than any other European capital. For this we have the Ottoman Empire, the Turkish Army and those two sieges to thank.

From the early Middle Ages the city of Vienna was a prize coveted by the Ottoman Empire. An emperor from the Habsburg family had first been elected to rule in Vienna in the thirteenth century, with the primary duty of defending the Roman Catholic faith. Successive emperors were crowned by the Pope in Rome, hence becoming Holy Roman Emperor of the Holy Roman Empire, ruling over vast territories of central Europe from the empire's capital, Vienna. To the Ottoman Turks, therefore, Vienna represented the centre of Christianity in Europe. Conquer Vienna and not only would conversion to Islam follow, but the Crusades of previous centuries would be reversed and avenged.

The first Ottoman ruler to attempt this was the impressively named Suleiman the Magnificent, who in 1529 led an army of over 100,000 soldiers north-west across the Hungarian plain and laid siege to the city. But it had been a long march in unseasonably wet weather. Heavy weaponry – cannon and artillery pieces – had to be abandoned in thick mud. Many soldiers were weak and in poor health, and the number of accompanying camels had been severely depleted. Food and water were in increasingly short supply.

Defending the city were civilians, farmers and peasants, reinforced by professional soldiers and mercenaries who hurried to their aid. Defensive walls were easily breached, but the defenders held the invaders off. Suleiman ordered a final all-out assault but it was beaten back. With winter approaching, sickness now rife in the ranks and supplies all but exhausted, Suleiman called off the siege and ordered a humiliating retreat.

Vienna had been saved, but there was general agreement that something had to be done to guard against any future attack. The flimsy and damaged medieval walls were pulled down and replaced by a high, dense, impenetrable city wall, with eleven fortified bastions jutting out from it. At ground level were gates, manned by sentries, providing the only access in and out of the city. Outside the wall and surrounding it was a wide expanse of grass, known as the Glacis, sloping away from the wall, giving defenders a spacious vantage point from which to repel any attack.

And a second attack, another attempt by an Ottoman Army to take Vienna, was exactly what happened a century and a half later, when Mustafa Pasha the Courageous led a force of around 200,000 men and many camels across the Hungarian plain and right up to the gates of Vienna. This time the situation was far more perilous. Mustafa Pasha had fortified his supply lines, heavy artillery had been sent on in advance so that it was already in place, and for the previous four years the strength of the people of Vienna had been depleted by fighting a different enemy – the plague.

Mustafa Pasha set up camp on the Glacis and prepared to starve the Viennese into submission. The city wall was now seen to serve a perilous double purpose. It kept the enemy out, as it was intended to, but it also kept the populace in. Mustafa Pasha had only to wait. For good measure his sappers dug beneath the wall to plant explosives – breaches in the wall would help a final assault.

Matters were certainly desperate; they might even be serious. Enter a colourful individual by the name of Georg Franz Kolschitzky, a Polish-born resident of Vienna, who had lived and worked in Istanbul. As a result, he spoke fluent and idiomatic Turkish and was familiar with the streets, cafés and restaurants of Istanbul. He persuaded the mayor of Vienna to allow him to get out through the city wall under cover of darkness, infiltrate the Ottoman camp, engage senior officers in conversation, establish the number of enemy forces and evaluate their equipment – and then, if he succeeded in gaining their confidence, persuade them he was a double agent, giving them false information about conditions inside the city wall. If he could convince them the Viennese were on their knees, it might forestall a full-scale invasion. In the meantime, he would make his escape through the camp and out along the Danube, where he would send word about the urgent need for military action to relieve the siege.

The plan was fraught with risk. Several previous attempts to send word out through the Ottoman camp to allies had resulted in a head on a pike at daylight. But none had the credentials Kolschitzky could boast. It was certainly worth a try.

And it succeeded. Kolschitzky, able to speak to the Turks in their own language, established that Mustafa Pasha was planning a final decisive assault – it was just a matter of when. He was able to get through the Turkish camp and join a small relief force stationed several miles west on the banks of the Danube. Told that the Polish king, Jan Sobieski, was marching south with a large army, he sent word of the grim state of affairs within the walls of Vienna. He was also able to give the king precise details of the Turkish Army and its plans for a final assault. Above all, he urged the king not to waste a moment.

Battle finally commenced on 12 September 1683, when the Polish king led his forces in a charge down the Kahlenberg Hill, the easternmost point of the Vienna Woods. Ditches with wooden spikes failed to deter the Polish Army. A fierce but short battle ensued. The Ottomans were overwhelmed and routed. When the dust cleared, it was found that the Turks had abandoned the battlefield. They had fled, leaving their tents and equipment behind on the Glacis. The siege, which had lasted for two months, was lifted. Tension and intermittent warfare between Habsburgs and Ottomans, which had endured for three hundred years, was finally ended. The Ottoman Empire never again marched to Vienna.[2]

Legend has it that Georg Franz Kolschitzky, in recognition of his heroic endeavour, was told to name his reward. He asked only for the contents of the sacks the Ottomans had left behind in their tents. 'Camel feed?' asked the incredulous mayor. 'Why would you want that?' But Kolschitzky, familiar with Turkish habits, knew what the small round beans were. With them he opened the first coffee house in Vienna and served up Turkish coffee. His clients hated it. Someone suggested adding cream. It still did not go down well. 'Why don't you whip the cream?' someone else suggested. And so *Schlagsahnekaffee* (coffee with whipped cream) was born, and Vienna began its rule, which continues to this day, as café capital of Europe.[3]

Beethoven, with his predilection for strong coffee – according to Schindler's biography he drank it every morning, counting out exactly sixty coffee beans – is certain to have been familiar with the heroic endeavour of Georg Franz Kolschitzky. And the inner city, surrounded by the impregnable wall and its bastions, with entrances and exits under armed guard in daylight and shut at night, is the Vienna Beethoven knew.

So what is the relevance, topographically, of the Turkish sieges to the city of Vienna today? Simply that, in the mid-nineteenth century, such was the growth of Vienna and its population that the huge city wall, which successfully kept the Ottoman Army out even if it trapped the citizens inside, was deemed too unwieldy and immovable to remain. And so the decision was made to pull it down. It took more than a decade to demolish the structure.

In its place a wide boulevard was created, surrounding the city, the Ringstrasse, which was opened with much ceremony by the emperor on 1 May 1865. Today this broad avenue is the site of many government buildings, including the Town Hall and Parliament. It is, in effect, a ring road, carrying buses, trams, coaches, cars, taxis and ever more bicycles and e-scooters – every mode of transport of a modern cosmopolitan city. I wonder how many travellers know they are moving along the site where once the city wall stood as a bastion against the Ottoman Army.

Beethoven, of course, knew the wall, not the Ringstrasse. Certain other locations he knew well still exist today, though not entirely as he knew them. St Stephansdom – St Stephen's Cathedral – had already stood in one form or another for several centuries. He would no doubt gasp in wonder at the steeply sided, decorative-glazed-tile roof with its double-headed eagles and city coats of arms, installed after a great fire destroyed the original at the end of the Second World War.

I imagine him today, heading with purposeful tread down the Kärntnerstrasse before turning left into the Himmelpfortgasse for refreshment in the Café Jahn. Here he, and Mozart before him, performed new chamber works in the small recital room upstairs. He is surprised to see it is no longer named after its owner, Ignaz Jahn, personal chef to Empress Maria Theresia, but gratified to see a plaque on the wall outside commemorating the fact that he, and his illustrious predecessor, performed in what is today known as the Café Frauenhuber – the oldest continuously working coffee-house in Vienna.

Fortified with a glass of red wine, Beethoven continues down the Kärntnerstrasse towards the Ringstrasse and a building he is most familiar with. But he will not find the Kärntnertor Theatre, where his opera *Fidelio* was premiered and where his Ninth Symphony, the *Choral*, was heard for the first time. On the site today stands one of the most prestigious hotels in Vienna, the Sacher. He could certainly pop in for a *Schlagsahnekaffee* and a *Sachertorte*, but would no doubt bemoan the fact that the famous chocolate cake was created in 1832, just five years too late for him.

Across the narrow street, and standing grandiloquently on the Ringstrasse – in fact it was the first major building to be constructed on the Ringstrasse – is the Vienna State Opera. Beethoven stares at it wistfully, wishing it had existed in his day. The Viennese were less admiring when the building was opened in 1869, and when the emperor himself expressed displeasure, it was too much for the architect, who took his own life.

We shall spare him that detail but urge him to cross the Ringstrasse and keep going straight for just a few hundred yards, where he will find a building that will make him gasp out loud.

'But where is the Wienfluss?' he asks.

Ah, now this will take some explaining. There is a small river, the River Wien, which rises in the Vienna Woods, flows round the inner city of Vienna (for which it is named) and out into the Danube Canal. Where it flows directly through the city, it is today underground. Above it, as it approaches the Ringstrasse, is Vienna's largest open-air market, the Naschmarkt. With more than a hundred stands selling fruit and vegetables, restaurants ranging from Viennese to Vietnamese, Indian to Italian, it is today a magnet for tourists and a fashionable place for the Viennese to meet.

Different, certainly, from in Beethoven's day, but maybe not too surprising for him. My 1827 map of Vienna shows the Wien, in blue, circling the inner city and there, off to the side, is clearly marked *Obstmarkt* (fruit market). So there was a market here two centuries ago, just as there is today. Beethoven will have undoubtedly bought provisions here, because in the years 1803 and 1804 he lived in a building just across the street, which still stands today. That is the building that causes him to gasp.

The Theater an der Wien, named for the river it stands alongside, played a greater and more important role in Beethoven's life than any other theatre in the city. It was built and owned by an eccentric musician and entrepreneur by the name of Emanuel Schikaneder, whose name is preserved in musical history for having written the libretto for Mozart's opera *The Magic Flute*, singing the role of Papageno at its premiere. The ornate entrance, the 'Papageno Gate', has a statue above it of Schikaneder as a cherub playing his flute, with cherubs each side of him.

Schikaneder opened the Theater an der Wien in 1801. For fifteen months in 1803–4, Beethoven was composer in residence and given a small apartment in the building. The contract was terminated when he failed to produce the opera he was contracted to compose.

Beethoven had a natural preference for the Theater an der Wien over other theatres for the fact that it was privately owned – therefore not state run – and that it stood outside the city wall. It was, in essence, the people's theatre. It was to the Theater an der Wien, free from the formalities of the state theatres, that the ordinary non-aristocratic citizens of Vienna would go for an evening's entertainment and enjoyment. No need to dress up, no need to bow in acknowledgement of those on a higher social rung than you.

It was here that Beethoven premiered his opera *Leonore*, and it was here that he held the single most important concert of his life. On 22 December 1808 he premiered his Fifth and Sixth Symphonies, as well as the Fourth Piano Concerto. Important beyond words, although not entirely successful. With other pieces the whole concert lasted for four hours on a freezing night. The heating system in the theatre had broken down, and the final piece, the *Choral Fantasia*, went off the rails.

Standing looking at that ornate and historic entrance today, he can see that it has not changed in more than two centuries. There, above the doors, is a cherubic Schikaneder playing his flute, amid his companions. Beethoven is however surprised to see that the original entrance is permanently closed. A new entrance on the main road bordering the Naschmarkt is where today's audiences come and go. One other element has not changed. For the most part, musicals and comedies are staged here. There is an informality about the Theater an der Wien now, just as there was two centuries ago.[4]

Informality is not a word to be used about another theatre that Beethoven knew well, the Burgtheater. This was, and is, Vienna's – and Austria's – national theatre, and it is where Beethoven gave his first public performance in Vienna. But the grandiloquent pillared building that stands today on the Ringstrasse is not the Burgtheater Beethoven knew. This building is a relative newcomer, having opened in 1888.

The Burgtheater that launched the career of the young man from Bonn stood alongside the Hofburg Palace, home of the emperor. This fact alone gave it a status unequalled by any other theatre. Here was formality, where rank and status were observed, a place to be seen, a theatre to which the lowly citizens of Vienna would not aspire – it was the Theater an der Wien for them.

Some years after Beethoven's death, as the wall came down and the city expanded, the old theatre was demolished. In its place an extension to the Hofburg Palace was built. The site of the old Burgtheater remains to this day a part of the Hofburg. Beethoven would recognise the Spanish Riding School on the other side of the Hofburg, which was already more than sixty years old when he arrived in Vienna. But nothing remains of the Burgtheater he knew, and which played such an important role in his early career.

He might be grateful for that, given what a traumatic debut he made there.

21

The Ludwig van Beethoven who stood in the wings waiting to walk out onto the most prestigious stage in Vienna on 29 March 1795 was a very different young man from the one who had arrived in the city only two years and four months earlier. Much had happened and much had changed.

In fact he had been lucky to arrive in one piece. If he had left Bonn a day later, he would have had to turn back. The French Revolutionary Army was marching through the Rhineland. The coach carrying Beethoven and his fellow travellers had to pass through Limburg and Weilburg, but the driver was informed, before crossing the Rhine, that the French were on the move and approaching Weilburg. Facing them was a small force of soldiers from the state of Hesse.

The decision was made to drive on, keeping as close to the Hessian soldiers as possible. To encourage the driver, the passengers reached into their pockets. 'The fellow drove us at the risk of a cudgelling right through the Hessian army going like the devil,' Beethoven wrote later. He was not exaggerating. On that same day the French Army took Weilburg. The career – indeed the life – of Ludwig van Beethoven could have ended on 5 November 1792, just short of his twenty-second birthday. He gives us no further details of the danger, but he does tell us how much he tipped the driver. 'Tip . . . one small Thaler.' We do not know how many passengers there were, but we can surmise that the driver, risking all the lives on board as well as his own, did not grow rich on the experience.

To say that Beethoven had a gilded start in the imperial capital might be an exaggeration, but only a small one. He had in his back pocket a letter of introduction to one of the wealthiest patrons of the arts in Vienna, Prince Karl Lichnowsky, conveniently a relative, albeit distant, of Beethoven's great

Bonn patron, Count Waldstein. Lichnowsky had known, and supported, Mozart, and was to become Beethoven's greatest Viennese advocate, both financially and musically, until a terminal falling out, but that lies some years ahead.

First things first. Rather as a university student might do arriving in a new city at the start of the first term, the young musician needed to equip himself with essentials. Showing an orderliness that would dissipate in later years, he made a list: overcoat, boots, shoes, laundry. And later: rent, food with wine, coffee, heating and lighting. Not just food, but food with wine! 'Piano desk', he notes down twice, and also the address of a dancing master. Being able to dance was an essential social attribute in Vienna – though he reportedly was not good at it and never pursued it, despite composing a number of dances at Haydn's instigation to be played at aristocratic balls.

Initially Lichnowsky gave Beethoven rooms in his palace, where the young man from Bonn had his first taste of Viennese formalities, such as meals at an exact time, with the diners always in formal attire. As soon as he could, Beethoven moved out to his own lodgings.

Lichnowsky maintained his own quartet of young string-players, and held a matinée of musical performance most Fridays, as well as regular soirées. It was at these recitals that Beethoven first showed his prowess at the keyboard, and word quickly spread. His most impressive talent was improvisation. Give him a tune, any tune, and he would take it, unpick it, put it back together, weave around it ever more impressively, with the original theme always discernible underneath. It was not long before the music-loving aristocrats of Vienna were competing with each other to set this young man challenges, and marvel at his handling of them.

But – and there is so often a 'but' in chronicling Beethoven's life – at the same time as acquiring a reputation for unrivalled musicality, he was attracting less adulatory notices as well. Lessons had begun with Joseph Haydn very soon after he had arrived in Vienna – that, after all, had been the reason for the move to the capital. Haydn, in his sixties now, venerated as the elder statesman of music in the city, had not found his young pupil easy to teach. From the start Beethoven was determined to forge his own path. He might turn up for a lesson; he might not. If Haydn pointed out errors in a counterpoint exercise, rather than accept the rebuke Beethoven would argue his case. Relations would soon become very strained indeed.

There was another musician whose name was much venerated in Vienna: Antonio Salieri, court composer and Kapellmeister, and therefore the most senior musician in the city. Soon after arriving in Vienna, Beethoven took lessons in vocal composition from Salieri, who was regarded as the finest living composer of opera, and who enjoyed giving free lessons to talented young musicians and singers. On one occasion he criticised a particular melody Beethoven had composed, saying it was not suited to the voice. However, the next day he told Beethoven he could not get the melody out of his head. 'Then it can't have been that bad after all,' Beethoven replied, no doubt with undisguised arrogance in his voice. Word quickly spread among the musical community. 'Have you heard what the young German had the cheek to say to Maestro Salieri?'

Beethoven was now composing at a rate unheard of in this city of musicians. Several rondos for piano, a number of trios for different combinations of instruments, a set of three piano trios, numerous songs and, most important of all, two piano concertos.

Most important, but not quite as straightforward as it sounds. The piano concerto Beethoven began composing back in Bonn had been abandoned, but he had begun work almost immediately on a new one. He had largely completed it before leaving Bonn – I imagine him clutching the precious manuscript close to his chest on that perilous journey to Vienna – but had revised it substantially over the next year or two, finally completing it in early 1795.

Well, not exactly. Beethoven was about to get himself mired in problems – most of them of his own making – as the most important day of his young life drew near. The dates of the annual concert for the Musicians' Widows Society were announced for 29 and 30 March 1795. Who was in charge of these concerts, determining the programme and engaging soloists? None other than Antonio Salieri. And Signor Salieri, putting musical talent before any reservations he might have in other areas, offered Beethoven the opportunity to perform his new piano concerto with full orchestra in front of a discerning audience in the prestigious Burgtheater.

It was a golden opportunity for Beethoven to establish his reputation once and for all. A successful performance in this, the most illustrious theatre in Vienna, would launch his career, giving him instantly a status it might otherwise take years to attain. As long as everything went smoothly.

There were, of course, problems. The most serious of these was that Beethoven had not actually finished composing the concerto. He was unhappy with the final movement, and kept revising it, right into the afternoon of 27 March, handing pages of manuscript to a team of four copyists. The tension in the room must have been excruciating: Beethoven composing in his notoriously haphazard manner, scribbling down notes, crossings out, rewriting, smudges, giving the copyists the almost impossible task of trying to decipher his writing.

You can imagine the effect all this had on the orchestral players. Beethoven already had a reputation for writing difficult music – musicians in Bonn had surely warned colleagues in Vienna that some of it was unplayable – and to think it was not even ready yet! Orchestral players today would be just as anxious, even uncooperative, under such circumstances.

There was worse to come. When soloist and orchestra finally gathered in the rehearsal room on 28 March, the day before the concert, the piano was found to be a semitone flat. Without thinking and at sight, Beethoven immediately transposed the solo part up. Anyone with even a rudimentary knowledge of musical theory will know how difficult that is.

Beethoven had another issue to contend with, something rather more personal, and we owe our knowledge of it to his old friend from Bonn Franz Wegeler, now Dr Wegeler, who happened to be in Vienna. For some days past Beethoven had been suffering from severe diarrhoea. 'I relieved him with simple remedies as far as I could,' writes Wegeler in his memoir. 'As far as I could' suggests it was not entirely successful. He does not elaborate, other than to say this was a condition that frequently afflicted Beethoven.

Thus the Beethoven who was about to give his first public performance in the capital city of music in front of a knowledgeable and discerning audience had completed the concerto he was about to play only two days earlier, had had just a single day's rehearsal with orchestra, during which he had to transpose his part up, had managed to upset all the players with his haphazard approach to the whole event and, to cap it all, was struggling to control a severe bout of diarrhoea. Given his reputation for bluntness bordering on vulgarity in his dealings with others more distinguished than himself, and despite his acknowledged musicianship, there are likely to have been some both on the stage and in the audience rather hoping that he might be about to get his comeuppance.

Frustratingly, I can find no contemporary account of how the concert went. But we can glean that it must have been a success, since the second performance took place, as planned, the following night, and on this occasion Beethoven improvised on the piano, as well as performing the concerto. On the night after that, 31 March, following the first act of a performance of Mozart's final opera *La clemenza di Tito*, arranged by his widow Constanze, Beethoven, in a moving tribute to the man he so admired, performed Mozart's Piano Concerto No. 20 in D minor, a particular favourite of his.

As if to set the seal on Beethoven's acceptance into the highest musical circles in Vienna in this his twenty-fifth year, his erstwhile teacher Joseph Haydn booked the young man to perform at a concert he was organising later in the year. At this concert, again in the Burgtheater, Beethoven would perform an entirely new piano concerto. It says much about the kindly character of the older man that he gave this opportunity to Beethoven despite their difficult relationship, which had culminated in the two exchanging words over the merit of Beethoven's newly completed set of three piano trios, to which he had given the opus number 1.

Haydn had the temerity to criticise the third of the set, which sent Beethoven into a rage. The rift was not long lasting. His very next composition, a set of three piano sonatas, he dedicated to Haydn. But one long-standing request of Haydn remained unfulfilled. Recognising the genius of his young pupil, Haydn asked him to put on the top of a new composition, any composition, 'by Ludwig van Beethoven, pupil of Haydn'. Beethoven never did.

22

What is the worst fate that can befall a musician? Beethoven tells us: 'I was deficient in the one sense that should have been more highly developed in me than anyone.'

Some years ago I was in a taxi on my way to give a talk on Beethoven in Inverness. 'Who are you giving a talk about tonight, then?' the driver asked me. I took a deep breath and answered in a fairly general way so as not to sound too academic. 'It's just about classical music. Very boring.' Realising that sounded pretty patronising, I added, 'Beethoven, I'm giving a talk about Beethoven.' 'Oh aye oh aye,' and he went quiet for a moment. A second or two later, sitting behind him, it was as if I saw a lightbulb go on in his head. 'Beethoven! I know him. He's the one who cut his ear off.'

He was on the right track. Beethoven went deaf. It is the one non-musical fact that (practically) everyone knows. I knew it too, long before I knew any music beyond *Für Elise* and the opening bars of the Fifth Symphony. But I always assumed – if ever I thought about it – that it must have happened overnight. That is how it happened in my family. My maternal grandmother went to bed at the age of twenty-nine with normal hearing. She spent a restless night with ringing in one ear. The next morning she was stone deaf in her right ear. That was the story my brothers and I grew up with, and we knew, as children, always to speak into Nana's left ear, and sit on her left at meals. The hearing in her right ear never returned.

When I first started researching Beethoven's life, I decided to try to learn about deafness, and the effect it has on a person's life. I did some work for a deaf charity and spoke to many deaf people. The first fact I was told that shocked me is that deafness is the one disability that every single person will experience to some degree as they become older. Deafness is a natural part of the ageing process. Writing this now, one month before entering my eightieth year, I can confirm it is true, although not always as you might expect. I am not losing my hearing. In general conversation I can hear every word that is said. What I am slowly losing, though, is the ability to process those words at the same speed at which they are being spoken. 'Sorry, could you just say that again?' or (particularly to the grandchildren), 'Could you speak a little more slowly?' If there is a slight and welcome pause after a question, I can quickly rerun the words in my head and get their meaning.

This, to put it at its most basic, is how Beethoven lost his hearing – slowly, gradually. The difference is that it began to happen to him in his mid- to late twenties.

I learned more from my deaf friends. Deafness is a disability that others cannot see. With advances in technology, modern hearing aids are tiny and easily hidden. They can now be controlled from an app on your mobile phone. There are no visual clues to tell you a person is deaf. When deafness first begins to take hold, there is often a natural tendency to try to hide it. Someone who thinks they are beginning to lose their hearing may well concentrate harder, possibly furrowing their brow. They might switch their gaze from the eyes to the lips of the person they are talking to – just for a second or two to begin with, then perhaps for longer. If the deafness worsens, there will eventually come a point when disguising it is no longer possible. Not so difficult for someone in their seventies or eighties, even sixties, to admit. But twenties? There is, inevitably, an element of embarrassment involved, simply because this should not be happening at such a young age.

We can easily imagine Beethoven, in his twenties, sitting with fellow exiles from Bonn who had come to Vienna to escape the French occupation of the Rhineland and their home town, sitting round a table at the back of the *Schwan* Inn, glasses of wine and beer regularly replenished, conversation becoming ever more animated, unstructured, interjections, words increasingly slurred, laughter – and Beethoven falling silent as he struggles to follow the fast-flowing and unruly words.

He might well have tried to hide it, disguise it, compensate for it, for as long as he could. But his close circle – his two brothers who had followed him to Vienna after their father's death in December 1792, and a small number of musical colleagues – would have noticed it long before he realised. Perhaps they discussed it among themselves. 'Should we tell him we've noticed something?' 'Should we ask him if everything is all right?' Most likely they decided it would be best to wait for him to say something himself.

Matters came to a head in the early part of 1802, a year that marked a turning point in Beethoven's life. Musically his reputation in Vienna was unequalled. Two piano concertos completed, published and also performed at the Burgtheater, a set of six string quartets, several new piano sonatas, violin sonatas, other chamber works and – most important of all – a first symphony published and a second nearing completion.

Beethoven's fame had spread. Not only a virtuoso pianist unlike any this city of virtuosos had seen – better than Mozart! – but a composer of extraordinarily complex works, and so difficult to play.

But – there is that 'but' again – he has noticed a problem with his hearing. A musician having trouble with his hearing. How can that be? What does it mean for his future? Could his career be over so soon after it had started? So many questions. And the biggest of them all: what caused Beethoven's deafness?

23

Some years ago I was invited to give a talk about Beethoven's health to the Medical Society of London. When I mentioned, almost in passing, that the post-mortem on Beethoven was carried out on his deathbed, there was an audible gasp in the room. Several doctors explained to me afterwards that a post-mortem is a messy affair, and they found it extraordinary that the procedure was carried out on his own bed in his apartment.

There is no recorded explanation for this. It is a fact that crowds began to gather outside the gates of the large apartment block – formerly a monastery – in which Beethoven died, and were already lining the streets in their thousands for the funeral procession, which had been announced for 29 March, three days after his death. To transfer Beethoven's corpse intact to Vienna General Hospital would have been difficult, nigh on impossible. When the coffin was brought down into the courtyard on the 29th, the crowd surged to the gates in such numbers that they had to be restrained by soldiers. And so the pathologist, Dr Johann Wagner, and his small team got to work in the privacy and calm, albeit primitive, conditions of Beethoven's apartment.

The question we still ask today exercised the minds of Beethoven's contemporaries too. What caused his deafness? We can set a date for when it began, but only a rough one. The first indication that he is experiencing any kind of problem comes on 29 June 1801, when he writes a long letter to his old friend Franz Wegeler back in Bonn. Wegeler is now a qualified doctor. No surprise that the first time Beethoven describes the problem, it is to a qualified doctor who lives several hundred miles away, distant from wagging tongues. The letter is warm and affectionate. He apologises for not writing before, and promises to write separately to Lorchen – Eleonore von Breuning, his first teenage love – who is now married to Wegeler. He asks Wegeler to remember him to all his friends in Bonn and assure them he has not forgotten a single one of them.

At the heart of the letter is an outpouring about his health. His career is going well; he is composing at a furious rate – 'as soon as I finish one piece I begin work on another' – but 'my wretched health has put a nasty spoke in my wheel'. He writes, 'For the last three years my hearing has become weaker and weaker.' He describes how he can no longer hear high notes produced by an orchestra, and in the theatre has to sit right up against the stage to hear what actors are saying. He has stopped attending social functions altogether, since in the buzz of conversation he cannot hear what someone is saying, and if he asks them to speak up it hurts his ears.

He begs Wegeler to tell no one, not even Lorchen. 'If my enemies, of whom I have a fair number, were to hear about it, what would they say?' He has been to see several doctors. One recommended cold baths, another prescribed 'tepid baths in the Danube'. Both remedies – despite the contradiction – improved his other perennial complaint, severe diarrhoea, 'which, as you know, was wretched even before I left Bonn, but has become even worse in Vienna'. But neither did anything to help his ears, 'which continue to hum and buzz day and night'.

Then, at the top of the fourth page of this long letter, three small words: *Ich bin taub* ('I am deaf'). You can tell he struggled to write the words down, actually see them on paper. There is a slightly larger gap before and after them. I imagine he fortified himself with a glass of red wine before putting pen to paper, then stared at the fateful words as the ink dried, before continuing to write.

Beethoven wrote this letter six months after his thirtieth birthday, and he says he has been having trouble with his hearing 'for the last three years'. Therefore we can date the onset of his deafness to around his twenty-seventh year, maybe slightly earlier or later. So what caused it? The short answer is, we do not know. Interestingly, for the summer months of 1797, when he was twenty-six, there is silence over Beethoven's activities. It was rumoured he had fallen seriously ill, possibly with typhoid fever contracted from contaminated food or water. Could that have led to the onset of deafness? It is possible. Deafness has been recorded as a possible consequence of typhoid fever, but it is extremely rare and symptoms would certainly have begun sooner than three years later. Beethoven was notoriously casual about dates, but it is unlikely he would have made a mistake over the timing of something so important to him.

As he wrote to Wegeler, he had consulted several doctors, who in addition to hot and cold baths had also recommended pouring almond oil directly into the ear, and even strapping the bark of the poisonous plant *Daphne mezereum* to the upper arm, then lancing the boils that formed. Nothing worked; nothing stopped the deterioration in his hearing.

Then one doctor, Dr Johann Adam Schmidt, came up with the only sensible suggestion. He recommended that Beethoven get out of the city, away from the noise and the dirt, and spend a few weeks in the calm and quiet of the countryside to rest his ears. That is how Beethoven came to spend more than a few weeks, in fact the late spring, summer and early autumn, in the little village of Heiligenstadt, less than an hour from Vienna via the public coach, in the foothills of the Vienna Woods.

There, on 6 October 1802, at the age of thirty-one and three-quarters, he wrote his Will, in the form of a letter to his brothers. It is more than that. It is a *cri de coeur*, an outpouring of the heart to humanity and posterity.

> Oh all you people who think and say that I am hostile to you, or that I am stubborn, or that I hate mankind, you do not realise the wrong that you do me . . . You do not know the secret cause of my seeming that way . . . For the last six [*sic!*] years I have suffered from a terrible condition made worse by stupid doctors . . . How could I explain that I was deficient in the one sense that should have been more highly developed in me than anyone . . .[1]

And those words again, so small but so full of portent: 'I am deaf.'

He talks of 'someone next to me who heard the flute in the distance and I heard nothing'. This happened when his young friend Ferdinand Ries came to visit him in Heiligenstadt. They had gone for a walk in the hills, and Ries had commented on the lovely sound of a shepherd playing his pipes. Beethoven could not hear the sound, which meant he could not hear music.

What was the point in continuing to live? He writes that he has contemplated suicide in the past. 'Only my art has held me back.' He acknowledges the possibility his deafness will continue to worsen and never improve. Taking his own life remains an option.

But – (once again) – Beethoven is a contradiction, an enigma. In Heiligenstadt he confronts his deafness; he acknowledges it. No more pretence, no more hoping for a miracle. He is a deaf musician. That is what he is. By confronting his deafness, he has overcome it. In the face of this supreme test of character, he has triumphed. The compositions flow from him. He completes his Second Symphony, composes three new piano sonatas, as well as a new set of piano variations, the main theme of which he will use in the opening movement of a work that has begun to form in his head – the ultimate expression of his triumph over deafness, Symphony No. 3, the *Eroica*.

Dr Wagner knew nothing of the Heiligenstadt Testament (as Beethoven's Will has come to be known) when he performed the post-mortem. The document was found amid a pile of papers when the apartment was cleared out. But he certainly knew about Beethoven's deafness. During the thirty-four years that Beethoven lived in Vienna, he was treated for the condition by at least six doctors. He was a difficult patient, disobedient and disrespectful. At least two of his doctors he had summarily dismissed, and one retaliated by refusing to come and see him in his final illness. No doubt Beethoven and his deafness were much discussed in Vienna's medical circles.

For that reason Wagner examined Beethoven's auditory system in some detail at post-mortem. In his report he wrote that there was some evidence of inflammation; the auditory nerves were shrivelled and lacking nerve tissue, with their blood vessels dilated. Such was the desire to establish what had caused Beethoven's deafness that Wagner made the decision to extract the auditory system as completely as possible from the skull. To achieve this, he cut right round the top part of the composer's head, lifting it off like a lid. A photograph of the skull, taken when the body was disinterred in October 1863, clearly shows the incision running laterally across Beethoven's forehead. The auditory nerves were extracted and put in a large jar of preserving fluid, which later disappeared. Legend has it that the jar found its way to London, where it stood on the windowsill of a room at University College Hospital, in a wing of the building that took a direct hit during the Blitz. True or not, the jar and its contents have never been found.

There are, however, several locks of hair, in both private and public hands, purporting to belong to Beethoven. This is not as surprising as it might sound. In the three days between death and funeral, so many admirers came to pay their respects at Beethoven's bedside, cutting a lock of hair for posterity – as was customary at the time – that Schindler reported that the corpse was almost bald at burial.

One such lock was scientifically tested and the results, announced in 2000, caused great excitement. Beethoven, it was revealed, had a concentration of lead in his blood one hundred times greater than commonly found in people today. He had, in effect, lead poisoning.

This is less dramatic than it sounds. Water in Beethoven's day was regularly contaminated, and he is known to have drunk a lot of it, especially when visiting spas. Kitchen utensils were made of lead, and paint was lead-based. If a dozen other Viennese citizens had been similarly tested (impossible at the time) they might too have been found to have levels of lead in their blood abnormal by today's standards.

We can, though, surmise that this will have affected his health, worsened his digestive problems and accounted to a large extent for his seemingly constant abdominal discomfort, irritability, sudden outbursts of anger, even depression.

But deafness? No. Lead poisoning does not contribute to a loss of hearing. The question the scientists – and owners – of that lock of hair were hoping to answer remained, and remains, unresolved.

Here is another question. Who are the owners of that particular lock of hair? Therein lies a fascinating story. It involves an American real-estate agent, an unexpected rejection, a California university – and a passion for Beethoven, the man and his music, that was both life-consuming and life-affirming.

❧

The village of Heiligenstadt is today a suburb of Vienna, easily reached on the U-Bahn, line 4. You emerge into a complex of modern buildings where you can take a taxi to Probusgasse in the old district. There, you will find calm and quiet, the Church of St Michael and a small park.

The cottage where Beethoven spent the summer of 1802 has been preserved, and recently underwent full restoration. It is today the most comprehensive museum to Beethoven anywhere in Vienna, containing portraits, facsimiles of letters and manuscripts, including of course the Heiligenstadt Testament, even a mock-up of Beethoven's 'chaotic' work room, complete with a fortepiano with five pedals from 1821. The gift shop, which did not exist when I first visited around thirty years ago, has a comprehensive selection of books, pamphlets, CDs, DVDs and myriad paraphernalia – including a Beethoven spectacle case (yes, I did).

From 1792 right into the twentieth century, the cottage served, uninterrupted, as a bakery. The baking oven was on the ground floor, there was a shop front, and a baker's apartment above. The small apartment Beethoven rented was on the side of the building, on the first floor looking over the garden. He must therefore have lived for the duration of his stay with the smell of freshly baked bread wafting up to his apartment, the comforting and nurturing aroma surely alleviating painful memories of a difficult childhood in the Rheingasse.

There is a small park a short walk from the cottage. In it stands a statue of Beethoven that I discovered by pure chance on my first visit to Heiligenstadt all those years ago. It is, in my view, of all the statues to Beethoven in both Bonn and Vienna, the most lifelike. He is depicted not as a god but as a human being. Short of stature, resolute, in full stride, hands clasped behind his back. This is, surely, the Beethoven that his friends and fellow musicians knew.

Unlike the sculptor. Extraordinarily enough, Robert Weigl made the statue in 1902, seventy-five years after Beethoven's death. Weigl's intention was that you would encounter the statue as if encountering Beethoven himself on one of his country walks. The only element that could have made it even more lifelike would be if Weigl had depicted Beethoven's arms waving around his head, pencil in one hand, notebook in the other, in full composing mode, his mouth wide open as musical phrases pour from him. Once, behaving exactly like this – striding across a field, arms waving, emitting coarse noises – he caused a small herd of oxen to stampede, to the farmer's fury.

Weigl's intention – encountering Beethoven on a country walk – was somewhat diminished when, in 1910 (after Weigl's death), it was decided by committee that the statue was not monumental enough. It was therefore raised on a plinth and half encircled by an open wall of columns. It now has more gravitas than the sculptor intended, but is no less accurate a depiction of Ludwig van Beethoven the man.

24

'My interest in Beethoven is like a fire burning inside me.' Not my words, but those of an American real-estate developer. Ira F. Brilliant, born in Brooklyn in 1922, resident of Arizona, had a passion for Beethoven, a passion that would lead us to an infinitely greater understanding of the man and his music, and provide an immeasurable, and unending, contribution to Beethoven scholarship.

Brilliant – his Russian émigré father translated the family name 'Diamond' from Russian into English – indulged his passion in every way he could as he built his business in Arizona. On his first date with the woman who would become his wife, he took her to a concert of Beethoven's music. Many more concerts followed. He bought recordings; he read books. But he wanted more, he wanted to get closer to the man whose music entered and enveloped him, and that always seemed to be playing in his brain, wherever he was, whatever he was doing. But how to do this?

Sometime in early middle age, in his forties, it came to him. He developed a burning desire to touch something Beethoven had touched, to touch it and own it. 'It was my way of paying homage to his greatness,' Brilliant said. He was about to embark on a journey that would last for the rest of his life, and beyond.

Brilliant became aware of a letter, signed by Beethoven in 1824, that was in private hands. He telephoned the owner and offered to purchase it. He was given a price of $7,500. He demurred. Almost a year later, on 1 December 1975, he made a second phone call, paid the asking price, and waited for the precious package to arrive at his home.

Then, not rushing things, staring at the unopened package for a full thirty minutes, carefully he opened it, took out its precious contents, unwrapped the protective covering and finally held in his hand a piece of yellowed paper dating back a century and a half, brittle now and delicate. He laid it down, and there, staring up at him, dancing in the light, was the instantly recognisable broad signature of Ludwig van Beethoven. This was paper that the great man himself had touched, and now Brilliant had touched it too. More than that, he owned it. His journey had begun.

Over the ensuing years more letters followed, along with first editions that had been corrected and approved by Beethoven, sketch leafs, handwritten notes and more. Soon Ira Brilliant had a unique collection of Beethoven artefacts sitting on shelves and worktops in his home. It was then that he decided to move to the next part of his project: to make this valuable material available to anyone who wanted to view it – musicologists, musicians, or simply those who, like him, shared a passion for the man and his music.

Brilliant offered his collection to the faculty of Fine Arts and the School of Music at Arizona State University. There was a condition. The university would have to create a special centre to house the collection, and also offer a course in Beethoven studies. The dean of the faculty and director of the school both turned him down. A few weeks later, Brilliant travelled to San Francisco to attend a conference, and stayed with a friend of his in San Jose, around fifty miles south of San Francisco. He told the friend of his ambition to endow a university with his Beethoven collection, housed in a Beethoven centre, but that Arizona State had turned him down. The friend happened to lecture at San Jose State University and asked Brilliant if he might approach the dean there. Brilliant agreed. And so Beethoven scholarship was changed forever.

On 7 September 1983, the Ira F. Brilliant Center for Beethoven Studies, known as the American Beethoven Center, was founded at San Jose State University, opening to the public in 1985. The Center supported an American Beethoven Society, of which I became a member in 1994. By the time of Ira Brilliant's death in 2006 at the age of eighty-four, he had seen his dream more than realised. The Center today possesses the largest and most important collection of Beethoven artefacts outside Bonn, including more than three hundred first editions, thousands of books and articles, items in Beethoven's handwriting, musical instruments from his time, and, of course, that famous lock of hair, which was acquired in 1994. A scholarly journal is published twice a year. The collection is constantly being added to and enhanced.

The lock of hair is the Center's most prized possession, yielding much valuable information about Beethoven's health – even if it failed to give us the cause of his deafness. But if a lock of hair, cut as a keepsake two centuries ago, remains a valuable source of information in the early twenty-first century, what might it be able to tell future generations? Where will science be two centuries hence? From 582 original strands of hair, 422 remain after testing. Surely these remaining strands will one day give us the answer to this enduring mystery: what caused Beethoven's deafness?[1]

❧

I cannot recall how I found out about the American Beethoven Society. In 1994 I was working furiously on my fictional biography of Beethoven, to which I gave the title *The Last Master*, quoting from the funeral oration delivered at his interment. My publisher had accepted my proposal for a novel based entirely on fact. He had not expected one volume to become two, then two to become three.

At one point I urgently needed the wording of a musical quip Beethoven had written for his stout violinist friend Ignaz Schuppanzigh. I knew the title, *Lob auf den Dicken* ('In Praise of the Fat One'), and the opening line, *Schuppanzigh ist ein Lump* ('Schuppanzigh is a rascal'). But what followed that? This was in the days before the internet, Google or email. I picked up the phone to the Beethoven-Archiv in Bonn, of which I was a member, and was told my query would be looked into.

After some days with no response, I dialled the American Beethoven Society in San Jose, California. I was not expecting much cooperation. If Bonn could not help, what help was a town on the West Coast of America likely to give? And who was I anyway, a television journalist with no musical qualifications? I expected short shrift. What I got was cooperation, genuine interest in what I was doing and a promise to look into the matter.

The next morning the words of *Lob auf den Dicken* were on my fax machine. I became a member of the ABS soon after, and remain so to this day.

25

It was no accident that the only cassette tape in my pocket on the ferry from Cyprus to Lebanon was Beethoven's Symphony No. 3, the *Eroica*. It was the only tape I needed, plucked from a shelf of Beethoven. I had been through a rocky period. My first marriage had ended, not swiftly and amicably but with much trauma. At the same time my professional life had imploded and come close to a full stop.

My journalistic career had begun in 1967, when I won a place as a graduate trainee at Reuters news agency in London. It was a close-run thing. I nearly became a professional musician.

In the interests of honesty, I should rephrase that. The strength of my desire to become a musician was not matched by musical talent, and deep down I knew it. There was a moment, though, when I thought it might.

My schoolboy conversion from violin to trombone had a lasting effect. A fellow pupil lent me his trombone and showed me the basic slide positions. I more or less abandoned the violin and taught myself to play the trombone. So passionate did I become about this ungainly instrument that I asked my mum if she would buy me a trombone. She looked at me bewildered. 'A what . . .?' Instead of telling me to come to my senses and stop wasting my time, she made enquiries, took a taxi to Bill Lewington's musical instrument shop in Shaftesbury Avenue, London, and came home with the most basic form of the instrument, a student trombone.

I fell in love with this four-foot contraption of shiny brass, and my devotion to her has not wavered. As I write this now, she sits on a stand in my living room, sixty-one years after I first raised her to my lips. I still give her the occasional toot, but strictly in private. Which was not the case on one night in early 1967, my final year at university in Dundee. I had formed a trad jazz group the year before. Two of the members were dental students, and they secured for us a most prestigious gig. We were to play at the dentists' graduation ball.

Panic set in, naturally. We rehearsed and rehearsed, and finally the big night came. Now it is possible that the passing of years has romanticised and exaggerated the event in my memory. But what I recall is that for four hours we played classic New Orleans jazz, number after number – *Savoy Blues, Tiger Rag, High Society, St Louis Blues, Muskrat Ramble, Bourbon Street Parade, Down by the Riverside* and the tribute to my trad jazz hero Kid Ory, *Ory's Creole Trombone,* and many, many more. It was one of those nights when everything came together, everything gelled. And there was not a single sheet of music between us. We busked, as they did back in New Orleans, and it worked.

At the end, exhausted and elated, we congratulated each other, and resolved to meet up again in the coming weeks to discuss whether we might take this new experience further. I packed up my trombone and walked back to my digs in the early hours of the morning. I knew now what I wanted to do in my life. I would study the trombone at the Royal Academy of Music in London, then turn professional and form my own trad jazz band, emulating my other jazz hero, the trombonist Chris Barber.

I did not know it, but I would not open my trombone case again for more than fifty years. My life was about to move in an entirely new direction, and it had nothing to do with music. That direction was the news, events happening in the UK and around the world. I found myself reading every newspaper I could get my hands on and listening to as much news on the radio and, increasingly, television as I could, at the expense of studying philosophical arguments over the theoretical separation of mind and body, or whether a table ceases to exist when you leave the room.

My only academic talent, and indeed interest, at Uppingham School in Rutland was modern languages. French came to me easily, German even more so, and I was the first boy at the school to pass Russian O-level. News and languages. And television. At news time I was glued to the screen, imbibing reports from around the world – the Six-Day War in the Middle East; dissent behind the Iron Curtain threatening to spill onto the streets of Prague,

Warsaw, Budapest; apartheid in South Africa. That was where I wanted to
be – with the camera crews reporting from the front line. And so I applied
to join the BBC trainee scheme and also the training scheme at ITN. I
also applied, given my facility for languages, for the Reuter trainee scheme,
though it was in television that my ambitions lay.

Three applications that would, I was confident, lead to three job offers.
Over pints of beer in the student union bar with friends I told them of the
luxury awaiting me of having to choose from three prestigious offers. How
would I decide? We toasted my glittering future.

The first to turn me down was the BBC. I was shocked. Had they
misread my application? Was the brief one-paragraph letter intended for
someone else? What more could they want than I had to offer? I was passionate about news, up to date on world events and proficient in modern
languages. There was no explanation. Just a formulaic 'We are sorry to
inform you that your application has been unsuccessful.' Just a few days later
an envelope dropped through the door of my student digs with the familiar
ITN logo in the top left corner. Truth be told, my first choice was the BBC,
with its prestigious reputation. But if it had to be ITN, that was fine. Two
paragraphs this time, but the same message: 'We are unable to offer you
a place on our graduate trainee scheme but wish you . . .' Something had
gone wrong, but I did not know what. I considered an appeal, two appeals,
but thought better of it. What if there was no mistake? The humiliation
would be all the worse.

That left Reuters. Again, in all honesty, it was number three on my wish
list. Television had been my goal. Suddenly, though, I wanted to join Reuters
very much indeed. Its application process had been very different from the
BBC's and ITN's. Whereas the broadcasting organisations had simply asked
for a form to be filled in with accompanying letter, Reuters had sent a written
test. On a single A4 sheet of paper were a dozen or more sentences describing
a fire in a store on Oxford Street. The sentences were badly written, repetitive
and in no particular order. The test was to write a 250-word news story based
on the information provided.

To this day I remember sitting at the tiny desk in my room, reading the
A4 sheet a couple of times, then folding a sheet of paper into the portable

Olivetti typewriter I had pleaded with my parents to buy me for my seventeenth birthday, and writing the story. It took me about five minutes. Something was wrong, surely? I must be missing something. It was all too easy. The basic facts were that the store had been full at the time, midday on a Saturday. At least two hundred people had had to be evacuated by firemen, who had struggled to bring the blaze under control. Among those rescued were the Soviet ambassador and his wife, who were in the store shopping at the time. One person had actually died in the fire and at least a dozen were injured, some seriously. A full investigation would be held into what caused the fire.

> One person died, and at least a dozen more were injured, some seriously, in a major fire in a store in Oxford Street in central London today. Police evacuated at least two hundred people, including the Soviet ambassador and his wife . . .

It was obvious that was the way to write it. Too obvious, perhaps. I showed it to two university friends. They both said the same thing, independently of each other. 'You've got the wrong lead. The most important fact is that the Russian ambassador was in the store. This is the Cold War we are living through. It could have major implications. Who knows the real reason he was there? There could be much more to the story . . .' or words to that effect.

Could they be right? I began to doubt myself. I rewrote the story, putting the Russian ambassador line at the top. It read well. I decided to wait a day or two, approach it afresh. When I did so, I was utterly in a quandary. I had two stories. Which one was right? My instincts told me the first version, my version, with the casualties at the top, was the right one. But it was two against one, and the two were adamant. There was no doubt in their minds, as there now was in mine.

I made my decision. I folded version two, the Russian ambassador version, and put it in the envelope. An hour later I made a new decision. I needed to trust my instincts. If I trusted theirs and Reuters turned me down, how would I feel? I would never know if my account had been the correct one. If I wrote it my way and it led to a job with Reuters, then it would show that my journalistic instincts were right. I took out the Russian ambassador version, put my original story in the envelope, stuck it down, stamped it and posted it.

Fifteen months later, in June 1968, I was a Reuter correspondent on the streets of Paris, covering the students' and workers' revolution that ultimately brought down President de Gaulle.

It was a golden start to a career in journalism, a career that nearly came to a shuddering halt a little over three years later. It seems the hubris of my late student years had not entirely left me. So keen was I to become a television news reporter that I resigned from Reuters and applied again to ITN, on the advice of the *Daily Express* correspondent in Paris who I had come to know and who knew ITN's editor-in-chief personally. Yes, in that order: I resigned first from Reuters and then applied to ITN. This time, with my matchless experience with Reuters, ITN would be certain to say yes.

The then editor-in-chief of ITN invited me to his office, was utterly charming, thoroughly complimentary, and before I knew it, I was back outside his office with his words – 'unfortunately there is nothing we can offer you' – ringing in my ears. He had, though, given me a name at the BBC. 'Ring him, he might have something for you.' I went into a public phone box, looked up the BBC in the phone directory, inserted four pennies (I think), pressed button A, to be told this particular gentleman was not available, and the one I needed to speak to was out to lunch. Could he ring me back? Yes, I replied weakly, recalling the old Reuter motto, 'They never ring back.'

But actually he did, and I remember his words exactly to this day: 'It just so happens you have come knocking on the door at the right time.' A month later I joined BBC TV News as a junior writer on the *Nine O'Clock News*, writing the weather forecast and football results. When I asked, repeatedly, to become a reporter, I was told, repeatedly, 'That's impossible, you're on MP3 grade.' And so, less than two years later, I tried yet again with ITN, and this time succeeded. I joined as a writer on *News at Ten*, again to begin with entrusted only with the weather forecast and football results. When I said my ambition was to become a reporter, I was told that was not where my future lay. Not that it was impossible, but that was not the career path I was on.

Three years later, it was. ITN put me in a studio and gave me a camera test, as a result of which the same editor-in-chief who had earlier ushered me out of his office with the advice to ring someone at the BBC, called me into the same office and told me I had won a coveted reporter's job. In the decade that followed I covered major stories at home and abroad – Northern Ireland, Rhodesia's fight to become Zimbabwe, the Bangladesh refugee crisis, the Iran Revolution, the Soviet occupation of Afghanistan, the Philippines Revolution. I interviewed any number of politicians, including Margaret Thatcher both as opposition leader and prime minister. Then, in 1981, the impossible happened. I was appointed ITN Washington correspondent, the most prestigious appointment it was possible for an ITN reporter to have.

That is when things began to go seriously wrong. In early 1982 it became clear that Argentina was preparing to take the Falkland Islands by force. Intense diplomatic efforts got under way to try to avert war, based on triangular diplomatic talks in London, Buenos Aires and Washington. As Washington correspondent it fell to me to cover the diplomatic angle in Washington. Diplomacy is a subtle activity. Words are carefully chosen; nuance matters. This did not come naturally to me. I attended regular briefings at the British Embassy. Whenever I asked a question, it seemed that the ambassador turned a withering eye on me.

There is a term for the kind of news reporter I was, and had always wanted to be: 'fireman'. A 'fire' breaks out somewhere in the world, I go there, report on the 'fire', and come back home. It was what I was best at. It was what got me the Washington job. Then the Falklands War happened and suddenly I was having to be a diplomatic correspondent. I was, to put it bluntly, out of my depth. I would have been better off on a British warship in the South Atlantic.

As 1982 turned to 1983, Britain basked in the glow of military victory; Margaret Thatcher won a landslide general election, and my career was imploding. The Falklands War had done for me. It did not seem to matter what report I satellited to London for *News at Ten*, it was not good enough. On 18 June 1983 America put its first woman, Sally Ride, into space. I filed a colourful three-minute report for *News at Ten*, using the sound of a song 'Ride, Sally Ride', which had been specially written for the occasion, over the actual launch footage. In London the *News at Ten* programme editor judged my report to be unusable. The piece was re-edited, revoiced by another reporter, the song was taken off, and this new version was run on *News at Ten*.

A day or two later the phone rang in the ITN Washington office. It was the editor-in-chief in London (successor to the one who had first refused and then given me a job). 'I want you in my office at two o'clock tomorrow afternoon.' I flew back to London, knowing what awaited me. On the flight I considered my options. Should I contact the BBC, or had I burned my boats there by leaving after such a short time? What about Reuters? I was a former graduate trainee, one of only about a dozen who had been taken on out of around two thousand university students who had applied. Would that give me a head start if I reapplied?

The following afternoon I sat opposite the editor-in-chief and waited for the axe to fall. After a formal dressing down – 'you seem to have lost your way', 'you haven't matched our expectations' – he said, 'There are those that want me to sack you, senior people, powerful voices . . .' I knew this, I had heard the rumours. '. . . But I am not going to. I still believe you can be a good reporter. I am taking you out of Washington, putting you back on the reporters' desk, and then it's up to you.'

Mentally I retreated into myself. I wanted to resign, take control, preserve my dignity. My soon-to-be wife Bonnie persuaded me not to. 'Fight back,' she said. 'You can show them.' I had risen to the top and then come crashing down. I needed help; I needed inspiration. I turned to Beethoven. I delved again into Thayer's *Life of Beethoven*, the book I had bought after that Beethoven concert in Washington. I wanted to know more. If Beethoven had overcome the worst fate that could befall a musician, could I overcome the worst fate that had befallen me? How did he do it? Could *I* do it? I bought more books on the composer who had lost his hearing but who never gave up.

The more I read, the more I listened, the more Symphony No. 3, the *Eroica*, spoke to me. It began with two chords of utter defiance, embarking on a vigorous, sometimes tortuous, journey of surprises and unexpected moments, the despair of a funeral march, but one that is overcome, and always building inexorably to a conclusion of triumph, pure triumph.

Listening to it inspired me and gave me courage and determination exactly when I needed every ounce. It became – and remains – my constant companion. That is how a badly worn cassette tape of it, played by the Berlin Philharmonic conducted by Herbert von Karajan, happened to be in my anorak pocket, along with my battered Walkman, as that ferry pulled out of Limassol en route to Lebanon.

26

'I am not very satisfied with the work I have thus far done. From this day on I shall take a new way.'[1]

Beethoven had come through the most difficult and testing period in his life. It was less than a decade since he had arrived in Vienna as a young man just one month short of his twenty-second birthday, carrying a battered case stuffed full of manuscript paper and sketchbooks and not much else, determined to prove himself in Europe's capital city of music. It had not been easy.

In the first place he simply did not look like a musician. Untidily dressed in clothes that needed repair, hair roughly cut and bristling shaggily about his head, frequently unshaven, a heavily pockmarked face and an accent from the Rhineland that was rough and harsh on the sophisticated and aristocratic ears of the Viennese nobility – how could such a figure be accomplished in the ethereal world of the sublime art of music? There is no question that had he not had the patronage of the highly respected Prince Lichnowsky he would not have been admitted through the doors of any palace music room or salon.

Lichnowsky himself, we can be sure, will have had his doubts when this somewhat uncouth young man first introduced himself and, the letter of introduction from Count Waldstein notwithstanding, must have wondered what he was about to hear when first Beethoven walked towards the piano. Once he sat at the keyboard, however, all doubts were dispelled. Well, maybe not quite all. Beethoven acquired his admirers, but also his detractors. It was not long before two distinct camps were formed: those who admired the delicacy and classical style required to play the music of Bach, Mozart and Haydn, and in the opposite camp those who could see that this young man was inventing a new way of playing. No longer holding the hands poised above the keys, fingers arched and pointing down, giving delicacy of touch, Beethoven held his hands low, fingers outstretched to give them more power.

From the start, Beethoven made it clear he disliked playing for an audience. His greatest skill was improvisation, and aristocrats were soon falling over themselves to give him a tune and then marvel at the way he would improvise on it. When, after such a performance, his listeners gasped in wonder, even sobbed with emotion, Beethoven would break into boisterous laughter and mock them. 'You are fools! How can I live amongst such spoiled children?'[2] Hardly the way to endear yourself to aristocratic patrons of the arts.

Beethoven performed in salons for one reason only: to introduce his own compositions to the Viennese nobility. Here again things did not go smoothly. There may have been those who sobbed with emotion, but others complained that it was simply wrong to begin a piano sonata with a loud chord, as Beethoven had done in the sonata known as the *Pathétique*. That is not sophisticated; it is rough and uncouth like its composer, said his detractors. And that new violin sonata that begins with the violinist double-stopping solo across all four strings – impossible to play without scraping rudely. There were plenty of chamber works for various combinations of instruments but, as there had been in Bonn, there were frequent complaints from performers that the music was too difficult to play, indicating that Beethoven did not fully understand a particular instrument's technical capabilities. As for the two piano concertos and two symphonies thus far composed and performed? Admired by some, tolerated by others, criticised by even more.

Then came Heiligenstadt. It was while he was there, away from the city and its distractions, that the germs of a new work began to form in his head. He had a theme that he had used before, twice, and it still would not leave him. He decided to use it for a third time, as the main theme for a huge set of piano variations, which would become known as the *Eroica Variations*, Op. 35. This he did, and *still* the theme would not leave him. In the piano variations he does something very different. He actually begins with several variations before stating the theme. In other words, not so much the standard theme and variations, rather the virtually unheard of variations and theme.

Typical Beethoven. He takes a familiar musical form and does it differently. And it works. So brilliantly that he decides he is still not yet done with this particular theme. In Heiligenstadt he jots down a few ideas. On his return to Vienna, emboldened, victorious, determined to take a new way, he works in earnest on the new composition.

He works quickly. He knows exactly what he is doing. He has embarked on what will become his longest, most complex, most ground-breaking work to date. He plays a piano version of it to Ferdinand Ries, who writes to a colleague, 'In his own opinion it is the greatest work that he has yet written. He played it for me recently, and I believe that heaven and earth will tremble when it is performed.'[3]

Beethoven had embarked on his Symphony No. 3, the *Eroica*.

27

Two blistering chords! In the first two bars! The main theme follows right away, no introduction, and then what happens only a few seconds later, in bar seven? A rogue C sharp – the wrong note in the wrong key in the wrong place at the wrong time.

This is how Beethoven opens his new Symphony No. 3, the *Eroica*, in E flat major. Over the next fifty or so minutes – twice as long as any previous symphony by Mozart, Haydn or anyone else – he will take you on a journey, a bumpy ride, with twists and turns, false starts and false endings, until finally, at the last moment, everything is resolved. But you are a changed person at the end from the one you were at the start.

Like the greatest works of literature that you return to again and again, there can never come a moment when you have heard everything there is to hear in the *Eroica*. But unlike words on a page, the notes on a piece of manuscript have to be played to come alive and you alone cannot achieve this. You need an orchestra and a conductor. So you have the composer's notes plus your own imagination, but you also need input from many other individuals. No two interpretations, therefore, will be precisely the same.

How, then, to perform those opening chords? There is no answer, or more accurately there are many answers. Otto Klemperer gives them such weight they act like two pillars on which the symphony will be built. Arturo Toscanini treats them like two whiplashes, starting pistols for what is to follow. For Wilhelm Furtwängler they are the conclusion, as if to forestall any doubt that may follow.

The chords are brusque, abrupt, yet affirmative. The obvious interpretation is that they are a call to attention. 'Pay attention! Listen!' To me, though, they are more than that. This is the new Beethoven, the composer who has accepted his deafness and, in so doing, overcome it. From someone who, at the age of thirty-one, has just written his Will, pleading to mankind to understand him, not to judge him cruelly, you might expect a morose – even self-pitying – opening to the *Eroica*. Not with Beethoven.

This, I believe, is Beethoven saying, 'Damn my deafness! It will not stop me!' But – there is that 'but' again – it is not that straightforward. Nothing ever is with Beethoven. Just when you think you know what he is saying, the direction he is taking, he subverts you. From those two chords the opening theme follows and should develop organically. That is what Haydn would have done, or Mozart. Not Beethoven. With the theme only half stated there then comes that unsettling, seemingly random, C sharp. Following that he develops the main theme, but again not in the obvious direction you would expect. 'Obvious': not a word ever to be used about Beethoven.

This is Beethoven, right at the start of the *Eroica*, saying, 'You think you know all about me? You are wrong.' So from the very opening of this mighty work you simply *have* to listen, you *need* to know what he is saying, what he is doing, where he is going.

Two-thirds of the way through the first movement he begins to bring things to an end. The huge development of the theme has been through all its stages and it is time to wind it down. This Beethoven does, and you begin to wind down with it. Time to take a deep breath before the second movement. But wait! What is he doing? With an almost silent chord in the strings, a lone horn sounds the opening four notes of the main theme, the whole orchestra joins in, and we are off again.

This caused a famous moment in the first rehearsal of the symphony, recounted by Ferdinand Ries in his memoir. He was standing with Beethoven, listening to the orchestra. Things were already going badly, with the usual complaints about Beethoven's music being unplayable. When that lone horn played those four notes, Ries said, 'That damned horn-player! Can't he count? It sounds terrible!' Beethoven was not amused. 'I believe I was very close indeed to having my ears boxed. Beethoven was a long time in forgiving me.'[1] Ries had a point. That moment comes suddenly and totally unexpectedly. To this day I know full well that it is coming, yet it still takes me by surprise. Twists and turns, false starts and false endings.

Who could have predicted that the second movement would be a funeral march? What does it mean and who is it for? Ries gives us a mighty clue. Napoleon was much on Beethoven's mind when he was composing the *Eroica*. The Corsican, the outsider, who had (thus far) proved invincible on the battlefield and had risen to high political office as consul-general of France. Beethoven was known to be an admirer, to the extent that he had considered leaving Vienna altogether and moving to Paris. But in 1802 Napoleon had proclaimed himself First Consul for Life after a plebiscite that had yielded a 99 per cent vote in favour. Of course it was rigged. The man who had risen from humble beginnings to rule France was now, in effect, a dictator.

Soon after Napoleon's self-elevation to consul-general, Beethoven had written a funeral march as the slow movement of a new piano sonata. Now, four years later, with Napoleon the all-powerful ruler of France amid rumours he might even go one step higher and assume the title of emperor, Beethoven writes a funeral march as the second movement of his new symphony, as if to mark this man's desertion of the ideal. When, nearly twenty years later, Napoleon died on the remote island of St Helena, friends asked Beethoven if he would write a funeral march to commemorate the French emperor. 'I already have,' he replied. And how does this movement, this funeral march, end? With the music disintegrating, just as Napoleon's life had.

The third movement of the *Eroica* comes almost as light relief, with a gentle theme high on oboe and flute. But beware. Relief and relaxation are not Beethoven's intention. The music builds and becomes more powerful until it reaches a natural climax. And then in come the horns with solo passages that stand alone almost as hunting calls. Remember, in Beethoven's day the horns had no valves; they were simply coiled brass tubing. The player had only their lips and a coiled fist in the bell of the instrument to control the notes. The sound was altogether rougher and more natural, so different to the slick sound of the modern instrument. So when the horns end their interjection on mighty discords, the sound will have shaken the listener to the core. Exactly Beethoven's intention.[2]

When it comes to the final movement, to say that Beethoven wrong-foots the listener is an understatement of gigantic proportions. When I listen to it,

I try to place myself in the audience at the first public performance. What must they have thought! A huge opening, the entire orchestra, in a downward sweep, pinning you back in your seat, followed by powerful chords. It's preparing you. For what? More power, more force, obviously. But that's not what comes next. What comes next is – silence. Then, plucked strings, the quietest sounds an orchestra can make. What on earth is Beethoven doing? I'll tell you what he is doing. He is doing exactly what he did in those piano variations he wrote in Heiligenstadt. He is writing a variations and theme. That's right. A variations and theme. Exactly the opposite of what every other composer writes, which is a theme and variations. Beethoven gives us a simple variation to begin, and then another slightly more complex, the next even more complex, building until finally, almost as a relief, in comes the main theme. But what is this? It is almost lightweight, punctuated by three chords, like a dance theme interspersed with stamping. Beethoven takes the relatively simple ingredients and slowly, almost without you realising, transforms and intensifies them. Midway through he provides some relief by slowing everything down, almost to a standstill. He knows we need to draw breath, re-compose ourselves. Then the journey begins again, building inexorably to a massive musical climax. You hold on for dear life. When the ending comes, with the upward rush to the final climactic chord, you cannot help but cry out.

Beethoven has taken you with him on a journey, his journey, from a musician's life crippled by deafness, to victory and glory. Who is the hero of the *Eroica*? Ries tells us Beethoven flew into a rage and scratched the name of Bonaparte off the title page of the manuscript on hearing that Napoleon had declared himself Emperor of France. 'So he is nothing but an ordinary man who will trample all human rights underfoot. All he cares about is his own ambition. He'll put himself above everyone else and become a tyrant!'[3] Yet he still dedicated the symphony to the memory of a 'great man', as if he could never rid himself of admiration for Napoleon Bonaparte.

You can see the *Eroica* as Beethoven's musical tribute to Napoleon if you want to. He might not acknowledge it, but I doubt he would deny it, if I say that for me it is obvious who the real hero of the piece is.

28

Beethoven is a difficult man to like. I struggle with this. To date I have written biographies of five composers – Beethoven (several times), Mozart, Tchaikovsky, Johann Strauss the Younger and Verdi. Of them all, Beethoven is the one I would least like to spend time with.

That's not quite right. He is the one I would *most* like to spend time with, since it is his music that accompanies me every day of my life, so I would want to talk to him, ask him questions, try to persuade him to play for me. But I would brace myself in advance. I would dread the encounter.

I imagine his deafness would not be easy to contend with. How deeply meaningful could our conversation be when I have to write down my questions? If he refuses to answer, waves away the question, how could I follow up? I will of course have spoken to his few close colleagues, and they will have warned me not to ask him anything personal – he could take offence at any moment. He is unlikely to respond to any question that is not music based, so how would I even begin to broach the identity of the Immortal Beloved, the only woman we know who returned his love but whose identity remains a mystery? Who was she, Ludwig? I hope you don't mind me calling you Ludwig, it's just that I feel I know you – ah, sorry, of course Herr Beethoven Sir. And your nephew, Herr Beethoven, why did you treat him so appallingly? You actually took his mother to court! That was a truly cruel—

And I have already been rudely and roughly shown the door, without even reaching the point of asking a musical question. No doubt he would have waved those away too, as being naive and amateurish. You have to feel sorry for his friends, that small circle of non-musicians who were close to him. A circle you could count on the fingers of one hand. Beethoven could throw his arms around a friend one moment, then shout dreadful insults the next. Each he loved like a brother, then offended to such a degree that he almost destroyed their friendship.

Take Prince Karl Lichnowsky. No personage was more caring of Beethoven in his early years in Vienna than Prince Lichnowsky. The prince gave him rooms in his palace. He introduced the young musician to other influential nobility at his weekly Friday concerts. He did all he could to make Beethoven's circumstances congenial so that he could compose. He was instrumental in securing theatres and recital halls so that Beethoven could direct performances of his larger works. And it was Lichnowsky who took Beethoven on his first foreign tour – Prague, Dresden, Leipzig, Berlin – only three years after the composer arrived in Vienna.

Lichnowsky's generosity towards Beethoven was extraordinary. When Beethoven published his first set of string quartets, Lichnowsky presented him with a valuable set of four Italian string instruments – two violins, viola and cello – which are today housed in a display cabinet in the Beethoven-Haus in Bonn. In an extreme act of faith and generosity, Lichnowsky decided to pay Beethoven an annuity of 600 florins, to continue until he found employment. Thus he need have no financial worries to impede his musical progress. In return Beethoven dedicated several early works to the prince, including the *Pathétique* Piano Sonata and the Second Symphony. This financial arrangement was to continue for at least six years, until a furious row erupted between them.

That row did not come entirely out of the blue. There had been moments of tension in their relationship, caused by Lichnowsky having a sense of humour but not always being able to gauge whether his young protégé shared it. There was the occasion when Lichnowsky spotted a manuscript on Beethoven's table, a song entitled *An die Hoffnung* ('To Hope'). On the top of the title page Beethoven had written the name of Josephine Brunsvik, a woman who had been his pupil and with whom he had fallen in love. Lichnowsky teased him about it, man to man, but Beethoven was not amused. He made Lichnowsky swear he would tell no one what he had seen, before smartly showing him the door.

A second miscalculation by Lichnowsky had rather more long-term consequences. Beethoven had composed a small *Andante* for piano. Ferdinand

Ries was in his apartment and heard Beethoven play it. He was utterly captivated, and asked Beethoven to play it again, and then again. He lauded
his master, praising the piece copiously. On his way home he passed Prince
Lichnowsky's palace and decided to pop in and tell him about this marvellous
new piece Beethoven had composed.

Lichnowsky asked Ries to play it, which he did. As he recounts in his
memoir,[1] the more he played, the more he remembered. Soon he was playing
the whole piece from memory, at which point Lichnowsky – a competent pianist himself – asked Ries to teach it to him. By the time Ries left, Lichnowsky
could play the piece pretty much in its entirety.

The next day Lichnowsky decided to have a bit of fun. He called in on
Beethoven and told him he had written a new piece for piano and wanted
to know what Beethoven thought of it. Beethoven was not interested. He
was busy. Lichnowsky, undeterred, then sat at the piano and began to play
the *Andante*. It took Beethoven just a moment or two to see through the
whole prank, and also to realise that it must have been Ries – for whom
he had played it the day before – who had taught it to Lichnowsky. He
exploded with rage, expelling Lichnowsky from his apartment. But that was
not the end of the matter, and it was not Lichnowsky who was to feel the
lasting effects.

Ries recounts how Beethoven never forgave him, ordering him never
to set foot in his apartment again. One day, after a morning concert in the
Augarten pavilion, a group including Beethoven, Lichnowsky and Ries were
breakfasting, and all decided to return to Beethoven's apartment to hear parts
of the opera *Leonore*, which he was working on at the time. Ries, because he
was at the breakfast table with Beethoven, must have hoped for a reconciliation. But the moment they reached Beethoven's apartment, the composer
barred Ries from entering and ordered him to leave. Ries turned and left,
deeply hurt and holding back tears. Lichnowsky, knowing this was all his
doing, hurried after him and tried to persuade him to return, saying he would
make it all right again with Beethoven, and – who could tell? – Beethoven
might suddenly forget about the whole thing and behave normally towards
his young friend again. But Ries, deeply wounded by the knowledge he had
upset the man who was to him a musical god, did not return.

Ries writes, 'I never heard Beethoven play again.' He left Vienna soon after, the young man whom Beethoven had taught as a boy in Bonn, who had performed Beethoven's piano concertos in public and in Beethoven's presence, and who would later come to London and be instrumental in securing a commission from the London Philharmonic Society for the Ninth Symphony. As for the *Andante*, when published it became so instantly popular that Beethoven himself named it *Andante favori*, a title it retains to this day.

Although it was Ries, rather than Lichnowsky, who had borne the brunt of Beethoven's volatility, it was Lichnowsky who was left with a permanent sense of guilt for having brought about the rift. His relationship with Beethoven, once so close, was never quite the same again. In fact, soon after the *Andante* debacle, his own relationship with Beethoven also came to an abrupt and sudden end.

It had not seemed that way, when Prince Lichnowsky took Beethoven under his wing after the failure of *Leonore*. The birth pangs of *Leonore* had been long and arduous. Beethoven had been appointed composer in residence at the Theater an der Wien, in residence literally, a small apartment provided, his contract requiring him to compose an opera. He made several attempts, several false starts, before giving up. The theatre directors gave up too. He was sacked. Then he found a story he liked – political prisoner saved from death by his wife Leonore, after she gets a job at the prison disguised as a boy, Fidelio. The story works on two levels: the triumph of freedom over oppression, and proof that true love conquers all.

On 13 November 1805, the French Revolutionary Army, Napoleon Bonaparte at its head, marched into Vienna and occupied the city. Napoleon installed himself in Schönbrunn Palace, the emperor's summer residence. Not a shot was fired. Exactly one week later *Leonore* opened at the Wien – to an almost empty theatre. Two more performances followed, before the opera was withdrawn.

It is not hard to see why *Leonore* flopped. The city was occupied by a foreign army. The nobility, who would be expected to make up the bulk of the opera-going audience, stayed behind their palace doors inside the city walls. To venture outside to the Wien would not be safe. The sparse audiences for the three performances were largely made up of French officers. The plot, of a man falsely imprisoned for his pursuit of freedom from tyranny, was hardly likely to appeal to foreign soldiers exercising a form of tyranny, and might even be expected to stir seditious feelings among the occupied citizenry of Vienna. *Leonore* had to go.

But there was another reason the opera failed, and no one understood it better than the musically sophisticated Prince Lichnowsky. The opera, in three acts, was too long, too unwieldy, with too many abrupt changes of mood and plot. Lichnowsky decided to do something about it, knowing he would have an uphill task on his hands. He summoned Beethoven to his palace. There in the music room, with his wife – a highly accomplished pianist – at the keyboard, and the tenor who had sung the lead role of Florestan, he told Beethoven the opera needed to be cut down and revised, and they would now go through it, aria by aria, chorus by chorus, line by line, making the amendments and cuts. Lichnowsky must have gasped out loud when Beethoven, albeit gruffly, consented.

After a long session of agreement and disagreement, they had a new version of *Leonore*, three acts reduced to two. This new version was premiered at the Wien three months later – during which time Beethoven had composed his most revolutionary piano concerto to date, No. 4 – and was a success. Everyone was happy – Lichnowsky, the theatre director, singers and players – except Beethoven. But instead of explaining that he felt it was still too long – the two acts were huge – and needed more revision, he flew into a rage, accused the theatre director of cheating him out of receipts, demanded his score be returned and stormed out of the theatre. That was the end of *Leonore* version two.

Things got worse for Beethoven on a more personal level. Against his orders, his brother Carl married Johanna Reiss. This was a young woman with a certain reputation, and word of it had reached Beethoven's ears. After their father's death, Ludwig was now paterfamilias and he forbade Carl outright to marry Johanna. Not only did Carl tell his elder brother to mind his own business, he made matters irretrievably worse by announcing that she was already pregnant. On 25 May 1806 Carl married Johanna and three months later their son Karl was born.

Beethoven was in despair. First, his opera had failed, and now his brother's immoral behaviour had brought the sacred name of Beethoven into disrepute. Something needed to be done to lift Beethoven from this trough of despondency, and Lichnowsky had the answer. He took Beethoven away to his country estate in Silesia – away from Vienna, away from the wagging tongues, away from the noise and tensions of the big city – to the calm of a rural idyll he knew Beethoven would love.

He was right – up to a point. Beethoven was again able to compose, writing the greater part of a new symphony, No. 4. His mood calmed. Lichnowsky congratulated himself on his successful tactic. Then he made a fatal mistake. He invited some French officers to come to his estate for dinner. As if that was not bad enough in Beethoven's eyes – French soldiers had occupied the Rhine valley and walked the streets of his home town of Bonn – the officers turned up in dress uniform. Lichnowsky, it seemed, either remained blind to the offence he had caused Beethoven or chose to ignore it as a trivial matter. He then compounded things disastrously by asking Beethoven to perform at the keyboard for his honoured French guests. It was a red rag to a bull. Beethoven refused point blank, insulted Lichnowsky, vilified the French officers and stormed up to his room.

There, he quickly gathered up his few belongings, scribbled a note to Lichnowsky that read, 'There have been and will always be thousands of princes. There is only one Beethoven,' and stormed off into the night. It was pouring with rain. Under his arm he had a folder of manuscripts, including a new piano sonata, which would be published as the *Appassionata*. The rain penetrated the folder. He later showed the sonata to some colleagues, laughing at how the rain had stained the paper. The autograph of the *Appassionata*, one of the greatest and most profound of all his piano sonatas, is now held in the Bibliothèque Nationale de Paris, and shows the water stains to this day.

Beethoven made it back to his apartment in Vienna, in ill health from the chill he had caught from walking for miles in the pouring rain, his mood once again despairing. Legend has it that he snatched up the bust of Lichnowsky he kept in the entrance hall and smashed it to the ground. In fact he smashed it to the ground two years later when Lichnowsky, appalled at Beethoven's behaviour in Silesia, and recalling earlier traumas over the

The font at which baby Ludovicus was baptised on 17 December 1770 in St Remigiuskirche, Bonn. The original church was destroyed by fire. The new church, a short distance away, bears the same name.

The site of the house in the Rheingasse, Bonn, where Beethoven spent his formative childhood and teenage years. The original house was almost as wide as these two postwar houses and taller with attic windows. To the left, one house further down, was the Rhine.

The bust of Beethoven taken from a life mask by Franz Klein in 1812. This is the only true image we have of Beethoven, showing pock marks and scarred chin, possibly from a fall, though the hair is unusually tidy and the clothing somewhat smarter than he was used to wearing.

After two centuries of ambivalence the city of Bonn has now embraced its most famous son, even adopting his name.

Up close with the great musician in the hall of Bonn's main tourist office.

Once Jahn's Restaurant in the Himmelpfortgasse in Vienna, today renamed Café Frauenhuber, the oldest continually functioning café in Vienna.

1788 gründete hier der Leibkoch der Kaiserin Maria Theresia, Franz Jahn ein Nobelrestaurant, eine sogenannte Traiteurie, wo berühmte Konzerte statt fanden.

Wolfgang Amadeus Mozart führte hier 1788 ein Pastorale von Händel und Ludwig van Beethoven 1797 ein Quintett für vier Bläser und Pianoforte auf.

A plaque on the wall of the Café Frauenhuber testifies to the fact that on this site Franz Jahn, personal chef to Empress Maria Theresia, opened a restaurant famous for its concerts. Here Mozart performed music by Händel and in 1797 Beethoven performed his Piano and Wind Quintet.

Zum Alten Blumenstock, 'At the Old Flowering Plant', a favourite tavern of Beethoven's in the oldest part of the city. For a time he rented rooms above it. Today's menu commemorates the establishment's most famous customer.

'You must write all this down,' said Nula as I regaled her with the story of how Beethoven wrote his Will at the age of thirty-one in this cottage in the village of Heiligenstadt outside Vienna.

Robert Weigl's 1902 statue of Beethoven in Heiligenstadt captures him perfectly, though the sculptor's intention of coming across him unexpectedly in mid-walk is somewhat diminished by the decision to raise him on a plinth.

Recreation of Beethoven's living quarters in the village of Mödling, south of Vienna, where he spent many summer sojourns. The chaos of papers and manuscripts is convincingly depicted. Bed and desk are together at one end of the room, a piano at the other. The portraits on the wall to the left of the cupboard are of his parents.

Meeting my trombone hero Chris Barber at Cadogan Hall, London, in 2016 when he was eighty-six. His band inspired in me a lifelong love of trad jazz and the trombone.

Schloss Breiteneich near Horn in Lower Austria, family seat of Pia Chelwood (direct descendant of Giulietta Guicciardi, dedicatee of the *Moonlight Sonata*), where Nula and I were guests in June 2024.

On the balcony of Schloss Breiteneich, the unique line-up of Austrian nobility with a connection to Beethoven. L–R: Countess Thun, Countess Waldstein, Princess Metternich, our hosts Dr Christian Lippert and Countess Gea Lippert, great-great-great-granddaughter of Giulietta Guicciardi.

Andante and *An die Hoffnung*, decided he needed to take action. He cancelled the annuity.

That marked the final rupture between Beethoven and his greatest early patron in Vienna. In later years the prince would climb the many stairs to Beethoven's apartment in the Mölkerbastei, sit by the door, listen to the composer playing at the piano and congratulate himself at having done so much to help him achieve greatness. But Beethoven refused to meet Lichnowsky again.

When Lichnowsky died in 1814, Beethoven wrote to the prince's brother, 'I have never forgotten what I owe to all your family, even if an unfortunate incident gave rise to circumstances in which I could not show it as I would have wished.'

'Unfortunate' is an understatement.

29

Bohemian aristocrat Prince Lobkowitz was born with a deformed hip, which gave him a permanent limp and left him walking with a crutch. As a boy, to try to keep him still, his father made him learn the violin. This sparked an early interest in music, which was to develop to such an extent that it came to dominate his life – and in the end ruin him. He would ultimately have several works dedicated to him by Beethoven, including the *Eroica* Symphony (after Napoleon's name had been expunged from the title page). In many ways he was more important in Beethoven's life than Lichnowsky, since he maintained his own orchestra and concert hall, which he put entirely at Beethoven's disposal. Beethoven owed him much, yet once again that would count for little when the composer's ire was up.

The family seat was, and is, in Bohemia, today the Czech Republic. The centre of its power and influence, though, came from its palace in the centre of the imperial capital, Vienna. The Lobkowitz Palace was the first palace of its kind to be built with private money after the second Turkish siege, and came into Lobkowitz hands half a century later. It stands today on the appropriately named Lobkowitzplatz, its baroque façade largely unchanged. The interior has changed greatly, and today accommodates the Austrian Theatre Museum. One room, though, remains today as it was more than two centuries ago, the Eroica-Saal, with its ceiling frescoes of naked nymphs depicting creative endeavours such as music, painting and landscape gardening. It is the room Beethoven knew, the room we can stand in today and sense filled with a new kind of music, and the room that contributed to Prince Lobkowitz's downfall.

Where Prince Lichnowsky's love of music inspired him to hold weekly recitals at his palace, Prince Lobkowitz's passion took him further. He decided to turn the largest and grandest of his reception rooms into a fully equipped concert hall so that the orchestra he maintained would always have a room at its disposal for performances. He installed fixed seating, the cushions upholstered in velvet.

It was in these ornate and comfortable surroundings that, on 23 January 1805, Beethoven conducted a performance of a new symphony that would stun the audience with its audacity, complexity, power and passion. It stunned the critic of the leading musical newspaper, the *Allgemeine Musikalische Zeitung*, also. 'This long composition, extremely difficult to perform, contains startling and beautiful passages, but often loses itself in lawlessness. There is too much that is glaring and bizarre, which hinders greatly one's grasp of the whole, and a sense of unity is almost completely lost.'[1] Hearing the *Eroica* for the first time today, you might expect a critic to use similar language. Is it possible that critic also believed the horn-player had mistimed his entry, as Ries had, but decided against mentioning it for fear of destroying the player's career?

Beethoven made good use of Lobkowitz's generosity. Who can blame him? An entire orchestra and concert hall at his disposal was more than any other patron could offer him. In return he dedicated not only the *Eroica* to Lobkowitz but also his first set of string quartets, Op. 18, the later String Quartet, Op. 74 – one of his sunniest, known as *The Harp* – the Fifth and Sixth Symphonies (jointly with another leading patron, Count Razumovsky, whose name will reappear later in the story) and the Triple Concerto.

Ah, the Triple Concerto. I shall take a small detour to give this work its moment in the Suchet spotlight. So there I was, on that midnight ferry from Cyprus to Lebanon, the *Eroica* blasting into my ears as we steamed silently towards the red glow of civil war. But the atmosphere in Beirut was strange. Shops, cafés and restaurants were open as usual. People walked the streets but it was eerily, dangerously quiet. We were warned to be careful. Kidnappings were taking place.[2]

A short walk from the hotel was a shop selling cassette tapes; I had seen it from our car. I needed more Beethoven. I told my camera crew I was going to walk to the shop, browse the shelves, then walk straight back. I told hotel reception too. At noon, the streets teeming with people, the traffic humming around me, I strode quickly to the shop. I was greeted with a warm smile, and in answer to my question – 'Classical?' – an arm was waved towards a set of shelves. I went straight to the letter B.

I had in mind a string quartet or piano sonata, something I did not already have at home. I quickly scanned the boxes – all the symphonies and piano concertos, obviously; there was the Violin Concerto, a box set of *Fidelio*, and – what's this? Triple Concerto? I had never heard of such a thing. Beethoven wrote a Triple Concerto? Did he really? For what instruments? I wonder if they've made a printing error on the box. Well, whatever it is, I think I'd better buy it. You never know, I might discover something.

Discover something is exactly what I did. Safely back in my hotel room, I took out the precious tape, unfolded the leaflet, and began to read. Beethoven wrote a concerto for three instruments – piano, violin and cello – in 1803 and published it in 1804. I thought immediately of the *Eroica* Symphony, which he had begun work on in 1803 and completed in 1804. He must have been working on this at the same time. Extraordinary, though not for Beethoven. Throughout his life he would work on several compositions at the same time, as if he had more inside him than he was able to get out.

I put the pristine cassette into my battered Walkman, prayed the tape would not snag or twist, and listened. Utter joy! This was not the Beethoven of the *Eroica*; it was a quieter, more meditative Beethoven, as if he needed respite from the turmoil of the *Eroica*. And the second movement! Oh my God, the second movement! A slow, short introduction from muted strings, and then solo cello enters, high on the top string, the cellist's left hand reaching down to the furthest extremity of the fingerboard, almost as far as the bridge. Piano and violin join, then the three rise together to a breathtaking climax. It is pure eroticism. I choose my words, and my analogy, deliberately.[3]

Many people, over the years, have told me they find Beethoven's music too full of drama, angst, violence even. My riposte (after resisting the urge to smack them) is to tell them to listen to the slow movement of the Triple Concerto. They have never heard of it, of course, as I hadn't either. I usually follow up with, 'Or try the slow movement of the *Pathétique* Piano Sonata.' Another blank stare. 'It was a smash hit for Billy Joel.'

But I digress. Beethoven dedicated the Triple Concerto to Prince Lobkowitz, obviously, because he was working on this gigantic new

symphony and the prince had told him his orchestra, and the newly fur-
bished concert hall in his palace, were entirely at Beethoven's disposal. And
then those other significant dedications followed. After the terminal breach
with Lichnowsky, Prince Lobkowitz could rightfully claim to be Beethoven's
most beneficent patron.

An orchestra, a concert hall, and then in 1809 came financial support
Beethoven could only have dreamed of. It arrived in an unexpected, and
rather bizarre, way.

The year 1808 was a difficult one for Beethoven. He was thirty-seven
years of age, his deafness now an open secret. The compositions kept coming. Two more symphonies had followed the *Eroica* – the Fifth and Sixth
(*Pastoral*), as unlike each other as it was possible to be – three more string
quartets (the Razumovskys) and a setting of the Mass, in C. But how much
longer would Beethoven be able to compose, given that his hearing was
inexorably worsening? He was in no doubt himself, but others certainly were.

This might be the reason that a benefit concert he had been long promised was postponed again and again and again. A benefit concert was the
highest accolade a composer could be given. He has the use of the hall, he
can select a programme entirely of his own music, he organises publicity –
leaflets and posters – he even sets ticket prices and sells them himself from
his apartment. After costs are deducted, all profits go to the composer.

It was exactly what Beethoven needed, to shore up his reputation as
Vienna's leading musical figure, both in composition and performance. To his
frustration and anger, the date kept being put back. In the summer of 1808
he received an unexpected visitor from the German city of Kassel, the capital
of the newly created kingdom of Westphalia. The individual was the emis-
sary of the ruler of Westphalia, King Jerome, younger brother of the military
colossus who was in the process of conquering Europe, creating this new arti-
ficial kingdom in the process, First Consul of France Napoleon Bonaparte.

His Majesty, Beethoven was informed, wishes to appoint you as his
Kapellmeister, to be at the head of all musical activity in the kingdom. The
salary would be the princely sum of 600 ducats. It was, to use contemporary parlance, a no-brainer. There was the obvious attraction of a regular,
and generous, income, but perhaps just as rewarding, he would carry the

elevated title that had been bestowed on his beloved grandfather. He would be Kapellmeister Beethoven.

He accepted the job offer and prepared to leave Vienna. That was when three aristocratic patrons – one very aristocratic indeed, the brother of the emperor, no less – decided to take action. They agreed to pay Beethoven an annuity of 4000 florins a year on the sole condition that he abandon his plan to relocate to Kassel and remain instead in Vienna. No further obligation, just stay put here in Vienna. At least that way, they surmised, they would be able to look after Beethoven's best interests. Strangers would likely be shocked and insulted by Beethoven's behaviour, however much they were impressed by his musical prowess. They might not appreciate the effect his deafness had on him. In short, they feared that if he moved to somewhere completely unfamiliar, the result would be a disaster.

The annuity, which Beethoven readily accepted, seemed to solve all his problems. Financially secure for years to come, if not for life, and free to compose not to order but when he wanted to. What could possibly go wrong?

Rather a lot, as it happens. The state of Austria was crippled by debt. Seemingly endless wars against Napoleon, with Austria almost guaranteed to come away the loser, had depleted not just the exchequer, but also the wealth of Vienna's senior aristocrats, who had been obliged to contribute financially to the war effort. Inevitably these aristocrats needed to divert funds away from the arts. Their plight was compounded disastrously in March 1811 when the government decided emergency action was needed to curb spiralling inflation, and devalued the currency by 80 per cent. Many aristocrats went from wealth to near bankruptcy overnight. Two of the three aristocrats who had contributed to Beethoven's annuity were seriously affected, and the composer was collateral damage.

One of these was a certain Prince Kinsky, who was a great admirer of Beethoven's music, though the two had never actually met. Kinsky promised, in writing, to adjust his contribution upwards to compensate for the devaluation, but, before anything could be signed, the prince – corpulent to a fault – fell off his horse while out hunting and was killed. The payments abruptly ceased. Beethoven took legal action against Kinsky's widow, which dragged on for three years before finally being settled in Beethoven's favour.

Arrears were paid and the annuity recommenced. Princess Kinsky received the dedication of a song in gratitude.

The second signatory to the annuity was none other than Prince Lobkowitz, who already had many more important dedications to his name. He was hit hard by the devaluation of the currency, but – loyal and loving patron of music as he was – did nothing to curb his extravagant expenditure, which was now about to catch up with him. Threatened with bankruptcy, he was forced to reduce drastically the size of his orchestra and cancel the regular concerts held in the Eroica-Saal (though the room had not yet acquired its name). The following year, 1813, he was made to resign his directorships of a number of theatres. With his finances spiralling out of control, he had no choice but to hand over his affairs to administrators. He re-enlisted in the army, albeit briefly, and in the summer of 1814 he left Vienna for his estate in Bohemia and never returned.

Beethoven had lost his most generous patron. Prince Lobkowitz's contribution to Beethoven's annuity ceased, and in an act of remarkable insensitivity and ingratitude Beethoven initiated legal proceedings against the humiliated prince. Once again, after protracted legal wrangling, Beethoven won, and the prince was ordered to resume his payments (which were the smallest of the three contributions). And once again, to express his gratitude, Beethoven dedicated his song-cycle *An die ferne Geliebte* ('To the Distant Beloved') to Lobkowitz. But the prince died before the printed edition bearing his name was published.

As evidence of Prince Lobkowitz's sincere and genuine admiration, even love, for Beethoven, he wrote from exile in Bohemia, while Beethoven was pursuing him in the courts, 'Although I have cause to feel anything but pleased with Beethoven's conduct towards me, I nevertheless rejoice, as a passionate music lover, that his undoubtedly great compositions are now beginning to be properly appreciated.'

It is surely not very wide of the mark to suggest that that appreciation was not entirely reciprocated.

❧

The Lobkowicz (modern spelling) family was, and remains to this day, one of the oldest and most distinguished noble families in what is now the Czech

Republic, dating back to the fourteenth century. Having recovered from the extravagances of two hundred years earlier, the twentieth century once again brought the family's status, wealth and influence crashing down, this time with more long-lasting and devastating effect. First, the invading Nazi forces confiscated all their property and possessions in 1939. At the end of the Second World War in 1945, these were returned to them, only to be seized again, this time by the Communists who came to power in 1948.

The Velvet Revolution of 1989 righted these wrongs, and the seat of the Lobkowicz family, Nelahozeves Castle outside Prague, was returned to them. One of the other possessions of the family is a beautiful palace set within the grounds of Prague Castle. In 1995, researching for my Beethoven trilogy *The Last Master*, my late wife Bonnie and I were in Prague. We visited the castle, and I enquired about the Lobkowicz Palace, which stands at the eastern end of the complex. Was it possible to visit the palace and have a tour? We were told that unfortunately the palace was used for government business and that was not possible. Did that stop us? Of course not. Having completed a tour of the castle itself, we walked over to the Lobkowicz Palace and marvelled at its beauty, standing alone by the Old Castle Steps.

The gates to the main entrance were open. We mounted the few steps and entered through the high-arched open front door. The interior was vast and largely empty. A desk stood by one wall and a woman was seated at it, sorting through quantities of paperwork. Expecting the firm hand of a security guard on our shoulder at any moment, we walked towards the desk. The woman did not look up, continuing to create piles of paper.

I coughed politely, and asked whether it would be possible to have a tour of the palace. I began to explain that I was researching for a book on Beethoven, and I knew that he had a close relationship with Prince Lobkowitz . . . She looked up, cut me short, unsmilingly pointed across the room and said, 'You sit, please.' We walked across and sat on a firmly upholstered sofa. The woman picked up the phone and had a brief conversation. At the end she nodded and put the phone down. She did not look up and continued working.

Smiling from ear to ear, I turned to Bonnie. I was genuinely excited. Why? It would teach me nothing about Beethoven. He visited Prague twice in the 1790s to give performances, but Prince Lobkowitz was not with him, and there is no record of Beethoven visiting the palace. Why would he? Again, he was in Prague for just three days in 1812, staying in a hotel en route to the spa town of Teplitz to take the waters. No mention of Lobkowitz or his palace. But here we were in Prague, in a palace owned by one of Beethoven's greatest patrons. If nothing else, I would experience an *atmosphere*.

We waited. The woman continued shuffling her papers. We waited and waited. All the while the woman, across the room from us, worked on her papers, arranging this sheet here, another sheet there, making notes on the pages. Slowly my heart began to sink. Prague had rid itself of Communist rule six years earlier, but this is what it must have been like. Regimented, unbending, rules, rules, rules.

We looked at each other. We both knew. We got up and, without a backward glance, left as silently as we had arrived. Still those papers were being shuffled.

Nelahozeves Castle, the family seat, was finally restored to the Lobkowicz family in 2002. Priceless works of art, including an invaluable collection of first-edition scores by Beethoven and many other composers, all previously dispersed, were returned to the palace. After nearly five years of restoration work the palace was opened to the public. There is now a Beethoven room, its most prized possession being a printed score of the *Eroica* with Beethoven's annotations in his own hand. How appropriate that the score is of the *Eroica*, which Beethoven dedicated to Prince Lobkowitz.

On 28 February 2017 an email dropped into my inbox from the House of Lobkowicz, inviting Nula and me to dinner in London with the prince and princess, William and Alexandra Lobkowicz. You could have knocked me down with a feather! A stimulating and exciting evening followed, with the prince telling a small group of guests of his plans for a new music education centre at Nelahozeves, with the emphasis firmly on Beethoven scholarship and performance. Beethoven was like a silent guest at the dinner.

The name of Lobkowicz once again rightfully sits at the centre of European culture.

30

The third signatory of the annuity promised to Beethoven was more than aristocratic; he was royal. Archduke Rudolph was the youngest brother of the emperor, and as such he was able to help Beethoven in ways others could not. Similarly, when Beethoven slighted or disappointed him, it was in a very different way from his attitude towards the Princes Lichnowsky and Lobkowitz.

Beethoven dedicated many more works to Archduke Rudolph – no fewer than fourteen in all – than to any other individual. They are among his greatest compositions and include the Fourth and Fifth Piano Concertos, the *Hammerklavier* Piano Sonata – the longest and most complex of all the piano sonatas – the *Grosse Fuge* for string quartet and his mighty choral work the *Missa Solemnis*.

It is not entirely certain when and how Beethoven first encountered the archduke. It was probably around 1808, when Beethoven was thirty-seven and Rudolph twenty, and most likely at a concert in Prince Lobkowitz's palace. Rudolph was an extremely gifted pianist, and he also already had several compositions to his name. He was a regular performer at these concerts, playing his own works and those of other composers, including Beethoven. It was inevitable the two would meet.

What was not so inevitable was that Beethoven would be seriously impressed by the young man's talent, so much so that when Rudolph asked Beethoven if he would teach him, Beethoven – normally thoroughly averse to teaching – readily agreed. In time he would take him on as a pupil of composition as well as keyboard, the only time he had ever done so. Recordings of Archduke Rudolph's compositions are available today on platforms such as Spotify and YouTube and on CD, but are very rarely performed in public. Among his compositions was a set of variations on the same waltz by Diabelli on which Beethoven composed his set of *33 Variations*, the greatest of all his piano variations.

There was, of course, an ulterior motive behind Beethoven's ready agreement to teach Rudolph. He appreciated his talent, but it will not have been lost on him that this was a member of the imperial royal family, and as such the young man was able to exert an influence not even the most senior aristocrat could match. No door would remain closed to Beethoven if Archduke Rudolph asked for it to be opened. To have an admirer, a patron, resident in the Hofburg Palace was a gift beyond measure. Beethoven went to the palace to teach Rudolph in his own apartment, and he could come and go as he pleased. The footmen knew that if a rather eccentric-looking, usually gruff and impolite individual calling himself Beethoven arrived at the palace doors, he was instantly to be admitted, unchallenged. Beethoven, of course, considered this to be entirely his due.

It was only around a year after they first met – it may only have been a matter of months – that Archduke Rudolph initiated the plan to prevent Beethoven leaving Vienna by granting him an annuity of 4000 florins. We can be in no doubt that it was Rudolph who summoned Lobkowitz and Kinsky and persuaded them to join him in making the payments. No aristocrat, however senior, would approach the emperor's brother with such a proposal. Probably Rudolph used flattery as much as anything. Why else would Prince Kinsky, who had never even met Beethoven, agree to the arrangement, particularly since his portion was more than that of the other two? Kinsky paid most, surprisingly, at 1800 florins, with Rudolph contributing 1500, and Lobkowitz's portion being the smallest at 700.

Beethoven was well aware, therefore, that Archduke Rudolph was not just a remarkably gifted musician, but also a supporter of the most extraordinary generosity. This was to inspire an immediate burst of creativity in Beethoven.

Just one month after Beethoven began receiving the annuity, outside events were to intrude on Vienna's musical world in the most brutal way. On 9 April 1809 Austria (yet again) declared war on France. This was a serious inconvenience for one Napoleon Bonaparte, who was fully occupied trying to quell opposition in Spain, having installed his brother Joseph on the Spanish throne.

Napoleon marched his Grande Armée to the banks of the Danube, where, in a manoeuvre that seriously rattled him, the Austrian army held him off, inflicting an unexpected defeat on the hitherto invincible French. Napoleon fell back, regrouped, rethought, replanned, then crossed the Danube, swatted the Austrian Army away, and marched straight for Vienna.

This was the second time in four years that Napoleon had the imperial capital in his sights. The previous time the invasion had been benign. Napoleon, on his grey steed Marengo, had ridden into Vienna at the head of his army and taken residence in Schönbrunn Palace. His officers had amused themselves by going to the latest opera at the Theater an der Wien, which had proved a little too close to the bone to be allowed to continue. Uniformed French soldiers had walked the streets. The Viennese retreated behind their front doors, firing off nothing worse at the French than insults.

This time it was going to be very different. The Austrians were proving to be a real nuisance that had to be stopped.

Panic descended on Vienna. The French Army, in full marching order and battle ready, was getting closer to Vienna with each passing day. Aristocratic families packed their belongings and fled to their country estates. The ordinary citizenry, if they had somewhere to go, loaded up carts and escaped as far away as they could.

Most important for our story, it was decided that the imperial royal family needed to leave Vienna for their own safety. That meant Archduke Rudolph. Beethoven decided to mark this by composing a new piano sonata, but a sonata unlike any other he had composed, or would go on to create.

Now, very often in Beethoven's life he would receive a commission to write a new piece of music, when he was actually already working on one. It happened with his Fifth Symphony, several earlier chamber pieces, and would happen later with string quartets. In other words, it was thoroughly opportune that he was being commissioned to write something new, because it meant he would now be paid for a piece he was already writing.

That was emphatically *not* the case with this new piano sonata. He wrote it specifically to mark Rudolph's departure, declaring that he would write the first movement immediately, and it would have the title *Das Lebewohl*

('The Farewell'). The second movement he would write while the Archduke was away in exile, and would be titled *Abwesenheit* ('Absence'). The third would be written only when it was certain Rudolph was returning, and this final movement would have the title *Das Wiedersehen* ('The Return').

Beethoven stuck to his plan. He set to work on the first movement immediately. It opens with three quiet, descending chords, above which he writes on the manuscript page, *Le-be-wohl*. A plaintive motif leads into much turbulence and agitation. This is not just sorrow at the departure of a dear friend; it is a graphic depiction of the danger at hand. The second movement is sorrowful, and redolent with fear and uncertainty. Will Rudolph ever be able to return to Vienna? While we languish in doubt, a sudden loud chord catapults us into joy at the realisation that the nightmare is coming to an end and yes, Rudolph and the royal family can return to the city and the Hofburg Palace. Above this final movement Beethoven writes the word *Vivacissimamente*. Not a word you encounter often. I am not entirely certain, but it is possible Beethoven invented it. The meaning is obvious: as fast and lively as it is possible to be. It is testament to the genuine joy and relief Beethoven felt at the prospect that the horror of the French bombardment and occupation would soon be over – not just for Rudolph, but for Vienna, its people, and indeed himself.

This piano sonata stands alone as the only one in which Beethoven tells us exactly what he is depicting through his music. It is one of only two compositions in his entire output in which he does this, the other being the *Pastoral* Symphony, each movement of which he describes in words. On the subject of words, Beethoven gave the title *Das Lebewohl* to the whole work. The publisher preferred a French title, no doubt considering it to sound more sophisticated, and so the sonata was published under the title *Les Adieux*, which infuriated Beethoven. To this day it is known as *Les Adieux*, which would infuriate him even more.

We therefore owe a piano sonata considered to be one of Beethoven's finest to his close friendship with Archduke Rudolph. We also owe another composition to that relationship, one of the greatest and most powerful of all his compositions. And this is where Beethoven pushed that friendship to its limits.

There were only two professions open to a member of the imperial royal family – the Army and the Church. Rudolph had always been in poor health, which ruled out military service, and so he took holy orders. His elevated status meant a swift rise through the ranks of the Church. In April 1819 he was made a cardinal, and two months later, on 4 June, he was elected Archbishop of Olmütz.[1] His enthronement as Cardinal Archbishop was set for 9 March 1820.

This was cause for much celebration in Vienna. Beethoven immediately promised he would compose a new work, a suitably religious piece, especially for the occasion, which delighted Rudolph and which was factored into the ceremony. Beethoven decided it would be a monumental work. He would set the Roman Catholic Mass for full forces of orchestra, choir and soloists, to be given the Latin title *Missa Solemnis*. It would be an epic undertaking, and he had nine months to complete it. He set about the task with relish, and then abandoned it. Other matters were pressing on his mind. He was deeply involved in a bitter court case he had brought against his sister-in-law over custody of her son, his nephew, and several lengthy letters testify to continuous wrangling with publishers. With only one section, the *Credo*, showing any substantial work, he put the whole thing aside.

We now know, of course, that Beethoven was in the final period of his life. The court case (which I will come to in more detail later) drained him emotionally and wrecked him physically. His deafness was profound, as near total as it is possible to be. Vibrations, or some sensations of sound, might be getting through, but to all intents and purpose Beethoven was stone deaf. His creativity, though, was in full flow – the final three piano sonatas, the Ninth Symphony, the late string quartets, the monumental *Diabelli* Variations, which, like the *Missa Solemnis*, he began then cast aside.

He returned to the *Missa* sporadically, and it is truly extraordinary that a work of such magnitude and such cohesion was composed almost piecemeal. It represents far more than a single burst of creative energy. Beethoven finally brought it to fruition, and delivered a presentation copy of the completed *Missa Solemnis* to Archduke Rudolph on 19 March 1823, precisely three years and ten days after his enthronement ceremony.

It is to his eternal credit that Rudolph accepted the manuscript, and dedication of the work, with good grace, showing how deeply he understood the vicissitudes of the man he held in such high esteem. Sadly, Archduke Rudolph died only four years after Beethoven, at the age of forty-three. His body lies in the Imperial Crypt in Vienna, alongside emperors and empresses. His heart is interred in the crypt of Saint Wenceslas Cathedral in Olomouc. His name is immortalised as the dedicatee of so many great works by his friend and teacher Beethoven.

31

Throughout the 1990s I laid my hands on every book on Beethoven I could find. There was certainly no shortage of literature on him. I began to get to know the people in his life. They are individuals whose names would be lost to history had they not come into contact with a supreme musical genius. But the more I delved into Beethoven's life, the more I absorbed the music and came to love it with an ever-increasing passion, the more difficult I found it to come to terms with the man himself. 'Why, Ludwig? Why did you behave like that? You took legal action against Prince Lobkowitz! The man who had probably done more to promote your music than any other individual, bankrupting himself in the process, and you tried to take him to court! What were you thinking?'

I increasingly found myself struggling to understand Beethoven the man. It is easy to say, simply, he was complicated and move on. But I am not sure that is right. He was not complicated. He was a musician. Music consumed him and it was the only thing he cared about. Everything else, everyone else, was ancillary. He was unpredictable. That is the correct, if rather unhelpful, word. That unpredictability caused immense hurt to almost everyone who came into contact with him.

In the case of Stephan (known as Steffen) von Breuning, the hurt was mortal. Remember Steffen? He was the younger brother of Eleonore (Lorchen), to whom Beethoven had taught piano in their home in the Münsterplatz in Bonn. Steffen came to Vienna three years after Beethoven, obtained a position at the War Ministry and remained in the city for the rest of his life. Beethoven was delighted to have his old teenage friend in Vienna, and the two quickly resumed their close friendship.

Steffen von Breuning was Beethoven's sole lifelong non-musical friend. He is the only person who entered Beethoven's life as a teenager, and was still in his life when he died. Do not, though, assume that the friendship was without its problems. Twice the two fell out, both times it was entirely Beethoven's fault, and it was without doubt a friendship that at the very least contributed, and at the most caused, the early death of this loyal, kind and forgiving man.

Having lost his position as composer-in-residence, with its living quarters, at the Theater an der Wien, Beethoven had taken an apartment in a large residential block named the *Rothes Haus* (Red House). Steffen already lived there. In fact it is likely he secured the apartment for Beethoven, since his friend needed somewhere to live rather urgently. But the loss of his grace-and-favour apartment meant Beethoven now had to find substantial money to pay rent, money he did not have.

In a remarkable act of generosity, Steffen, a bachelor of thirty, and four years younger than Beethoven, suggested his friend move in with him. He must have known this might cause issues, domesticity not being Beethoven's strong point, but his kindly nature and loyalty to an old friend were paramount. Might cause issues? Little could he have known. Beethoven gratefully accepted Steffen's offer and moved in. What he had forgotten to do, though, was cancel the lease on his old apartment, which meant he was obliged to continue paying rent. A difficult situation, made worse by the fact that soon after moving in with Steffen, Beethoven fell ill. Steffen looked after him, cared for him and summoned a doctor to attend to him.

I remember the sympathy I felt for Beethoven when I first read of this episode. His wretched health so often compounded his problems. But as I researched more, I learned that at this point, when Beethoven needed Steffen's help most, he openly accused Steffen of interfering in his affairs and trying to cheat him out of money. There was a furious and heated row between them. Beethoven, still in poor health, immediately moved out and took cheaper rooms down in Baden, and the two did not see each other again for several months. It was resolved as suddenly as it had begun when Beethoven – with a touch of arrogance he was no doubt oblivious to – presented a miniature portrait of himself to Steffen, as a token of their special friendship and as if nothing had happened.

Only a year later, further proof of Beethoven's respect for Steffen came when he entrusted Steffen – an amateur and gifted poet – with the task of providing the libretto for the revised version of *Leonore*. This was the version hammered out at that meeting with Prince and Princess Lichnowsky, that would be a success when premiered at the Theater an der Wien the following spring, but which Beethoven then withdrew, accusing the theatre manager of cheating him out of receipts!

However, a much more serious breach between the two Bonn friends occurred around a decade later. The cause of it is not known with certainty, but Schindler suggests, with some credibility, that it probably happened during the court case, that long, draining court case that Beethoven brought against his sister-in-law to try to win custody of her son, his nephew Karl. Steffen, we can be certain, advised Beethoven to drop the case, for the sake of his own health as much as anything else. It was causing him to suffer physically, and was also stunting his creativity. We can be equally sure Steffen felt the full force of Beethoven's anger in response, and decided to step well back. He was not alone. During this awful period of the numerous court hearings, lasting in all for nearly five years, there is practically no mention of any of Beethoven's friends or colleagues. For them all, discretion proved to be the better part of valour.

The rift between the two old friends this time was serious, and showed every sign of being terminal. There is no word of them having anything to do with each other for the best part of ten years. But reconciliation eventually came, and in the most unexpected – and most Beethovenian – of ways.

Steffen's twelve-year-old son Gerhard, in his memoir of Beethoven, tells us how it happened. He was walking with his parents along the avenue that encircled the city wall, when they spotted, coming towards them, 'a powerful-looking man of medium height, vigorous in his gait and in his lively movements, his clothing far from elegant or conventional; and there was something about him overall that did not fit into any classification'.[1] Is that not a perfect description of Beethoven, particularly those final words marking him out as somehow different?

Gerhard, although only a boy of twelve, recalls that he had already many times asked his parents to introduce him to this great musician about whom he had heard so much. He also was well aware of the serious falling out between his father and Beethoven, and a pang of apprehension shot through him as he realised the two men, fast approaching each other on the avenue, would come face to face. He need not have worried.

Beethoven flung his arms round Steffen's neck, embraced him, asked how the family was, enquired after relatives back in Bonn, then – a delicate moment – berated Steffen for not coming to visit him for so long. But without waiting for an explanation, he talked on and on, giving Steffen no time to reply. He even told them he was shortly to move into a new apartment in the *Schwarzspanierhaus* ('House of the Black-Robed Spaniards'),[2] which was diagonally opposite the *Rothes Haus*, where the Breunings still lived and where Beethoven had lodged briefly before the first rift between them. Gerhard says his father struggled to get a word in, but when he did, he spoke very loudly and distinctly, gesticulating animatedly to overcome Beethoven's deafness, assuring him that they would get together soon for a proper catch-up.

They did more than that. The chance encounter, which healed relations between the two friends, took place in August 1825. Beethoven's health was already in terminal decline. He had little over a year and a half to live. His life was spiralling downwards, even as he was working on some of his most intense and profound compositions, the Late String Quartets. Recognising his friend's great genius as well as his failings in practical matters, Steffen once again took it on himself to care for Beethoven, dealing with the day-to-day paraphernalia of living, so the composer – now famous in Vienna and beyond – could devote himself to his work. This took an enormous toll on Steffen, who was not in good health himself.

In the final weeks and days of Beethoven's life, Steffen spent many hours by Beethoven's deathbed, helping to control the ever-growing stream of admirers who had come to pay their last respects. Steffen was with his boyhood friend when he died on 26 March 1827. What followed distressed him deeply. Only a few days later, Gerhard recalled, the room in which Beethoven had died, that was 'so sacred' for us, was 'desecrated' by a miserable collection of second-hand dealers, sorting through old clothes, tugging them this way and that, labelling up his pieces of furniture, pushing and thumping them, getting everything ready for auction.

Steffen had been taken ill several times with a recurring liver complaint during Beethoven's final illness, but still forced himself to attend the auction, to ensure that there would be no cheating and that Beethoven's effects were treated with respect. Steffen died just two months and nine days after his lifelong friend, at the age of fifty-two – 'one mourned by his family and all who knew him, the other mourned by the world'.[3]

Gerhard von Breuning, christened *Hosenknopf* ('Trouser Button') by Beethoven in the final weeks of his life, went on to study medicine, qualifying as a physician and serving as a doctor in the Army, before setting up in private practice in Vienna. He wrote his valuable memoir at the age of sixty-one. He makes it clear that, in his professional opinion, the strain of caring for Beethoven in those final years of his life caused his father's early death.

32

I have mentioned the court case Beethoven took out against his sister-in-law to try to gain sole custody of her son, his nephew Karl. It is time to explore this further, and for me to brace myself. This prolonged legal action lasted for over four years, and it stands as the single most damaging, most draining, most hurtful and harmful episode in Beethoven's life. And it was also entirely unnecessary. By pursuing his ill-conceived and unthought-through ambition in the courts, he hurt himself, he hurt others, he damaged his reputation, he ruined his health, he stifled his creativity – and he left people like me, his lifelong admirers, struggling two centuries later to understand why he did it, and struggling even harder to forgive him.

The final ruling of the Court of Appeal was delivered on 8 April 1820. The story begins, though, several years earlier. Beethoven's younger brother Carl suffered the cruellest fate that could befall the sibling of a musical genius: he was a mediocre musician. Having tried, and failed, to make a career out of music, he gained employment as a clerk in the Department of Finance, but also took it upon himself to manage his brother's affairs. He soon upset publishers with his greedy haggling and duplicitous methods, playing one off against another. He alienated those close to Beethoven: his pupil Czerny couldn't stand him, and Ries wrote to one publisher that Carl 'for the sake of a single ducat will break fifty promises, and as a result make bitter enemies for his brother'. When Beethoven then discovered that Carl was actually trying to palm off some pieces by Ludwig as his own, it was the last straw. Beethoven forbade Carl to have anything more to do with his affairs.

As if Beethoven was not already heartily sick of his wayward brother, Carl then made matters irretrievably worse by informing his elder brother he was engaged to be married, and the object of his affection was one Johanna Reiss. Beethoven was appalled. He had heard of this young lady, as had much of Vienna. As a teenager she had accused the family's housekeeper of stealing something from her parents, when she was herself the culprit. The housekeeper was actually charged with theft and put on trial, and it was only during the proceedings that Johanna was forced to confess. She was fortunate that no action was taken against her. The case, not surprisingly, was widely reported.

It is a fairly safe assumption that her moral life was not of the highest standard either, and that this was also common knowledge. In both areas – honesty and morality – she was to fall well short in later years, and get herself into considerable hot water. If Beethoven needed any further proof that Johanna Reiss was an entirely unsuitable bride for his brother – to bear the exalted name of Beethoven! – it was the fact that she was already three months pregnant when they married. But marry they did, against Beethoven's explicit instructions as paterfamilias, and their son Karl was born on 4 September 1806. Beethoven knew there would be trouble ahead, and trouble there was.

Five years after she married Carl, Johanna committed an act of extreme folly. A friend asked her to sell a three-string pearl necklace worth 20,000 florins on her behalf on commission. Johanna then hid the pearls, faked a burglary in her home, opening cupboards and drawers and scattering belongings, and – in an echo of her teenage offence – accused her former maid of stealing the necklace. This young woman, one Anna Eisenbach, was interrogated for several days by police before being released for lack of evidence.

In an inexplicable display of arrogance, misplaced bravado and downright stupidity, Johanna was spotted days later wearing one of the strings of the supposedly missing necklace. She was swiftly arrested, and under police interrogation confessed that she had sold two strings for 4000 florins and kept the third. She stood trial four months later and was found to be thousands of florins in debt to various individuals. Her defence was that her husband did not give her enough money to keep house and live on. She was found guilty of embezzlement and making a false accusation, and handed a severe sentence of one year's imprisonment, placed in leg irons, forced to sleep on bare boards, restricted to a meatless diet and not allowed to converse with anyone but her jailers.[1]

This sentence was eventually reduced substantially to just one month's house arrest, but the damage was done. Johanna van Beethoven was a convicted felon. Even worse in her brother-in-law's eyes, she had brought the name of Beethoven into disrepute, just as he had predicted she would.

Her moral life was no better. At the age of thirty-nine, Carl fell seriously ill with consumption, to the extent that it was believed he would die. Rumours abounded of Johanna's behaviour while her husband was bedbound. She apparently did little to hide her philandering, nor indeed to deny it. Word reached Beethoven's ears and he was predictably outraged. In a letter he accuses Johanna of behaviour tantamount to prostitution:

> Last night the Queen of the Night[2] was at the Artists' Ball until three a.m. exposing not only her mental but also *her bodily nakedness*[3] – it was whispered that she – was willing to hire herself – for 20 gulden! Oh horrible![4]

I should note here that there is absolutely no evidence from any other attendee at the ball that Johanna behaved in this way, or even that she was there. Why would she be there? Her husband was a civil servant. But it is the final sentence of Beethoven's letter, referring to his nephew Karl, that carries most import:

> Into such hands are we to entrust our precious treasure even for one moment?[5]

Here we come to the crux of the matter. Carl van Beethoven recovered sufficiently to leave his sickbed, but two years later suffered a relapse, and this time it was clear to everyone he would not survive. Just two days before his death he signed a Will appointing his elder brother Ludwig as sole guardian of his son Karl. We can be in no doubt that Beethoven coerced him to do this, reminding him of a written promise he had made to that effect when he had first fallen ill two years earlier.

Beethoven was determined to exclude that wicked woman Johanna from the upbringing of her son. But to his utter shock and bewilderment, when the Will came to be read following Carl's demise, there was a codicil, properly signed and witnessed, naming his wife Johanna as co-guardian of Karl. Beethoven could not believe his ears. Had he not prevented precisely this situation by forcibly persuading Carl to name him as sole guardian? What had happened was that in the final hours of Carl's life, Johanna, by his bed-side, had seen the Will, realised that it excluded her from Karl's upbringing, and persuaded her husband to add the codicil. Carl, the arch manipulator, on the point of death is manipulated first by his brother and then by his wife.

In a moving coda to the Will, Carl states: 'God permit [my wife and brother] to be harmonious for the sake of my child's welfare. This is the last wish of the dying husband and brother.' He could not have imagined how far from being realised this last wish would be.

Johanna, 'Queen of the Night', now co-guardian of Karl, the sole Beethoven of the next generation, the boy chosen by the gods of music to carry the name Beethoven to future glory? Beethoven was having none of it. There was no attempt at discussion, mediation or reconciliation. Beethoven decided to throw the book at Johanna. With his brother gone, here was his opportunity, once and for all, to exclude Johanna from the Beethoven family, to banish her, and to do it with the full force of the law behind him. Beethoven took Johanna to court.

It was the start of a long-drawn-out process, with unexpected moments of high drama, beginning four days after Carl's death, when Beethoven peti-tioned the Landrecht, the court of nobility, to appoint him as Karl's sole guardian. Unsurprisingly, the meat of his argument was that Johanna had a criminal conviction and was therefore not of sufficient moral rectitude to be entrusted with Karl's future. Or, to put it in his language, how can such a precious treasure be placed in such hands even for a moment? On 9 January 1816, the Landrecht ruled entirely in Beethoven's favour, and ten days later he stood before the court and took solemn vows as sole guardian of the child.

A famous victory for Beethoven, but not the end of the story. Beethoven enrols nine-year-old Karl in a boarding school in Vienna, which Johanna is expressly forbidden to visit. An anguished mother, she makes several attempts to see her son, but is rebuffed each time by the school's director, who has the weight of the law behind him. In desperation she disguises herself as a man to try to get through the school gates, which is the last straw for both the director and Beethoven. The court grants him an injunction under which Johanna will be allowed to see Karl on rare occasions, but only with Beethoven's consent.

Here is where I find myself shaking my head in disbelief. If I struggle to understand how he could take Johanna to court in the first place, how could I possibly begin to forgive him for putting a mother through such misery, whatever her crimes and misdemeanours? Beethoven is wilfully depriving Johanna of the right to see her own son. In my eyes, a mother's natural desire to be with her child outweighs anything of which she may be guilty, particularly petty theft. The fact that she actually wore a single string of the pearls in public suggests she was not acting logically or calculatedly. Is that not a mitigating factor? To use this episode as the basis on which to exclude Johanna from her son's life is surely a step too far. But (but!) I think to myself, I must be wrong. I am allowing sentiment to get in the way of the facts. She broke the law. The court ruled in Beethoven's favour. He had justice firmly behind him.

To accord Beethoven the slimmest shred of forgiveness, there is evidence he himself is feeling shards of guilt. In his diary he appeals to God to understand his behaviour, to recognise that he has sacrificed everything for the sake of his 'dear Karl'. God must know how it pains him to cause another to suffer, and implores Him to 'bless the widow'![6]

Matters are far from over. To remove the boy still further from his mother, Beethoven takes Karl out of the school in Vienna and enrols him in a school run by the parish priest in Mödling, a village some miles south of Vienna, on the way down to Baden. There are problems from the very start. To use unsophisticated but painfully direct modern vernacular, Karl is by now a thoroughly messed-up teenager – not even that, being barely twelve years of age. For the past three years he has been pulled this way and that by his mother and his uncle. Towards one he has the natural love of a child, while his relationship towards the other has been dominated by fear and the desire to please, if only to avoid outbursts of anger.

In his new school Karl soon begins to misbehave. Turning up late for class, playground high jinks, answering back in class – nothing too serious, but the priest reports to Beethoven that the boy is becoming increasingly unruly and this is having a deleterious effect on other pupils. Beethoven attributes Karl's bad behaviour to the evil influence of his mother. He berates Karl, pleading with him as a wounded uncle to put that wicked woman out of his mind. He begins now to assume the role of father. If he has been de facto father for some time, he wants the boy to recognise that he has taken the place of his dead father psychologically as well. He implores Karl to call him 'father' and refers to the boy as 'my son'.

This has the unsurprising effect of confusing Karl even further, and the conflict of emotions leads, naturally, to ever more wayward behaviour. After Karl has been at the school for just one month, the priest informs Beethoven he is expelling the boy. Beethoven, mortified, accuses the priest of secretly plotting with Johanna, and lays the blame entirely at her feet. She, using the turmoil of her son's life as grounds for a legal appeal, twice petitions the Landrecht to grant her reasonable access to her son, and twice her appeal is rejected.

Then, on being told that Karl had stolen some housekeeping money to buy sweets, Beethoven flies into an uncontrollable rage. Karl, now aged twelve years and three months, for the first time takes matters into his own hands. On 3 December 1818 he runs away to his mother. Beethoven is wounded to the core. Instead of rage, he feels uncontrollable hurt. Through tears he cries that Karl must be ashamed of him. In a surprising move, he goes to Johanna's lodging and pleads with her to return Karl to him. If she was surprised to find her brother-in-law outside her front door, she must have been dumbfounded when Beethoven informs her, through his tears, that he has reported her to the police for breaking the court order, and they will be coming to collect Karl later that evening.

Johanna has lost her son yet again, but this time she has strong grounds for another appeal. Not only has Karl exhibited his own natural desire to be with his mother, but the condition he was in showed total neglect on Beethoven's part. Johanna was appalled to find that Karl's hands and feet were frostbitten, that he was wearing light clothes in a bitterly cold December, that his underwear needed changing, and he clearly had not taken a bath for some time. This time the Landrecht could not summarily dismiss Johanna's appeal. The tribunal needed to sit and hear evidence.

The court summoned Beethoven, Johanna and Karl to a hearing on 11 December. Yes, Karl too. Still only three months past his twelfth birthday, he took the witness box and testified – against his mother. You can imagine the conflict of emotions in the poor boy's head, whether to confess his longing to be with his mother and unleash a storm from his uncle, or praise his 'father' and cause suffering to his mother. He testified that he would rather live with his uncle than his mother, even though Beethoven's deafness made conversing with him difficult (a brave and rather grown-up thing to say). He admitted that Beethoven often punished him, but only when he deserved it. And only once had Beethoven really frightened him, when he threatened to strangle him for running away to his mother.

Johanna testified that it was obvious Karl wanted to live with her rather than with his uncle, because why else would he have run away to be with her? She also referred to Beethoven's deafness making normal conversation impossible, and said Beethoven was incapable of looking after Karl's domestic needs, such as cleanliness, clothing and washing. Her lawyer argued that her conviction over the pearls happened some years earlier, Johanna deeply regretted it and had served her sentence, and it was no reason to deprive a mother of her natural right to see her son.

When it came to Beethoven's turn to take the witness stand, he testified that there was no need to spend time on trivial matters such as clothing, since Karl's leisure time was taken up entirely with French, piano lessons and drawing. Then the tribunal asked about Karl's education. Given that he had been expelled from the school in Mödling, what plans did Beethoven have for future schooling? In her evidence Johanna had asked for Karl to be sent to a local day school in Vienna. Beethoven rejected this because he had heard that discipline at this particular school was lax. So what, he was asked, did he suggest as an alternative?

It was the turning point in the trial, a moment that would reverberate down the years. It would, not to overstate facts, determine the course of Beethoven's life from now until his death. Similarly for Karl. And it all happened in a single sentence. 'If he were only of noble birth, I would give him to the Theresianum,' said Beethoven.[7]

As courtroom dramas go, it can have few equals. The dramatic staple of modern life, whether on the large or small screen, where always there comes a moment, the sudden revelation, the unexpected twist, that causes those in the courtroom, as well as those in the audience, to gasp out loud. That is what must have happened in the austere Landrecht in Vienna on that December day two centuries ago. The Theresianum was an academy founded by, and named after, Empress Maria Theresia. It was exclusively for sons of the nobility, and open to no one else. The Landrecht was likewise a court reserved exclusively for the nobility. And here was Beethoven implicitly admitting that Karl was not of noble birth, which must surely mean that he too was a commoner, that the entire Beethoven family did not belong to the nobility.

The court immediately ordered Beethoven to produce a diploma or patent proving he was of noble birth, to justify his decision to bring this case before the Landrecht, rather than the lower court. Is it too fanciful to imagine Beethoven's lawyer shouting the judges' order into his ear, and his eyes widening at the realisation of what he had done, that an almost throwaway line was about to land him in enormous trouble?

Why had Beethoven brought the case to the higher court, when he must have known he was not entitled to? And how was it possible the court did not check his eligibility? The simple answer in both cases is that the Dutch prefix 'van', relatively uncommon in Vienna, was generally assumed to be the equivalent of the German 'von'. Given that 'von' denotes nobility, it was assumed that 'van' also signified noble rank. But it did not. Throughout his years in Vienna, Beethoven was variously addressed both as 'von' and 'van', with his membership of the nobility being taken for granted. Given the respect it brought, Beethoven never thought of correcting those for whom he was 'von'. It was also well known, given his fame, that he moved in aristocratic circles, that his many patrons were of noble rank, that he was even close to the emperor's brother, Archduke Rudolph. Why should the Landrecht judges pause to question his eligibility to appear before them?

Now Beethoven had answered the question for them. Relieved to get the whole matter off their hands, the Landrecht – no doubt admonishing

Beethoven and telling him he was lucky not to be punished for falsely claiming to be of noble birth – handed the case down to the court of the common people, the Magistrat.

Imagine the humiliation for Beethoven! He is now in his mid-forties, the most famous musician in Vienna. He takes his sister-in-law to court to try to exclude her from the upbringing of her own son, the testimony from all sides is riveting and, to crown it all, the case is thrown out because – can you believe it? – Beethoven is not a member of the nobility. It was the talk of Vienna. Today we think of Beethoven as a champion of the common man, but he certainly did not behave that way when it came to the court case. It suited him very nicely to be considered an aristocrat, until he was brought crashing down by his own words.

The Magistrat, predictably – and certainly with an element of revenge that Beethoven had not come to them in the first place – threw the case out. Johanna had won. But Beethoven was not finished. A friend tells Beethoven it is obvious why the Magistrat threw the case out. He hadn't bribed them. 'The Magistrat are always trying to fish in troubled waters. Anyone, even with the most just cause, who does not bribe, loses his case. If you had used bribery, you would have won your case long ago.'[8] Beethoven hires a new lawyer and lodges an appeal. This time he does not repeat his mistake. He and another friend have private talks with two of the judges. Does money change hands? Suffice it to say, on 8 April 1820 the Appeal Court, the highest court in the land, reverses the Magistrat's ruling and finds in Beethoven's favour. Johanna makes one last desperate appeal to the emperor, but he refuses to intervene. Beethoven has, at last, won. Karl is his.

But at what a cost. And now Beethoven truly discovers what it is like to be a single parent.

33

Beethoven and his nephew Karl – 'my beloved son' – are now living under the same roof, and it is not a harmonious existence. Beethoven has just turned fifty years of age and is in poor health. He suffers first from rheumatic fever, and no sooner has he recovered from that than he develops jaundice. The stress of the four-and-a-half-year legal battle is taking its toll, and is exacerbated by the news that Josephine Brunsvik, with whom he had been in love and hoped to marry, has died. He is composing, though. In the course of the year he completes the Piano Sonata No. 31 in A flat, Op. 110, and embarks on its successor, which will become No. 32, Op. 111. He does not know that this new piano sonata will be his last utterance in the form that, of all musical forms, is closest to his heart, the only form in which he composed throughout his life without a significant break, the form that was his voice. Illness and sadness, combined with an unpredictable and volatile personality, make for a decidedly difficult atmosphere in the Beethoven residence.

Karl van Beethoven is fifteen years of age in 1821, the first full year after the conclusion of the torrid and terrible court case. He is damaged beyond repair, torn between his instinctive love for his mother and a duty towards his 'father', which, if nothing else, is necessary to ward off outbursts of anger and misery. Karl's physical health, too, is fragile. He develops a hernia. He undergoes surgery, after which he wears a truss and is under doctor's orders to take total rest. Beethoven insists he come down to Baden with him, where he takes the boy hill walking in the Helenental, a thickly wooded trail that rises to the Rauhenstein ruins, a medieval monastery whose damaged and decayed towers stretch up to the sky like broken fingers. Later, lying in his sickbed, the pain of the operation compounded by the enforced hill walking, Karl tells Beethoven he wants to see his mother. Beethoven flies into a fury. Karl, fearing Beethoven will hit him, lashes out and scratches Beethoven's face.

Two years later, in an obvious bid to distance himself from Beethoven, Karl enrols at the University of Vienna to study philosophy and languages. It does not go well. He fails the end-of-year exams and has to repeat the first year of studies. Midway through he abandons university and enrols in the polytechnic institute to study business and commerce. Still he cannot settle. Both at university and polytechnic Karl is aware Beethoven has asked friends to spy on him, to report back on how he spends his time. Does he drink too much? Is he wasting too much time playing billiards? Is he in the library studying?

Karl is stifled by his overbearing – and famous – uncle. Finally he understands what he needs to do. He needs to get away, far away. In the summer of 1824, only weeks after Beethoven has premiered his Ninth Symphony, Karl makes a decision and delivers the devastating news to Beethoven, knowing the torrent it will unleash. He has decided on a military career. Beethoven is shocked to the core. The sole Beethoven of the next generation, destined to carry the flame of the most divine of the arts, is to become a soldier? He orders his pupil Carl Czerny to give Karl instruction on the piano. When Czerny reports that Karl has no musical talent whatsoever, Beethoven refuses to accept it and orders him to teach harder.

Extraordinarily, it is in this period – the years between the end of the court case and his death – that Beethoven composes his greatest body of work, compositions of more emotional intensity than any that have gone before: the final three piano sonatas Opp. 109, 110 and 111, the Late String Quartets in which Beethoven bares his soul to us, the *Missa Solemnis*, the most spiritual of any of his works, and the *Diabelli* Variations. His deafness is now total; he senses nothing more than vibrations. His health is in terminal decline. Yet his creative genius has never been stronger.

The turmoil in his domestic life, though, has never been more tempestuous. Beethoven simply cannot come to terms with Karl's wish to join the military. From Baden, where he now spends much of his time – the Ninth Symphony was largely composed there – Beethoven bombards Karl, in Vienna, with messages that alternate between anger and despair. 'My Beloved Son! Stop, no further – Only come to my arms, you will not hear a single hard word,' reads one.[1] I imagine Karl howling with rage: 'I am not your son! You are not my father! Leave me alone!' Beethoven accuses Karl of secretly seeing his mother, which may be true. Why should he feel guilt over that?

The constant haranguing, combined with the knowledge his every move is being watched and reported on, finally overwhelms Karl. He decides he has had enough. On 5 August 1826 he pawns his watch and buys two pistols and gunpowder. The following day he climbs the Helenental, the hike he has so often taken with his uncle, and enters one of the ruined turrets of the monastery. He loads the first pistol, puts it to his temple, and fires. The bullet misses completely. He puts the second to his temple, fires, and this time the bullet grazes his skin, giving him a flesh wound. He is found, bleeding and in despair, by a wagon driver. He asks to be taken home – to his mother. The effect on Beethoven is devastating. Not just the shame of Karl attempting to take his own life, but also that he seeks comfort from his mother! Everything Beethoven had striven for in those fraught years of the legal battle had ultimately come to nothing.

Under Austrian law a potential suicide must be reported to the police. In hospital, Karl is legally required to receive religious instruction. On his release from hospital he is brought before a magistrate. 'My uncle has tormented me too much. I became worse because my uncle wanted me to be better,' he says in his defence.[2] He is released without charge. Vienna is awash with the news. This is an even bigger story than the court case. Beethoven takes Karl – head still bandaged from the bullet wound – to stay at his brother Nikolaus Johann's estate in Gneixendorf, two days' carriage ride west along the Danube. Karl spends much of the time out of the house, drinking in taverns in the small town, keeping his distance from his uncle Ludwig. He combs his hair forward to hide the scar and must wait for it to be invisible before being accepted into the army.

Beethoven is now terminally ill. That allows Karl at last to make decisions for himself. When they return to Vienna, Karl arranges medical help for Beethoven, then leaves to join his regiment in Bohemia. The day after he leaves, Beethoven draws up a Will, leaving his entire estate to Karl. Once Karl has gone, Beethoven's health quickly deteriorates. Word is sent to Karl to come as soon as possible. The end is imminent. Karl arrives three days after Beethoven has died. A final gesture of defiance? If so, who can blame him?

34

What, then, of the third person in this psychodrama? It would take a psychiatrist many hours of listening, analysing and assessing before coming to a clinical diagnosis that explains Ludwig van Beethoven's relationship with his sister-in-law Johanna. On a superficial level, he despised her as an immoral woman. She was a philanderer with a criminal conviction. But his antipathy towards her clearly went much deeper than that. Beethoven harboured a 'hatred and distrust of his sister-in-law that can only be regarded as an obsession bordering on the insane', writes one biographer.[1] I have already quoted from the letter where he effectively accuses her of prostitution. In other letters he uses words to describe her that range from relatively mild to utterly scathing: poor, unworthy, vicious, bestial, depraved, malevolent, treacherous.

There is no question that Johanna did little to endear herself to her famous brother-in-law. Beethoven knew of an affair she was having while her husband lay on his deathbed, and she did nothing to disabuse him of his antipathy. Shortly after winning the legal battle in the lower court she became pregnant, giving birth to an illegitimate child two months after the Appeal Court ruled against her. The father's name in the church register was left blank. As if to exact some form of revenge on Beethoven, she named her daughter Ludovica.

I can understand Beethoven's hostility towards her. What I struggle to comprehend is Beethoven's obsessive desire for Karl to feel the same way. Karl was just nine years of age when Beethoven launched the court case against his mother, and he had lost his father only thirteen days earlier. That would play havoc with the emotions of a teenager twice his age. Ultimately, by fair means or foul, Beethoven won custody of Karl, but he had not won Karl's love. Despite Beethoven's clear instructions, Karl frequently mentioned his mother, or said that he wanted to see her, each utterance of her name a barb to Beethoven's heart.

Beethoven can blacken Johanna's name as much as he likes, but the truth is she was a mother who loved her son. Several appeals to the law, repeated attempts to see her son, Karl's reciprocal desire to see her – why else would he run away to be with her? – testify to maternal love. It is not normal to behave in the way Beethoven did, and I find it hard to forgive him.

There is evidence he too found it hard to forgive himself. There is that plea to God to bless the widow, which is followed by the words: 'Why cannot I obey all the prompting of my heart and help the widow?'[2] Just a few years later he did indeed help the widow. Knowing she was short of money, he allowed her to keep for herself the half-portion of her widow's pension that she had undertaken to contribute to Karl's education. It was a small gesture – she had asked him to advance her money but he had refused – but it reveals underlying feelings of guilt.

Could it be that that guilt was actually larger than anyone – even Beethoven himself – could know? I have seen it suggested that a hatred as intense as his is akin to love.[3] To put it another way, was Beethoven in love with Johanna? Did he harbour intense feelings of desire for her that – even if he was unable to acknowledge them – disgusted him? We can be in no doubt about his deep sense of morality, something that was alien to Johanna. If he had such feelings, instinctively he would need to suppress them, even kill them off. How better to do this than to transfer his guilt to Johanna herself, to blame her for the way he felt? To me this theory seems barely credible, but then I am not a psychiatrist and Beethoven is not lying on my couch.

Little is known of Johanna's life once the court case was settled. She does not feature again in Beethoven's life. Five years after Beethoven's death, Karl married and went on to have five children. Did she enjoy a happy relationship with her son, daughter-in-law and grandchildren, now that the main source of her unhappiness had been removed? I would like to think so, but can find no evidence either way.

Karl van Beethoven himself, the sole offspring of the three Beethoven brothers, had a short and undistinguished career in the military before marrying and managing his uncle's legacy and the estate he had inherited from his other uncle Nikolaus Johann. He died aged fifty-one on 13 April 1858, his life, I believe, irreparably damaged by an obsessive uncle.

There is a sad coda, though. Johanna lived long after all the other players who had so influenced her life. Karl suffered from liver disease (as had Beethoven), and his mother outlived him by ten years. She outlived her husband by more than fifty years, and her brother-in-law, who had gone to such lengths to vilify and discredit her, by forty-one years.

Am I wrong to lay the blame entirely at Beethoven's door for his unrelenting efforts to keep Johanna and Karl apart? Possibly. Certainly, contemporary accounts hold her at least partly, if not greatly, responsible. Steffen von Breuning is unsparing in his opinion of her innate immorality. The lawyer (a distant relative) who represented her in the court case wanted nothing more to do with her once he discovered she was pregnant with an illegitimate child. Perhaps I am guilty of judging her by today's very different standards. Nula and I have discussed this many times late into the night. She reminds me that a woman who behaved as she did – the criminal conviction, the affairs, the illegitimate child – would have been universally ostracised, and by the standards of the day would certainly not have been judged of suitable moral rectitude to be allowed to bring up her son alone.

I cannot help, though, but look at the big picture. Beethoven's patrons, his friends, and now his family – all suffered in some way from having had dealings with him. Some carried the pain for life. Beethoven, it seems, was oblivious to the hurt he caused. He had higher objectives, which were not to be impinged on in any way by matters as trivial as human relationships. I can admire, even worship, Beethoven as the creator of music I simply cannot live without but, try as I might, and I have truly tried, I find it difficult to like him as a human being.

35

The court case against Johanna drained Beethoven physically and emotionally, wrecked his health – he was never again free of illness for the remaining seven years of his life – and, most important of all, blocked his creativity. In that (almost) five-year period he composed nothing of importance, with one monumental, gigantic exception.

'I am writing a sonata now which is going to be my greatest,' Beethoven wrote to his pupil Czerny.[1] He was not guilty of overstatement. He had embarked on a new piano sonata, which would be the longest, most complex, powerful and most deeply emotional of any he had hitherto composed, or would go on to create.

Given the circumstances he was facing at the time, the only explanation for his ability to do this is his unique genius. He has won the first round of the legal battle against Johanna for custody of Karl. But he knows it is not the end of the story. Johanna is making repeated attempts to see her son and has already lodged two appeals against the judgment. Karl, now living with him, has had to undergo surgery for a hernia, which has left Beethoven helpless as a carer, inflicting more pain on Karl rather than helping him heal. Tension between the two frequently erupts into fierce arguments, even violence. Beethoven's own health is poor. He describes it himself as 'severe inflammatory catarrh', causing him to remain bedbound for a considerable period of time and unable to go out. He complains of acute attacks of colic, as well as rheumatic pains and 'one head cold after another'. It is more than mere pessimism that causes him to speculate that 'perhaps I will never be better'.

It is against this background that he embarks on a new piano sonata, which will change the sonata form for ever and fulfil his prediction that it will be his greatest. From his words written at the top of the title page,

Grosse Sonate für das Hammerklavier, it has come to be known as the *Hammerklavier* Sonata.[2]

In a fortunate coincidence, as he begins to shape the first movement Beethoven receives an unexpected visit from an English gentleman by the name of Thomas Broadwood Esq., of the London firm of piano manufacturers John Broadwood & Sons. Broadwood is on a tour of European capitals, probably to secure orders, and is delighted when Beethoven agrees to see him. Broadwood tells us that the meeting was convivial but not easy, Beethoven's deafness combined with language problems making conversation awkward. Seated at the keyboard, he can see how different Beethoven's style of playing is to the conventions of the day. There are no arched fingers delivering a delicate touch; rather Beethoven's fingers are almost horizontal to the keyboard, and he uses the strength of his forearms and wrists to push them down on the keys.

We can assume there is discussion, with a colleague acting as translator, of the difference between the hammer action of English pianos compared with those made in Vienna or Paris. The English action, Broadwood explains, is much heavier, giving a more solid sound, which he thinks will suit Beethoven's playing much better than the instruments he currently uses, and in an extraordinary act of generosity he promises to send a Broadwood piano from London to Vienna as a gift for Beethoven. The familiar name of Ferdinand Ries comes up. He has now settled in London, and is a member of the London Philharmonic Society. Broadwood will get him to arrange things.

We can forgive Beethoven if he soon forgot about the encounter, and the promise. But Broadwood was as good as his word. In late January 1818 Beethoven watched workmen unpack a large wooden box reinforced with tin to reveal a beautiful instrument built of Spanish mahogany, with a solid steel frame, triple-stringed throughout, inlaid with marquetry and ormolu, the brass carrying-handles formed of laurel leaves. To the right of the keyboard, in black ink, were the signatures of five prominent musicians active in London, including, of course, his long-suffering – and clearly endlessly forgiving – young friend Ferdi Ries.[3]

It is difficult to see how any fortepiano could have coped with the opening of the *Hammerklavier* Sonata. A single extra-loud note deep in the bass followed by gigantic thundering chords in both hands. The leap in the left hand from that low note to the first chord is practically impossible at the metronome speed Beethoven has marked. That means he could do it. Others have tried and come close. The renowned Austrian pianist Artur Schnabel, the first to record all the Beethoven sonatas, by playing the opening of the *Hammerklavier* at the speed Beethoven marks, produces a splash of sound rather than distinct chords. I suspect Beethoven would have smiled and told him to keep trying. The fourth chord in the right hand is a deliberate discord.

What, then, inspired such an epic, defiant, triumphant opening? It's tempting to say this is Beethoven shaking his fist at Johanna and the whole legal system, shouting at them that he will prevail. Actually, there may be a much simpler, more prosaic, explanation. Beethoven wrote in a letter that the sonata was long intended 'in my heart' for his royal patron and friend, Archduke Rudolph, to whom it is dedicated. He also states that the first two movements had been written in time for Rudolph's nameday on 17 April 1818. It is a fact that the words 'Vivat, vivat Rudolphus' fit perfectly with the opening chords.[4] Is that what lay behind that most exultant of openings? Beethoven does not enlighten us. The first movement is peppered with moments of chaos – organised, but only barely.

The second movement is built around a fragmentation of those opening chords, with a haunting passage in which Beethoven echoes the opening theme of the *Eroica* Symphony, but in the minor key. It is as if he is preparing us for the third movement, the slow movement.

Here now we come to the heart of the sonata. The longest, most emotional, ethereal, melancholic movement for piano he would ever write. In fact only the *Cavatina* of the Late String Quartet in B flat, Op. 130, can compare. Of that Beethoven said he wrote through tears, and a friend said no composition had caused him such pain. Understandable, given that Beethoven's health was in terminal decline and Karl would shortly attempt suicide.

But the slow movement of the *Hammerklavier*? There is nothing like it, before or since, in the piano repertoire. Wilhelm von Lenz, friend and student of Liszt, described it as 'a mausoleum of collective sorrow'.[5] The early twentieth-century German music critic Paul Bekker, using remarkable imagery, writes that it is 'the apotheosis of pain, of that deep sorrow for which there is no remedy, and which finds expression not in passionate outpourings, but in the immeasurable stillness of utter woe'.[6] For the great twentieth-century pianist Wilhelm Kempff, a noted Beethoven specialist, the slow movement of the *Hammerklavier* was reportedly the most magnificent monologue Beethoven ever created.

This is Beethoven talking quietly to us, telling us of his innermost despair, so deaf now he can no longer converse, struggling to save his beloved 'son'. He writes at the top of the manuscript page, *Adagio sostenuto e con molto sentimento*. He wants us to be in no doubt. It begins in a fashion that is as extraordinary in its own way as the opening chords of the first movement. Just two chords, only three notes in each, all an octave apart so the sound is almost hollow, to be played with the soft pedal down. Only in the second bar, with a full chord, does the movement properly begin.

The mood is sombre and filled with pain, hauntingly expressed in a falling motif. Even moments of relative levity quickly yield once more to sorrow. And when we think Beethoven is bringing the movement to an end, no, he has more to tell us, more to help us understand his deep despair. But we do not linger in anguish. Just as in the original version of the string quartet he follows the despairingly emotional *Cavatina* with the thunderous *Grosse Fuge*, so in the *Hammerklavier* the despondency he has plunged us into is followed with an enormous exultant fugue, which he marks *Allegro – Fuga: Allegro risoluto*; *risoluto* being the all-important word.

Beethoven was himself deeply affected by what he had created. He must have carried it in his mind for some time before setting pen to paper – how else would he be able to predict it would be his greatest sonata? And he clearly thought about the sonata even after its completion. It was due to be published in London slightly ahead of Vienna, and only a few short weeks before publication date he wrote to Ries in London, telling him to add those two hollow chords at the very start of the slow movement. Poor Ries! Imagine his dash to the publisher to tell them to hold everything. As it happened, he was able to make the addition just in time. Similarly in Vienna, Artaria added those two extra chords before the first bar.

Why do these seemingly random chords matter so much? They fulfil three purposes, according to Professor Barry Cooper. They form an essential

bridge between the two very different keys of the second and third movements; they echo the opening leap of the first movement, and they anticipate
an important motif that is to come later in the movement.[7] Beethoven never
does anything by accident. There is always a reason, and Ries knew better
than to question it. But it is an example of how the compositional process
never stops in Beethoven's head, even when it is seemingly completed.

There are two ways of looking at the *Hammerklavier* Sonata. It is the
most technically demanding of all Beethoven's piano sonatas; in fact it is one
of the most challenging in the entire repertoire. That deep heartbreaking
motif is played by the right hand crossing over the left, low on the keyboard.
In the very same bar the right hand has to repeat it at the top of the keyboard.
The performer has to accomplish this technically while investing the passage
with the utmost emotion. The sonata is complex and elaborate, using practically every key signature, ranging from six flats to six sharps. But it is also
the most deeply personal of all his sonatas. Beethoven is talking to us in the
language he understands best. He is sharing with us his pain, his conflicting
emotions – moments of joy vanquished by anguish – and, overriding everything, the scourge of his deafness, which by now has robbed him of the one
sense he needs the most.

36

I want to go back in time now around fifteen years for Beethoven, and nearly thirty for me, to tell an extraordinary story, which, I am afraid, does little to enhance my admiration for Beethoven the man, but which has enriched my life incalculably.

It is a barely credible story of insults and coincidences, and I shall start at the beginning. In 1803 a brilliant young violinist by the name of George Bridgetower – of mixed heritage, mother Polish, father West Indian, born in Poland but resident in England – arrived in Vienna and was very swiftly accepted into the highest aristocratic circles, given that he had performed for King George III at Windsor Castle and the Prince Regent at the newly built Brighton Pavilion. Prince Lichnowsky arranged a meeting with Beethoven. The two men met, hit it off, and Beethoven agreed to Bridgetower's request to compose a new violin sonata that the two could perform together at a recital Bridgetower was due to give in a month's time in the Augarten pavilion.

Beethoven being Beethoven, he immediately turned his attention to other matters. Bridgetower enlisted the help of Ries and the violinist Ignaz Schuppanzigh, who was organising the concert, to put gentle and flattering pressure on Beethoven, pointing out Bridgetower would need rehearsal time, given the technical mastery he was sure to need to play music by the great Beethoven. Leaving matters until only a week or so before the scheduled concert, Beethoven finally began work on the new sonata, taking the last movement of a sonata he had composed the year before and attaching it to the new work, so Bridgetower at least had something to work on. He composed a new first movement, which opened with devilishly difficult solo chords on violin requiring double-stopping across all four strings, which would stretch Bridgetower's virtuosity to the limit. To his consternation, the opening movement grew to a formidable length of a greater complexity than any sonata Beethoven had hitherto written for the violin. As for the second movement, Beethoven was still composing it the night before the concert. No time for the violin part to be written out, so Bridgetower would have to read it at sight over Beethoven's shoulder at the concert. The scene was set for potential disaster.

Concerts in the Augarten began at eight o'clock in the morning and were highly prestigious. Thus it was the cream of Viennese aristocracy, including the British ambassador in honour of Mr Bridgetower, that gathered on 24 May to hear the premiere of a new violin sonata, with the composer himself at the piano.

The performance began, and just a few minutes in something extraordinary happened. In bar 18 of the *Presto* Beethoven had written a huge run just for the piano, just for himself. It comes in a section he had marked to be repeated. In the repeat, Beethoven played the run, and Bridgetower immediately imitated it on the violin. Beethoven looked up in utter astonishment. The audience held its breath. Then he leapt up, threw his arms round Bridgetower, and shouted, *Noch einmal, mein lieber Bursch!* ('Again, my dear fellow!') And the two played their runs again.

The performance, with Bridgetower sight-reading the complex second movement, a theme and variations, over Beethoven's shoulder, was a triumph. At the celebration lunch Beethoven announced he was dedicating the sonata to Bridgetower, and wrote flamboyantly on the title page of the manuscript, *Sonata mulattica composta per il mulatto Brischdauer, gran pazzo e compositor mulattico* ('Mixed-race sonata composed for the mixed-race Bridgetower, madman and mixed-race composer'). He also wrote what was intended as a good-natured insult, *Sonata per un mulattico lunaticco.*

Bridgetower knew his name was made, forever to be linked to a composition by this greatest of composers. But then he made a mistake, the mistake of his life. He made an off-colour remark about a lady Beethoven knew and respected. Beethoven's mood changed in an instant. No man who could allow such language to pass his lips could have his name inscribed on a work by Beethoven, the great moralist. Beethoven immediately withdrew the dedication and sent the manuscript instead to the celebrated violinist

Rudolphe Kreutzer in Paris, whom he had met briefly some years before in Vienna. How grateful was Monsieur Kreutzer to receive this masterwork by the great Beethoven? He looked at the manuscript, saw those opening double-stopped chords, and looked no further. Declaring Beethoven did not understand the violin, he never once performed it in public, the sonata that to this day bears his name.

As for Bridgetower, he left Vienna soon afterwards and never met Beethoven again. He had a successful career, settling in London, but old age and arthritis in his fingers put an end to his playing days. He died at the age of eighty-one in some poverty in Peckham, south London, the witness to his death signing her name with a X. He is buried today in Kensal Green Cemetery just off the A40 flyover west of London, his name forgotten to history.

It is a remarkable story, telling us much about Beethoven, his volatility, his high morals preventing him from enjoying a bawdy joke, and his instant willingness to sacrifice a valuable musical friendship for the sake of probity, in the process elevating an unmerited name to musical history while obliterating a worthy one.

The story is recounted in bare detail in Thayer's *Life of Beethoven*, which is where I first encountered it. A footnote states that further details of Bridgetower's life can be found in an edition of the *Musical Times* dated May 1908.[1] At the time, in the mid-1990s, I was researching and writing my trilogy on Beethoven's life, *The Last Master*. The Bridgetower story captivated me, I had to know more. It must have been such an extraordinary moment – the cream of Viennese aristocracy, the British ambassador, all gathered over morning coffee to witness the first performance of a new work by Beethoven, with the always unpredictable composer at the piano and the rare sight of a mixed-race violinist.

Unpredictable? They could have no idea what was coming. Yet it is Bridgetower who proves to be the unpredictable one. Taking his musical life in his hands, he improvises a virtuoso run across all four strings – up, down, up again, ending on a single low C on the G string, in exact imitation of the run Beethoven has just executed on piano. All eyes are on Beethoven, whose face is frozen in astonishment. What would be a normal reaction? A smile between the two players, and they play on. But Beethoven leaps up from the piano stool, embraces Bridgetower, praising him to the roof! What normal musician would behave like that, interrupting the performance, actually stopping it, to throw his arms around the violinist?

I had to know more, but in those pre-internet days, how on earth do you track down an edition of an obscure musical journal dating back almost a century? I had an idea. At the time I lived in a block of flats in central London just round the corner from the Royal Academy of Music, the august institution I had once considered joining to study trombone after that sem-inal night of trad jazz at the dental students' graduation ball. Would they have a library? Probably. Would they have a copy of the *Musical Times* from May 1908? Highly unlikely, if not impossible. Would someone there, if I could get to speak to anybody, be able to give me some advice, point me in the right direction, so I might be able to see the article on microfiche or slide or something? Possible. It was worth a try. What was the worst that could happen?

The next morning I mounted the steps to the main entrance of a frankly rather forbidding building – at least forbidding to someone who had no right entering it. In the main lobby was not one security desk but two, one on each side of the hall. I thought about turning round and heading straight back out, but I was inside now; I had no choice but to go on. I walked to the desk on the left, and muttered to a stern-looking security guard, 'Er, could I possibly go to the library, please?'

'Certainly,' he said. 'Do you know where it is?'

'Er, no, I'm sorry.'

'Down the stairs, turn left at the bottom, it's at the end of the corridor. You'll see the sign on the door.'

I was in! That at least was a start.

I found the door and rather gingerly opened it. A woman was stacking papers on a small counter, behind her rows of packed shelves. She looked up at me enquiringly, her face clearly registering mine was not a face she recog-nised. I explained, haltingly, that I was researching for a book on Beethoven, and was trying to track down an edition of the *Musical Times* from May 1908. 'I don't suppose . . .'

She frowned, I braced myself for the worst, and she said, 'Do you know, I think I might just be able to help you there.' She vanished between the rows of shelves. I could see her taking volumes out, putting them back. Finally, she held on to one. 'There you are. This what you are looking for. This has all the editions for that year.' And that is how I came to know so much about Bridgetower and the *Kreutzer* Sonata.

The first volume of my trilogy was due to be published in 1996, and my editor asked where I would like to hold the publication party. The obvious answer was a reception room at a hotel, or a private room at a restaurant. Then I had a sudden thought. I wonder if the Royal Academy of Music would let me hold it there. It would give a wonderful musical feel to the evening, and it would also give me a chance to express my gratitude for how helpful they had been.

In those pre-email days, there was no alternative but to make a phone call. I looked up the number and rang. A female voice answered. I said this was a slightly unusual request, but I don't suppose there would be any chance of holding a small reception at the Academy to mark the publication of a book I had written on Beethoven?

There was a rather long pause, then she said, 'I'm sorry, that's not the sort of thing we do. I've never heard of us doing that before.'

I apologised profusely, saying I fully understood. 'Thank you anyway,' I said, and moved the phone away from my ear on its way back to the cradle.

As I did so I heard her say something else. 'I'm sorry, I didn't catch that?'

'You could always ask the principal, I'm sure he'd love to do something like that.'

I thought about it for a day or two then, emboldened, picked up the phone, dialled the number, and asked for the principal's secretary. A month later I entered the Academy for only the second time, this time to hold the launch party for the first volume of my Beethoven trilogy.

Over the next few years my late wife and I attended concerts and recitals at the Academy, and were frequently invited to special events. It gave me an enormous feeling of pleasure and satisfaction that I was now involved with this distinguished institution that it had been my early ambition to join, before life took me in another direction.

Sometime in the spring of 2000 the principal, Professor Curtis Price, asked me to come to his office. 'Would you be our Orator at graduation?' I was, literally, speechless. He smiled and explained that each year, at graduation, celebrated musicians were honoured. I would read the citation in each case. 'Don't worry, we'll write the citations. All you have to do is read them.' Knees knocking, I did it. I have been Orator now for nearly twenty-five years, reading the citation and shaking hands with some of the most celebrated names in the world of music – Sir Colin Davis, Sir Simon Rattle, Christoph von Dohnányi, Valery Gergiev, Dame Kiri Te Kanawa, Renée Fleming, Sir Elton John and Annie Lennox, who were both students at the Academy, George Martin – the fifth Beatle – Sir Mark Elder, Sir Peter Maxwell Davies, Pierre Boulez, Denis Wick the legendary trombonist who had been an early idol of mine; more recently Lin-Manuel Miranda, creator of the hit musical *Hamilton*, actor and musician Matt Lucas. The list goes on. In 2001 I received my own honour, an Honorary Fellowship of the Royal Academy of Music, for my involvement with the Academy and my work on Beethoven.

It all began because George Bridgetower improvised at that first performance of a new violin sonata with Beethoven. It was written up in the *Musical Times* of May 1908, and the Royal Academy of Music had a copy.

37

What connects Beethoven's *Moonlight* Sonata with a risqué gynaecological joke about childbirth? 'A publishers' lunch' is the answer. Soon after the first volume of my *Last Master* trilogy was published in 1996, my editor asked me if I would give a short talk at a publishers' lunch in Manchester, along with three other well-known names who had just published new books. The event is seared on my mind, since it was the first of many, possibly hundreds of, talks I was to give on Beethoven, and am still giving, with results ranging from brilliant to calamitous.

The event was well attended, with possibly twenty or more large round tables and a top table of the four authors and the host publisher. I was told to speak ideally for not more than five minutes, and definitely not more than ten. I would be third speaker, following the humorous Australian writer Kathy Lette. I had never spoken about Beethoven in public before. I sensed instinctively that a lunch gathering, with wine flowing, was not the ideal occasion. In that, at least, I was spot on. With wine glasses being emptied and refilled, teaspoons jangling against coffee cups, Kathy Lette got up to speak.

The next ten minutes sped by in a whirl of laughter. I remember her closing line as if it was yesterday. 'And so, girls, if you want to avoid sleepless nights, next time you give birth, when your gynaecologist tells you he's just going to put a couple of stitches in, tell him to keep going!' The room imploded. Screams of delight. A tsunami of laughter. The host of the event rose to his feet, cheeks tinged with pink. 'Thank you, Kathy. Hilarious. Now, to talk about Beethoven, here is John Suchet.'

There was a faint murmur of applause, and a tangible sense of disappointment that they weren't getting another ten minutes of Kathy Lette. I apologised at the start for the fact that Beethoven was not a man who inspired many laughs, told the story of how the most famous piano sonata ever written had acquired its name, a name that the composer himself never knew, and sat down as swiftly as I could.

It was an early lesson in public speaking, or at least in public speaking when the subject of your talk is something as innately serious as Ludwig van Beethoven. When did you last see a portrait of Beethoven smiling? Always the downturned lips and permanent scowl. The lesson? Avoid invitations to give an after-dinner speech about Beethoven, because your audience will drink during the dinner, and when you get to your feet they will expect you to make them laugh.

Alas, I did not fully learn that lesson until a year after that publishers' lunch. I was asked to give an after-dinner speech about Beethoven at the Christmas dinner of a local law firm at the Grand Hotel in Brighton. There would be a piano in the room, and my pianist would play short pieces to illustrate my talk. For instance, I'd tell how the piano sonata published as the *Sonata quasi una Fantasia* became the best-known sonata ever written. My pianist would then play the famous opening bars of the *Moonlight* Sonata, and blank looks in the audience would turn to smiles of recognition.[1] Just one thing, the organisers said: they won't know what your talk is going to be about, so it'll be a wonderful surprise for them. If there was the smallest feeling of apprehension stirring inside me, I admit it was outweighed by the flattery of being the evening's star turn with a mystery subject.

Those small stirrings of apprehension became full fear midway through the dinner. 'I bet you've got some hilarious stories to tell,' said the chap sitting next to me, 'all the things that must have gone wrong when you're reading the news. You're going to have us in stitches,' he said, draining his glass and refilling it. I went into silent panic mode. Could I switch from Beethoven to stories of my career as reporter and newscaster for ITN? I had nothing prepared. It was too risky. Also, it had already been announced there would be words and music after dinner from our special guest speaker. There were not too many music-based anecdotes about a life in television news.

I began to recast the top of my talk in my head, in between carrying on a conversation with the man to my right and the woman to my left. It was impossible to think it through properly. Why was I even here? I made a vow there and then never again to accept an after-dinner invitation to give a talk about Beethoven – or that if I did, I would certainly not participate in the dinner.

I was not introduced but simply given a nod from somewhere at the back of the room. I walked to a central spot and my pianist took his seat at the piano. It took a moment for the room to calm down. I gazed out over a sea of expectant faces, braced to burst into laughter at the hilarity about to unfold. 'Good evening. There aren't too many jokes about Beethoven. Of all the many people who have come up to me to tell me their Beethoven joke, I have so far collected just two.' I then told the feeble 'rumbling noise in the churchyard is Beethoven decomposing' joke, and the marginally better one where the punchline is Beethoven's wife denying she is his inspiration and laughing in imitation of the opening of the Fifth Symphony – *Ha-ha-ha-Haaah*. (Followed by the anti-climactic addendum: 'It can't be true, of course, because Beethoven never married.')

My pianist and I made it to the end with no calamities, no moments of hilarity. I dropped a couple of stories to tighten things up, and restructured the ending, replacing the normally emotional moment of the funeral oration with a request for more jokes to add to my puny collection. I did not ask in vain.

A group of four solicitors came up to me afterwards and one said, 'Thank you for a great talk, though we didn't hear a word of it. When you said you'd only collected two jokes, we spent the rest of your talk trying to come up with a new one. And we have! Ready for this? Beethoven goes into a newsagent and buys a lottery ticket. The chap hands it to him and says, "You could soon be very rich because this week it's a Rollover Beethoven!"' I confess I laughed my head off, more at the release of tension than anything else. I have dined out many times on how a disastrous talk yielded one positive result – a brand new Beethoven joke.

I feared I might hear a new Beethoven joke, at my expense, when I was giving a talk at a school somewhere in the Home Counties. There was no dressing room and only one gents' toilet. In the interval I hurried into the gents, head down, and shut myself in a cubicle.

'What do you think?' said one man to another as they stood at the urinals.

'Well, it's better than I thought it'd be,' said the other. 'But I hope he doesn't go on too long. I've got an early start tomorrow.'

Then there was the ancient and illustrious Worshipful Company of Musicians, who around the turn of the century asked if I would propose the loyal toast at their annual dinner in a liveried hall in the City of London. 'That's all you'll have to do, just stand up, raise your glass, and say, "Please join me in the loyal toast to Her Majesty the Queen."'

I agreed to do it, flattered that my work on Beethoven had reached such an esteemed organisation. I took my place at the top table, to find the menu and evening's running order on a card in front of me, declaring, 'Guest speaker John Suchet'. The *Moonlight* Sonata story got another outing. It was greeted with polite laughter, though I suspect it was well known to most of those present.

One venue somewhere on the south coast produced a portable keyboard on spindly legs that threatened to collapse under the furious inverted double fugue that closes Piano Sonata, Op. 110. On another occasion my pianist had a long-standing engagement he could not relinquish so I had to hum the opening of the *Moonlight*.

There were nice moments too. Midway through a talk in Exeter, I said, 'I would like to tell you the story of Beethoven and his nephew Karl but I'd keep you here till midnight.' A man in the audience called out, 'Please do!' And one of the most stressful evenings of my life: after trying and failing to get round Birmingham in rush-hour traffic for a talk at Theatre Clwyd in Mold, North Wales, I had no choice but to phone ahead to say we would have to put the start time back from 7.30 to 8 p.m. There would be no time for rehearsal or a sound check. At 8 p.m. I introduced myself breathlessly to a full house by saying, 'Beethoven had many problems in his life, but he never had to cope with the M6 round Birmingham in the rush hour.' Afterwards I was swamped with audience members apologising to me for what I had gone through, when it should have been the other way round.

Travels with Ludwig. Never a dull moment.

38

Easter 1995, my final research trip to Vienna with my wife Bonnie before the publication, due the following year, of the first volume of *The Last Master*. I decided to commemorate it in two ways. First, we were staying at the Ambassador Hotel in the Neuer Markt, formerly the Mehlgrube performance hall known to Beethoven, and outside which the centrepiece of the fountain shows the naked man aiming his bare rump at that shopkeeper's window. We could ill afford the Ambassador's prices, but I somehow felt it gave me a connection to Beethoven, to be sleeping in the same spot where he, and Mozart before him, had performed. Even less could we afford the half-bottle of champagne I insisted on extracting from the minibar in our room. Bonnie thought I was mad, but she understood.

There was something else I wanted, and I expected it to be fairly simple to achieve. I wanted a small bust of Beethoven to stand on my desk at home. Not one of the ubiquitous and tacky little things in numerous tourist shops, alongside Mozart and Johann Strauss, but a bust modelled on the life mask taken by the sculptor Franz Klein in 1812. This is the truest representation we have of what Beethoven actually looked like, since it was taken from life. Such a treasure was most likely to be found in an antique shop, or at an art dealer's, and so we set out on a tour of Vienna's museum and art quarter.

I prepared my enquiry in advance. *Grüss Gott. Haben Sie eine Büste von Beethoven?* It would be too complicated to ask for a bust based on the Klein life mask, but I would know it as soon as I saw it. I also expected a knowledgeable antique dealer to understand exactly what it was I wanted, and gladly produce it for me. *Leider nicht* ('I'm afraid not') was the response in the first shop we entered, and the second, third, fourth, and every other shop we tried. I was baffled. Here we were in Vienna, Beethoven's adopted home city, and no one could offer me a bust of Beethoven. Maybe the clue was in the word 'adopted'. Not one of us. Now if it's Johann Strauss you want . . .

We gave up and went and had a coffee. We had left the museum quarter and were walking back to the hotel, when we passed an antique shop. Should we have one last try? Why not, we were passing it anyway. In we went, and the familiar exchange took place.

Leider nicht, said the shopkeeper. *Aber Moment mal!* He bent down, pulled open a drawer behind the counter, and lifted out, cradling it gently with both hands, a bronze life mask of Beethoven.

I gasped out loud. It was the Klein life mask. I recognised it instantly. I stood rooted to the spot. He held the mask so that it was looking at me. I was gazing at the face of Ludwig van Beethoven.

⁂

The year is 1812. Beethoven is forty-one years of age and at the height of his fame. To date there have been a number of portraits of him, the best known of which, dating from eight years earlier, shows him in idealised form, left hand resting on a lyre, right arm outstretched, hand open, fingers extended, with a sylvan scene behind him. His strong unsmiling gaze locks eyes with ours. This is the artist as god. A powerful and striking image that looks nothing like the real Beethoven.

It is time, Beethoven's closest associates decide, to do something about this. Coincidentally Andreas Streicher, the piano manufacturer, wants a bust of Beethoven to stand in the recital hall attached to his workshop, where Beethoven frequently performed. And so Franz Klein, a well-known sculptor, is commissioned to create a bust of Beethoven that would accurately represent his features.

In order to achieve a true likeness, Klein needed to make a life mask of Beethoven. From this he could take a mould to use as template for the bust, guaranteeing the accuracy of the final sculpture. A straightforward process, but one that would require the full cooperation of the sitter. Therein, they all knew, lay the problem.

Straightforward the process might be, but not comfortable. Klein would have to begin by tilting Beethoven's head backwards, at right-angles to his shoulders. He would place cotton wads over Beethoven's eyes, then spread wet plaster of Paris over his face, pressing it into every contour and crevice. Finally he would need to insert two straws into his nostrils so he could breathe, and instruct him to remain as still as he possibly could for at least ten minutes to allow the plaster to set.

We do not know exactly how Streicher set about persuading Beethoven to submit to the process. Probably he used plenty of flattery, with the practical argument that no artist had thus far managed to capture Beethoven's true likeness on canvas. At any rate, no doubt to Streicher's astonishment and delight, Beethoven agrees.

So far so good. Beethoven sits in Klein's chair, and the sculptor stirs the mixture in a bowl. On it goes, wet and heavy, pressed firmly onto his forehead, cheeks, nose and chin. The problem comes when Klein inserts the straws into Beethoven's nostrils. The straws are the last straw. Beethoven has had enough. He sits bolt upright, tears the plaster off his face, flings it to the ground and heads for the door. Streicher hurries after him, brings him back, sits him down, makes light of the whole thing, no doubt pours him a glass of wine, and when he has calmed down, persuades him to give it another try.

Klein is no doubt over-cautious for fear of upsetting Beethoven again. As gently as possible he inserts those straws, all the while cajoling Beethoven and imploring him to relax. Maybe the wine made him soporific, maybe he actually fell asleep, but however it happened, Beethoven acquiesces and Klein gets his mould. From that original 'negative', Klein creates a small number of 'positives', which he uses to make the bust. To that bust he adds a luxuriant head of hair swept back, a neck scarf knotted at the front, and the top part of a double-buttoned jacket turned up at the collar. The pockmarks are clearly visible on his cheeks. The skin has many blemishes. Across a cleft in the chin is a deep horizontal scar, most likely caused by a fall. This is, and always will be, the closest likeness we have of the real Ludwig van Beethoven.[1]

It was a small version of that famous bust that I was looking for on my trawl of antique shops in Vienna. It was a re-creation of the original life mask that I found. In the years and decades following Beethoven's death, many bronze copies of the life mask were made, with laurel leaves adorning his head as if he were an emperor. But beneath the laurel leaves is the face of a real man, pock marks clearly visible on the cheeks. The grim expression and the downturned lips are evidence of the discomfort of having his face smeared in plaster of Paris, but forever define a humourless and angry man, depriving us of the other side to his character – flashes of humour, which we know from his friends could break out as unexpectedly as his anger.

The heavy bronze life mask of Beethoven that stared at me across the counter in that antique shop in Vienna had hung for half a century on the wall of a lawyer's office in the city. On his death his family disposed of it along with his effects. That severe countenance has gazed down at me now for almost thirty years, witnessing every word I have written about him. I'm still waiting for a smile and a nod of approval.

39

If the Klein bust is guilty of one thing, it is that it gives Beethoven an unmistakable air of sophistication. That elegantly coiffed, swept-back hair. The neatly tied neckerchief and close-fitting formal jacket. That is not the Beethoven his contemporaries knew. Here is a vivid first-hand evocation of Beethoven the man, with his scruffy unkempt appearance, and behaviour bordering on paranoia.

> Before walking into the room to join us, he would usually stick his head round the door first to make sure no one was there that he did not like. He was short and unremarkable, with an ugly red face full of pockmarks. His hair was very dark and hung fairly tousled about his face. His clothing was very informal and paid no attention to the formalities that were customary at the time, and particularly so in our aristocratic circles.[1]

In an extraordinary passage, the writer of these reminiscences, a young woman renowned for her performances of Beethoven's piano works, describes how she saw a high-born lady, Countess Wilhelmina Thun, the mother-in-law of Beethoven's great patron Prince Lichnowsky, prostrate herself on the ground before him, pleading with him to play something at the piano for her. Beethoven, seated on the sofa, refused to move. (She absolves Beethoven slightly by pointing out the countess was well known for her eccentricity.)

She goes on to describe how, at a musical gathering, she distinctly remembers seeing Haydn and Salieri sitting on one side of the salon, 'most carefully dressed in the old-fashioned style with wig, hair tied neatly at the back, buckle shoes and silk stockings', while on the other side was

Beethoven, 'casually and carelessly dressed in peasant clothes from the Rhineland'.

It is not difficult to understand why Beethoven cut such an unconventional, and indeed largely unloved, figure in the highly stratified social system in Vienna, how he stood apart from everybody else – aristocrats, fellow musicians or simply admirers. Every personage in early nineteenth-century Vienna knew their place, their standing in society, the unspoken rules that governed behaviour and etiquette. Everybody except Beethoven. When he sat at the keyboard, his preternatural talent simply overrode everything else. His compositional skills alone would not have been enough to guarantee acceptance in the highest circles – even with his musical reputation firmly established, there was unrelenting criticism of his compositions. But allow him to take his place at the keyboard, and any sense of disquiet simply melted away.

Once established in Vienna, Beethoven lived a somewhat solitary life. It was not entirely out of choice. His worsening deafness made an ordinary social life increasingly difficult. Those who had been involved with him tended to give him something of a wide berth, simply because his eccentricities made any normal kind of friendship nigh on impossible. He was utterly unpredictable. Share a table with him in a restaurant and he could be the perfect companion. In an instant, though, that could change. On one occasion, not being satisfied with the lamb dish served him at an inn in the foothills of the Vienna Woods, he picked up the plate and hurled it at the waiter. Only the good nature of the waiter, licking his lips as the gravy ran down his cheeks into his mouth, saved the day. Beethoven's eccentricities extended into his private life. Ferdinand Ries recounts how he would arrive at his master's apartment for a lesson at 1 p.m., to find him still in his night clothes, his face peppered with bloodstained pieces of cotton wadding where he had cut himself shaving. On the whole, it was simply safer to stay away.

Not that this was always possible. Ignaz Seyfried, concert master at the Theater an der Wien, gives a detailed, absorbing and amusing account of dinner 'chez Beethoven'. The composer had gone to the market and chosen all the ingredients himself, 'undoubtedly paying anything but the most reasonable prices'. In other words, stallholders had seen the perfect opportunity to relieve an eccentric customer of as much money as they could. Then came the invitation to dinner, to be prepared with his own hands, which, said Seyfried, left us with no choice but to accept, and appear at the appointed hour, 'full of expectation as to what would happen'.

The first surprise came when Beethoven's housekeeper opened the door to them. 'We found our host dressed in a short evening jacket, a stately nightcap on his bristly shock of hair, and his loins girded with a blue kitchen apron, very busily engaged at the hearth.' I find it interesting that eyewitness descriptions of Beethoven always seem to comment on his hair, how full and unkempt it was, clearly indicating he was never seen in a wig (unlike Haydn and Salieri). It was never tied back in a bow, and it probably never saw a brush or comb – something portraitists and sculptors invariably chose to correct.

Now imagine Beethoven, that nightcap perched on his untidy mane, standing at the oven, busily cooking – for an hour and a half! That is how long Seyfried and his colleagues waited, 'the turbulent demands of our stomachs assuaged with increasing difficulty by cordial dialogue'. When, finally and with much self-praise, Beethoven placed the food in front of them, they reacted with extravagant compliments to a meal that bordered on the inedible.

> The soup recalled those charitable leftovers which are ladled out to beggars in the taverns. The beef was half cooked and fit to be eaten only by an ostrich. The vegetables floated in a mixture of water and grease. The roast seemed to have been smoked in the chimney. None of this stopped the giver of the feast praising every dish, and our applause put him in such good humour that he named himself after the cook in the latest burlesque, *The Merry Nuptials*. The fact is we could barely choke down more than a few morsels, managing to fill ourselves with a healthy mixture of bread, fresh fruit, sweet pastry – and the unadulterated juice of the grape.[2]

There was relief all round when, after this 'memorable banquet', Beethoven declared himself exhausted and returned to his desk to work. His house-keeper took over duties, forbidding him to eat any of the food he had himself cooked for fear of it giving him indigestion! Imagine the scene. One moment Beethoven the chef is regaling his guests with laughter and anecdotes; the next he gets up from the table and returns to his desk to work, as if they do not exist. This will not have surprised them. They knew full well how unpredictable he could be.

Seyfried tells us more. Among Beethoven's favourite dishes, which his housekeeper prepared for him every Thursday, was 'a kind of bread soup, cooked like mush'. When it was ready, his housekeeper had to present to him ten large eggs on a plate. One by one he would hold them up to the light to check the contents, then decapitate them and anxiously sniff them to ensure they were fresh. Inevitably one or two of the eggs would have gone off, and then the storm would break. Beethoven would shout at his housekeeper in a voice of thunder. She, knowing exactly what was coming next, would turn and hurry away, as Beethoven hurled the offending eggs at her back. They would 'pour out their yellow-white, sticky intestines over her in veritable lava streams'.[3]

Beethoven told a colleague he never ate lunch or dinner at home, unless he was entertaining. This caused something of a problem for the establishments he chose to frequent. Some even were known to keep a small table at the back reserved for him, so any outbursts that might occur could be contained, with the least disruption to other diners. Two establishments, the *Roten Hahn* ('Red Cockerel') and the Prater Kaffeehaus, had suffered the same indignity as Beethoven's housekeeper regarding eggs that were not fresh. In the case of the Prater Kaffeehaus the eggs were overcooked. Instead of throwing them at the waiter, Beethoven hurled them through the window, where they landed on customers dining al fresco. Diners at the *Römischen Kaiser* ('Holy Roman Emperor'), one of the most exclusive restaurants in Vienna, asked to be seated well away from Beethoven, after seeing him 'investigating the contents of his nose'.[4]

A regular meeting place was the *Weissen Schwan* ('White Swan') in the Neuer Markt, next to the Mehlgrube. There, with the Rhineland now occupied by Napoleon's Revolutionary Army, Bonners-in-exile would regularly meet to discuss events in their home town, and how their families had written to them of French soldiers patrolling the streets. Vienna too would twice suffer the same fate, in late 1805 and then again, with devastating damage from cannon fire, in 1809. Thereafter, with Klaus Metternich first as foreign minister and later as chancellor, Vienna was in virtual lockdown. Spies were everywhere. At tables at the back of the *Weissen Schwan* the Bonners would speak in hushed tones – except Beethoven, whose deafness led him to declaim in full voice, his words potentially seditious and dangerous. At first this was a problem. Soon the spies at other tables came to know this was just that eccentric musician spouting off. 'Take no notice, he's not dangerous.'

Several establishments frequented by Beethoven are still there to be enjoyed today. The Café Jahn, where both Mozart and Beethoven performed their music, is today the Café Frauenhuber in the Himmelpfortgasse, just off the main pedestrianised Kärntnerstrasse. Beethoven was particularly partial to the red wine in the *Schwarzen Kameel* ('Black Camel'), where he would not only dine but also buy provisions at the delicatessen counter. The *Kameel*, on the same site in the Bognergasse, still serves excellent lunches and dinners, though the deli counter is long gone, and I can personally vouch for the quality of the red wine.

Another favourite was the *Alten Blumenstock* ('Old Flowering Plant') in the narrow Ballgasse, a short distance from St Stephen's Cathedral. For a time Beethoven lived in rooms above the *Blumenstock* and would regularly go downstairs for meals. Today the *Blumenstock*, in the oldest part of the city, still does brisk business, the back of the menu paying tribute to its famous guest, noting that his favourite dish was roast lamb with gravy. Every Friday Beethoven would eat fish at the *Braunen Hirschen* ('Brown Deer') in the Rotenturmstrasse, and in his later years he would frequent the *Brandstätte* ('Fireplace') on Stefansplatz on a Saturday evening to enjoy a meal of blood sausage and potato, after which he would smoke a pipe that could be bought, ready filled with tobacco, at the counter.

We can glean from entries in the so-called Conversation Books (notebooks Beethoven carried with him to compensate for his deafness) a fascinating insight into how Beethoven managed an average day in the final years of his life, when not stepping out to cafés or restaurants. He rose early, around 5 a.m., and went straight to his desk. He worked for as long as he could, without interruption, for the main part composing, but also writing letters and jotting down lists of errands and shopping. Coffee time ensued after two or maybe three hours, with Beethoven meticulously counting out sixty coffee beans, according to his secretary Schindler. Around noon he might step out to run a few errands, or meet a musical colleague, before returning for lunch around 2 p.m. Frequently he asked friends or colleagues to join him, with lunch being prepared by the housekeeper. The afternoon was spent catching up on paperwork, with more shopping if necessary, followed by a late-afternoon visit to a café to drink coffee, read newspapers, smoke a pipe. Evenings, if there were no formal engagements or musical performances, were spent quietly in his apartment, with a light supper, some reading, and then to bed by 10 o'clock.[5]

This was by no means a set pattern. Mealtimes could vary enormously. He might go without food when in the white heat of creativity, often working well into the early hours. Or he would feast on huge meals shortly before retiring, and pay the price with indigestion and the need to get up in the night.

The Beethoven I have described is not the sophisticated Beethoven of the numerous portraits done during his lifetime, nor the heroic Beethoven of the many statues that stand in Bonn and Vienna to this day, nor the coiffed Beethoven of the Klein bust. It is Beethoven the man.

40

Beethoven's eccentricities extended into his musical world as much as into his private life, something that we might struggle to comprehend, given the sublime certitude of his music. In the first place, composition did not come easily to him. Even a cursory glance at autograph manuscripts reveals an indecisive, even tortured, mind. Compare a Beethoven manuscript with a Mozart manuscript. Mozart's notation is neat and tidy, no second thoughts or amendments. It is – as Salieri memorably says in Peter Shaffer's play *Amadeus* – as if the music has been put into Mozart's head by God; it simply flows down his arm, into his pen and onto the paper. Beethoven's manuscripts, by contrast, are redolent with crossings out, whole sections obliterated by an angry pen, blotches of ink testifying to Beethoven's frustration.

To a modern eye many of Beethoven's manuscripts are indecipherable. Even in his own day copyists struggled to render his markings accurately. Several copyists would work on a large-scale score at the same time. When a particularly problematic passage occurred, they would confer among themselves and reach a consensus, rather than risk the wrath of the composer by asking what he meant. This, naturally, could lead to mistakes. In a letter to Ferdinand Ries on 9 April 1825, Beethoven enclosed a second, corrected copy of a song because he found the first one to be full of errors. Only one copyist did he trust implicitly, and that was one Wenzel Schlemmer, who was adept at deciphering exactly what he meant. Sadly Schlemmer, ten years older than Beethoven, suffered failing eyesight in his later years and was forced to retire. Beethoven bemoaned the fact that now there was not a single competent copyist left.

We might naturally assume today that Beethoven scores used in concerts and recordings are thoroughly accurate, and that therefore the music produced is as Beethoven intended. That is not always the case. A mistake can creep into an early edition, which is subsequently reproduced by a publisher as authoritative, and then copied by later publishers. This is exactly what happened to Beethoven's Piano Sonata No. 15 in D, Op. 28, the *Pastoral*, a new edition of which was brought out by a highly regarded publisher in the early 2000s. It showed, as had many previous editions by different publishers, a *staccato* mark at a particular point.

This puzzled the British Beethoven scholar and music editor Jonathan Del Mar, who was at the time preparing an *Urtext* (original edition) of the complete piano sonatas, in which he went back to the original autograph scores, where possible, and first editions. The *staccato* mark sat oddly with him – it bore no relation to the music around it. Close study of the original autograph score, which is held in the Beethoven-Archiv in Bonn, revealed that the *staccato* mark, which had been accepted as made by Beethoven, was in fact a tiny hole in the original paper. Del Mar has, to date, produced *Urtext* editions of the complete symphonies as well as the piano sonatas, also of the string quartets and cello sonatas, and is currently working on the piano concertos. Along the way he has corrected many errors that had crept into published editions of Beethoven's works down the years, and his scores are now accepted as the closest it is possible to get to Beethoven's original intentions, and are regularly used for performances and recordings.[1]

If we frequently find it difficult to render Beethoven's music exactly as he intended, a fair share of the blame has to be laid at the feet of the composer himself. He did not make it easy, and this extends beyond his pretty appalling handwriting. Sometimes he simply wrote nothing down at all. Remember the *Choral Fantasia*, premiered at the Theater an der Wien, going off the rails at that four-hour-long concert on 22 December 1808 in the unheated hall? It would have helped if Beethoven had written the entire piece down.

The *Choral Fantasia* is a curious composition, rarely performed today, mainly because of the enormous forces it requires – solo pianist, full orchestra, mixed chorus, and six solo singers (soprano, two altos, two tenors and bass, though that is normally reduced to the standard four of soprano, alto, tenor, bass). It is therefore expensive to put on, particularly when it is generally regarded as a rather lacklustre piece, the theme of the final section being an early, and inferior, version of the main 'Ode to Joy' theme of the *Choral Symphony*. The piece opens with a lengthy solo improvisation on piano. The problem lay in that word 'improvisation'. Beethoven took it literally. He had written nothing down, and so when he played it at the premiere, the orchestra had no idea when to come in. Only later, when preparing it for publication, did he write that piano part down, and that is what is played in concerts and recordings today. Is it exactly, or largely, or even just a little, similar to what he played at the premiere? We cannot know.

The likelihood is you do not have the *Choral Fantasia* (often called *Choral Fantasy*) in your music collection, which made it all the more surprising when, as the conversation turned to Beethoven early in our relationship, Nula told me her favourite piece was the *Choral Fantasia*.

'You mean the *Choral* Symphony,' I said patronisingly.

'No, the *Choral Fantasia*. James had just been diagnosed with dementia. I was in a bookshop and there was this amazing piece of music playing. I asked what it was. Beethoven's *Choral Fantasia*, I was told. I bought the CD and listened to it again and again.'

As dementia overwhelmed James, the music became indispensable to her. She listened to it last thing at night and every day in the car. It is still her favourite piece of Beethoven, alongside the *Emperor* Piano Concerto, which is the first piece of Beethoven she ever heard.

∽

A comparable situation arose over a much better-known piece. We owe our knowledge of this to Ignaz Seyfried, the same colleague who enlightened us about Beethoven's skills in the kitchen. The premiere of a new piano concerto, Beethoven's third, was scheduled for 5 April 1803, with Beethoven himself as soloist. Seyfried had agreed to turn the pages for him. As was so often the case, recalls Seyfried in his memoir, Beethoven had not had time to write everything down. Seyfried felt physically sick with nerves when Beethoven put the piano part on the stand and Seyfried saw little more than a collection of 'Egyptian hieroglyphics'. Beethoven played the solo part mostly from memory, aided by a squiggle or two on the page. Seyfried had no idea when to turn. Beethoven took great delight in throwing him a secret glance at the appropriate point. At the celebratory supper afterwards, Beethoven teased Seyfried 'heartily'.

Beethoven's Piano Concerto No. 3 in C minor, Op. 37, I regard as the finest of the five. After a long orchestral introduction, the piano enters with a double run of a C minor scale. A simple scale, nothing more. But that scale comes to define the first movement, and it reappears, slowly and poignantly, at the close of the sublime, hymn-like second movement. Except that here, towards the top of the scale, Beethoven flattens a note. I remember the very first time I heard Piano Concerto No. 3. It was on the radio in my hotel room in Belfast in the 1970s, where I was reporting for ITN's *News at Ten*. The soloist was the renowned Russian pianist Emil Gilels. That flattened note hit me like a thunderbolt. I sat bolt upright. He's hit a wrong note! A simple upward scale and he's hit a wrong note! In the very next bar the same thing happens again; that same note is flattened. And I relaxed, realising I had just reacted exactly as Beethoven intended. That is not a wrong note, he is saying, it is exactly what I have written, and here it is again to prove it.

Beethoven's musical eccentricities extended to conducting. On several occasions he conducted performances of his symphonies, and the orchestral players dreaded it. The violinist and composer Louis Spohr was in the orchestra for a performance of the turbulent, driving Seventh Symphony conducted at a charity concert by Beethoven himself. During a quiet passage, 'the poor deaf Maestro . . . crept completely under the desk. In the *crescendo* he reappeared, climbing continually higher and higher, and then sprang right up off the ground'. Seyfried echoes this:

> He was accustomed to indicate a *diminuendo* by trying to make himself smaller and smaller, slipping completely under the conductor's desk. As the music got louder again, he too seemed to swell, and on the entrance of the whole orchestra he rose on the tips of his toes, grew to well nigh giant size, and swaying in the air with his arms, seemed to be trying to float up into the clouds.[2]

There are numerous accounts of eccentricities during concerts. When the *Choral Fantasia* went off the rails, Beethoven leapt up from the piano, strode into the orchestra ranks and accused certain wind-players of ruining the performance. At a performance of one of his piano concertos, Beethoven gesticulated so wildly at the keyboard that he swept the candelabra off the top of the piano, requiring someone to hurry on stage to stamp out the flames.

His most legendary act of eccentricity on the podium is remembered as one of the more poignant moments in the history of classical music, one that I relate in talks, interviews and discussions, but which I struggle to complete due to a lump in my throat and the pricking of tears behind my eyes.

Beethoven insisted on conducting the premiere of his Ninth Symphony, the *Choral*, despite his profound deafness making it impossible for him to hear the orchestra. It was only the latest in a series of muddles and mishaps that nearly caused the abandonment of a concert at which the audience would first hear the work that represented the pinnacle of Beethoven's achievements. First the censor banned the concert because the *Missa Solemnis* would also be receiving its first performance: as a religious work it was forbidden to perform it in a theatre. A compromise was reached: only three of the five movements would be performed. As for the concert hall, Beethoven rejected the one offered to him. A second was offered and also rejected. Finally Beethoven agreed to the Kärntnertor Theatre, but plans were now so far behind, the scheduled date had to be put back. The concert would take place on 7 May 1824.

Then things really did start to go wrong. Only two full rehearsals were scheduled for what was – no surprise here – fiendishly difficult music requiring orchestra, chorus and four solo singers. The little rehearsal that did take place did not go well. In particular, the four singers complained bitterly about what was required of them. The bass said his part was too high, the tenor that his was too low. The soprano was brought in late in the day and complained she did not have time to learn her part, and the contralto sided with her. The contralto, Karoline Unger, was deputed to complain to Beethoven the night before the performance that the parts were unsingable as written, and could they please be allowed to sing within their range. Beethoven would not budge: 'You will sing exactly what I have written.' Karoline Unger remonstrated with him, calling him 'a tyrant over all the vocal chords'. The bass singer quit, and was hurriedly replaced by a member of the chorus.

On the night the theatre was relatively full, but with the wrong kind of audience. Summer had come early to Vienna, and the aristocrats, the patrons of the arts, had left the city for the comfort of their country estates. The royal box was empty, which piqued Beethoven. He had expected his great patron and friend, Archduke Rudolph, brother of the emperor, to attend. Beethoven was still adamant that he would conduct, but friends decided to take evasive action, and hired a professional, Michael Umlauf. All agreed that there was no point in trying to talk Beethoven out of conducting. Umlauf would stand slightly behind him and to the side. The orchestra would follow his direction, not Beethoven's erratic beat.

As if to set the tone for what was certain to be a disastrous, even comical, evening, Beethoven strode into the hall wearing a green frockcoat. Black was de rigueur, but he did not own such a thing. There was a ripple of laughter from the audience. Umlauf followed Beethoven onto the stage, staying discreetly out of sight behind him. Another ripple of laughter as Umlauf visibly made a sign of the cross in front of the orchestra. The players and singers would need all the divine help they could get.

In Vienna there was no such thing as a musically unsophisticated audience. They knew from the opening hushed chords of the symphony that they were hearing something unsettling, mysterious and unnerving, something clearly ahead of its time. Where would it lead them? Massive affirmative chords followed, but then more question marks. Umlauf, using all his professional skill, brought out the best from the players, who concentrated on his every gesture, ignoring the flailing arms of the composer. The second movement stunned the audience with what amounted to a solo role for timpani. At the end, a hint of the great theme that was to come in the final movement. They could not help themselves. An eruption of cheers and calls for an encore. But Umlauf raises his baton and ushers in the divine calm of the third movement.

By now the audience know they are hearing music that is entirely new. Beethoven, always the innovator, has created a new sound world. At the start of the final movement he quotes from the three previous movements, but cuts each theme off abruptly. A *crescendo*, and then the bass singer comes in with a plea to banish these sounds and hear instead more pleasant tones.

Voices in a symphony! No one had done that before. Relentlessly Umlauf drives players and singers towards the huge musical climax of the work, but suddenly – silence. Everything stops. The audience hold their breath. Just small beats on bass drum and deep wind. Syncopated dotted rhythm. Martial music, and the rise to musical climax begins again.

The final chord sounds, there is a moment of stunned silence, and then the theatre erupts. Hats and handkerchiefs are raised in the air. Shouts of 'Bravo! Bravo! Bravo!' alternate with 'Beethoven! Beethoven! Beethoven!' And Beethoven? He is still conducting the imaginary orchestra, the one he hears in his head. Leaning forward, Karoline Unger – she who had accused Beethoven of being a tyrant – touches him on the shoulder and gently turns him round to witness the cheering audience. At that moment he knows the gift he has given to the world.[3]

41

Beethoven loved the trombone. I did not know this when I fell in love with the trombone. You'll remember that, as a schoolboy, I gave up the violin and turned instead to the more forgiving trombone, but that was not the full story.

My conversion came about more than six decades ago because a fellow pupil persuaded me to listen to an LP of Chris Barber and his trad jazz band. It took considerable persuading. I was in my Tchaikovsky phase. Classical music was the only music that interested me. I listened grudgingly, screwing up my eyes at the noise and mentally going through the prep I needed to do that evening. Then, suddenly, I realised I was tapping my feet. I was rather enjoying the sound. I was enjoying it very much. A couple of tracks later and I had fallen in love with trad jazz, a love I carry with me to this day. If I am not listening to Beethoven, Wagner or Johann Strauss, you might well catch me listening to Kid Ory or Chris Barber.[1]

But listening was not enough. I wanted to create that sound. I decided, on the spot, to form a jazz band. Ambitious? Certainly. Crazy? Definitely. I could play violin to Grade Three and piano a little better, well enough to play hymns at evening service. But jazz? Where do you start? I had two good friends at Uppingham School, one of whom played the trumpet and the other the banjo. That was a start. All we needed was a clarinet or trombone and we'd have two-thirds of a front line and a very small rhythm section. It was, as I said, a start – and an end. I could not play either clarinet or trombone. I knew enough to know that both were fiendishly difficult. The clarinet required precision fingering. The trombone? That slide and its strange movements were a complete mystery.

I knew that another pupil, with whom I was in German class, was learning trombone. Dare I ask him to teach me the basics, then actually lend me his trombone to see if I could get any sort of sound out of it? It was a long shot. I asked, tentatively, and he said yes. On a quiet Saturday morning we went into the music school building and shut ourselves in a practice room. For the first time in my life, I held a trombone in my hands. He explained the six positions on the slide, which you would find only by feel and instinct, told me to keep the slide locked at all times when I was not playing, or it would slide right off and crash to the floor, and left me to it.[2]

I was in trombone heaven. Within half an hour I could get a tune out of it; after another thirty minutes I could play 'When the Saints Go Marching In' well enough for me, at least, to recognise it. I had found my musical home. We would have our jazz band – or at least three-fifths of it. And that was a brave thing to do. On the wall outside the practice rooms, pinned to a notice board, was a handwritten note by the school's music director. 'The playing of dance music on school premises is forbidden,' it said. *Dance* music! What it meant was that any kind of music that was not classical was not allowed. To form a jazz band, therefore, and play this seditious, salacious music in any building belonging to the school was against school rules. By decree of the music director.

Rather than stopping us, it had the opposite effect, as banning something always does. And so that beautiful piece of brass – somewhat tarnished now as I look at her fondly across the living room – arrived at Uppingham with my name on the packaging. All that was left was for the three of us – trumpet, trombone, banjo – to jam it up. But where? There was an answer. A small room at the back of the school hall was named the 'band room' because it housed a selection of brass instruments. Technically this was school premises, but on a Sunday morning surely all would be quiet.

In we went. Six decades later I can still smell the mustiness of the wooden floor, the slightly stale aroma of brass and the damp breath that had dried inside. 'A-one, a-two, a-one-two-three-four' – and we were away. Now I do not wish to exaggerate. The sound was pretty dreadful, but we were loving it. We were making music. On and on we played, marginally improving as the minutes went by. I waved my slide at the other two to indicate I would take a solo riff. Away I went, eyes screwed tight, slide pointing to the ground one moment, high in the air the next. I put in a growl in imitation of Kid Ory.

As I reached the end of the solo I pointed the slide at the other two and opened my eyes, but they were not looking at me. They were looking at the door. There, framed in the doorway, was the music director. He was not a big man, but in my mind's eye I see him filling the door frame, an outsized ogre whose enormous body shut out any chink of light. I, as the known ringleader, received a Saturday afternoon detention for playing 'dance' music at school.[3]

My trombone had got me into trouble, but that is not the reason I did not pursue my desire to study it. Life just moved in a different direction. But my love of the trombone stayed with me, and in later years the more I learned about Beethoven, the more I discovered how much he liked the trombone too. Yet in the countless biographies and musicological analyses I have read about his music, I have never encountered a section exploring this aspect of his music. So I shall do so now.

On 5 April 1803, while he was composer-in-residence at the Theater an der Wien, Beethoven put on a concert of his own music. The programme included a new oratorio he had written, entitled *Christus am Ölberge* ('Christ on the Mount of Olives'). The days leading up to the concert had been fraught. The programme was enormously ambitious, with the premiere of his Second Symphony as well as the Third Piano Concerto also scheduled, and there was nowhere near enough rehearsal time. On the morning of the concert itself, at around 5 a.m., Beethoven summoned Ferdinand Ries to come to his apartment immediately.

Ries gives us a compelling account of what he found. Beethoven was sitting up in bed, writing on separate sheets of manuscript paper, which were strewn around him. Barely glancing up – and certainly with no apology for disturbing Ries at such an early hour – Beethoven said he had decided to add tenor and bass trombone to *Christus* and told him to find two trombonists. Ries was dumbfounded. The final rehearsal was in three hours' time. Not only would it be impossible to find trombonists in time for the rehearsal, but that rehearsal would be the only opportunity they would have to learn the score. Things were difficult enough already; was it really necessary to add this additional challenge to a concert that was surely already doomed to failure?

Ries gives us no further details, but he must have remonstrated as tactfully as he could. However, Beethoven was adamant. 'Get me trombones!' he shouted at Ries's retreating back as the hapless young man left the bedroom. How he did it we do not know, but Ries must have found his trombonists, because a full orchestra and voices performed in the concert. To this day tenor and bass trombone feature in the score, giving a portentous and otherworldliness to the rising motif of the opening two bars in which they play alone with deep horn and bassoon.

❦

A more familiar work, Beethoven's Fifth Symphony is known for many things. The opening motif of three short notes and a long one forms what are rightfully called the most famous bars in all classical music. They occur, in one form or another, through all four movements of the symphony, the first time a composer had done such a thing. The transition from third to fourth movements occurs without a break, an eerie passage slowly building until the full orchestra explodes in a blaze of light to usher in the final movement. 'Full' includes trombones. Beethoven is the first composer to use trombones in a symphony, and he does so in the final movement of the Fifth. He does not make it easy for them though. They have to sit through three movements without playing a note, then enter for the first time in that opening chord of the final movement – the first trombone having to hit a perilously high note. Go to a performance of the Fifth in the concert hall and you will see the trombonists silently blowing into their instruments, slides pointing down, during that eerie passage, just to ensure they are warmed up for that enormous entry.

In the autumn of 1812, the traumatic year that begins with Klein taking the life mask from which he created the famous bust, and includes the brief love affair with the woman known as the 'Immortal Beloved', Beethoven is recuperating in the Bohemian spa town of Teplitz, taking the waters, attempting to relax away from Vienna, while writing out the autograph score of his Eighth Symphony, when he receives bombshell news from his brother Nikolaus Johann in Linz, where he has established an apothecary shop. Johann invites him to join in celebrating the wonderful news that he is to marry Therese Obermayer, his housekeeper.

Beethoven is utterly appalled. Johann is to give the glorious name of Beethoven to a housekeeper? The indignity! The insult! He already has one brother married to an immoral woman and they have a son conceived out of wedlock, and now another intends to demean the illustrious family name. Johann has to be stopped. Beethoven leaves Teplitz for Linz, two hundred miles to the south, where he is even more appalled to find that Therese has an illegitimate daughter by a former employer. He confronts his brother and several furious rows ensue. Beethoven then approaches the local police, arguing that Therese, on account of her immoral behaviour, should be barred from Johann's house. Unsuccessful in this tactic, he demands to see the local bishop and argues that Johann should be forbidden to marry Therese on account of her immorality and the existence of an illegitimate child. The bishop points out that since neither party has been married before, there is no impediment to their union. There are more altercations between the two brothers, in one of which it is believed they actually come to blows. Beethoven is powerless to stop his brother marrying Therese and adopting her daughter Amalia, and remaining married to Therese until she died sixteen years later. Johann outlived her by twenty years.

Extraordinary though it may seem (if there is such a thing as 'extraordinary' in chronicling Beethoven's life), while this family drama was playing out, Beethoven immersed himself fully in the musical life of Linz, which was rich and varied, thanks to the efforts of the town's Kapellmeister, Franz Xaver Glöggl. Glöggl welcomed Beethoven to Linz as a musical god, describing him in his own musical journal as 'the greatest composer of our time'. Local musicians were summoned to perform for Beethoven, and Glöggl ensured he was feted wherever he went.

There was a motive behind this behaviour, which bordered on sycophantic, but that naturally appealed to Beethoven's own sense of self-importance. Choosing his moment, Glöggl asked Beethoven – no doubt using language redolent with flattery – if he would be disposed to composing a series of small pieces to be used at funerals while he was in Linz. Traditionally these were played by trombones, the sonorous tone appropriate to the occasion, and Glöggl was clearly particularly proud of the city's trombonists. He had pitched his request perfectly. Nothing too grand or time-consuming, just a few small pieces that should not inconvenience Beethoven too greatly. Given that Beethoven was in a state of emotional turmoil trying to deal with his brother's amorous intentions, it is truly remarkable that he acquiesced to Glöggl's request. Clearly the sombre nature of the music he was asked to write suited his own feelings of sadness, even despair, but he was also undoubtedly captivated by the thought of composing for solo trombones. Why else would he agree?

Beethoven composed a set of three *Equali* for four trombones, the name signifying the equal role of the four instruments. Played together, the trombones produce chords in imitation of a church organ. The sound is deep, mellifluous and resonant. Glöggl was overjoyed, and classical trombonists ever since have reason to be grateful to Glöggl for inspiring Beethoven to increase the trombone repertoire. At Beethoven's own funeral two of these *Equali* were arranged for four male voices and sung at the funeral mass, accompanied by trombones.

Some years ago I presented a concert of Beethoven's music at Glasgow Royal Concert Hall, performed by a youth orchestra from the Royal Conservatoire of Scotland. I told the story of how Beethoven came to write the *Equali*, and four young trombonists stepped forward to play them. One of them cracked on the opening chord. He swiftly recovered, but seated behind them I saw the blood rise slowly up the back of his neck and into his close-cropped hair, turning a vivid purple as it rose. The quartet proceeded to give a perfect rendition of the pieces, but I suspect that young trombonist will ruefully remember that opening chord of Beethoven's trombone *Equali* for many years to come.

42

In 1979–83 the Lindsay Quartet, in my view the finest string quartet this country has ever produced, recorded the complete set of Beethoven string quartets. There has been no better recording of the sixteen string quartets, either before or since. Even the Lindsays themselves, in their second complete recording a decade later, did not match the sheer emotional intensity of the earlier recording. This recording holds a deeply personal resonance for me, and if that has influenced my accolade, I make no apology.[1]

To me, the deep poignancy of the slow movement of the *Hammerklavier* Piano Sonata is equalled only by the *Cavatina* of Op. 130, the fourteenth of the sixteen string quartets.[2] What a misnomer '*Cavatina*' is, a name usually applied to a simple, melodious, expressive air. Why Beethoven chose such an inappropriate name for this extraordinarily profound piece of music, we cannot know. Maybe he was simply being ironic. From the opening bars of the movement, we are instantly aware that Beethoven is baring his soul to us.

Above the stave Beethoven writes *Adagio molto espressivo*, and under each of the four parts *sotto voce*, followed by *p* to stress to the players that he wants this to be played gently, softly, with as much emotion as possible. After a calm opening from second violin, viola and cello, the first violin enters on the final beat of the first bar with a rising sixth on the low strings. It is a lift redolent with poignancy, like a measured intake of breath. A plaintive melody ensues, as if the violin is a human voice expressing sadness and despair. The voice is telling a tale of woe, and the other three voices are accompanying it and comforting it. That lift is then reversed, with a fall of a fifth that takes your soul with it.

There then comes a passage, a brief passage, that is more than heart-rending. Beethoven takes us into his innermost sanctuary, his most private thoughts and emotions. Second violin, viola and cello play *staccato* triplets marked *pianissimo*, and on the second beat of the following bar – second beat, in other words *off* the beat, so already unsettling – first violin plays a long, low note, again marked *pianissimo*, and then . . . and then . . .

Beethoven describes it himself for us. He writes on the manuscript paper *beklemmt*. The word does not translate easily from the German: oppressed, anguished, tortured, overcome by grief and heartache. All of these and more. And the way Beethoven writes the word gives us its meaning. Untidily placed, brushing up against the stave above it, he writes in a way he never, ever writes: small, tiny, cramped; the letters tightly packed together. Beethoven always writes in a scrawl, the words spreading across the page, imprecise. Yet here the word is so small that it is hard to find. I have a facsimile copy of the autograph score of Op. 130. Even knowing where the word comes, I have to hunt to find it, and then use a magnifying glass to read it. It is still practically illegible, almost obscured by the bottom line of the stave above. By contrast, on the stave below he writes *Sempre pp*, the six letters of the word '*Sempre*' expansively written, easy to read, taking up far more space on the page than the eight tiny, cramped letters of '*beklemmt*'.

So what exactly is the music that Beethoven marks *beklemmt*? Technically it is a passage in which, over a steady beat in the three lower strings, the first violin plays a disjointed series of quavers, semiquavers, slurred demi-semiquavers, redolent with accidentals and tiny rests, conveying the impression of intensely suppressed emotion. That is exactly how it is always played.

The Lindsay Quartet, led by Peter Cropper, go further. While the other three voices with their regular rhythm attempt to console him, the top voice weeps. This is Beethoven sobbing, catching his breath. This is more than a passage of short notes played over a steady beat; this is a human being weeping without restraint. That is what Beethoven is conveying to us in the only language in which he is able to do so. Words, for Beethoven, are never enough. Peter Cropper understands this. His rendition of this passage transcends the sound of the violin. Through him, we hear Beethoven's sobs. I have never heard this passage played as he plays it, and I doubt I ever will.

Just nine and a half bars, and the rising sixth that opened the movement returns. Nine and a half bars that are unique to Beethoven, and unique in music. Nine and a half bars in which we see into Beethoven's soul.

∽

Learning the violin at Uppingham was always something of a struggle – that score of the Tchaikovsky Violin Concerto was never going to be much troubled by me – but I did progress to somewhere around Grade Three, to a point where I would soon be ready to make the leap to more positions on the fingerboard. One day (I can't remember if it was before or after she found the Tchaikovsky score) my violin teacher told me she was going to form a school string quartet, and she had decided I should play second violin. My pride was somewhat piqued. I asked, tactfully, if I could be first violin, the leader, since the name of any boy more proficient than me did not immediately come to mind. She told me bluntly a new boy had arrived at the school on a music scholarship. He was a much better violinist than me, and he would be first violin, leader of the quartet. I would meet him at first rehearsal, she told me. His name was Peter Cropper.

When the time came, I was in the rehearsal room a little early, polishing my violin to a deep sheen, tuning it to within an inch of its life, when the door opened and in walked the scruffiest teenager I had ever seen. His hair was all over the place, his shirt collar stuck out over his jacket, his tie was askew. The immediate thought that went through my mind, as I felt the knot of my tie to ensure it was centrally placed in the shirt collar, was that I would soon see him off. Our violin teacher introduced Peter Cropper to us.

We took our seats and began to play. I cannot remember the piece – it certainly was not Beethoven. Nor can I recall a single note. All I can remember is that the other three reached the final chord together – I had no idea where we were on the manuscript page and I had not played a note for a full minute. One of the reasons I had lost my place was that I could not take my eyes off Peter, this scruffy new boy. I had never heard playing like it. The energy, the emotion, eyes half closed, jaw jutting. He can have been only thirteen or fourteen years of age, yet he played as if he was imbued with the music, his violin an extension of the music on the stand. I was sacked after that first rehearsal; Peter went on to better things.

We lost touch after we left Uppingham, but I read about the Lindsay Quartet in the 1980s and swiftly acquired their complete recording of the Beethoven string quartets. When I began researching for the *Last Master* trilogy, I contacted Peter through the Old Boys' network and invited him out to dinner. We talked Beethoven over several bottles of wine. It was fascinating to hear a musician's perspective on this man whose music I loved so much. I mentioned the passage in the Op. 130 Cavatina that Beethoven had marked *beklemmt*. Another string quartet had recently recorded the complete set and I asked Peter what he thought of it, particularly of that passage. He was unstinting in his praise. He acknowledged that they approached it in a slightly different way from the Lindsays, but it was every bit as valid. I probed just a little harder. Finally, with a smile, he leaned forward conspiratorially and said, 'They play from here [hand on head]. We play from here [hand on heart].'

The Lindsays recorded the *Cavatina* in a single take, which makes it all the more remarkable. It is music to listen to in a darkened room with headphones on. The original recording of the complete quartets was on the ASV label. It was re-released in 2021 on the Eloquence label and I was delighted to be asked to write a personal memoir of Peter in the booklet. It is a set that every lover of Beethoven's music should have in their collection.

Peter died suddenly of a heart attack in 2015, aged sixty-nine. At his funeral, as the wicker coffin was lowered into the grave, a cockerel crowed in the distance as though applauding Peter. It put a smile on every face, exactly what he was used to seeing after each performance.

43

What was happening in Beethoven's life that caused him to write the *Cavatina*, and that remarkable and astonishing *beklemmt* passage? Troubles with nephew Karl, of course. And his deafness. And his inexorably worsening health. No wonder he himself said he wrote it through tears, and a friend said nothing had caused him more anguish. Beethoven composed the String Quartet in B flat, Op. 130, as well as the Ninth Symphony and several other works, in the spa town of Baden, a half-day's carriage ride south of Vienna.

This elegant town, famed then as now for its natural springs, was a favourite resort of Beethoven. He spent no fewer than fifteen summers there over a period of twenty-two years. It was in the final stay, in 1825, that he composed Op. 130, and also the *Heiliger Dankgesang* of the following quartet, Op. 132.[1] This 'Holy Song of Thanks' is as extraordinary, in a different way, as the *Cavatina*. The four strings play block chords, no *vibrato*, thus imitating the sound of a church organ. At the top of the movement Beethoven writes 'Heiliger Dankgesang eines Genesenen an die Gottheit' ('Holy Song of Thanksgiving from a convalescent to the Deity'). This is a man who is not known ever to have expressed religious beliefs, giving thanks to the *Gottheit* for his recovery from what he believed to be a terminal illness. Tellingly he chooses the word '*Gottheit*' rather than '*Gott*', evidence I believe of an increasing spirituality as his life begins to ebb, while at the same time distancing himself from any religious commitment to a supreme being.

In April 1825, at the age of fifty-four, Beethoven falls seriously ill with stomach pains. At the time he is going through all kinds of turmoil with Karl. The summer before, Karl had informed him of his desire to pursue a military career, which plunged Beethoven into despair. Long and heated arguments follow over the ensuing months, at the same time as he is working on the first three of the late quartets. As a compromise, Beethoven agrees Karl can leave university and attend business school. Maybe that will rid his mind of this absurd idea of becoming a soldier.

Hardly surprisingly, the tension and turmoil in his life affects his health. His deafness is now total. He has long since accepted this and has at least come to terms with it. But other issues are now afflicting him. For a couple of years past he has suffered from problems with his eyes. Now they are inflamed again. He tells his doctor they are painful and he cannot bear bright light. The doctor's advice is to cover his eyes at night to be sure of resting them, and also to rest them as much as possible during the day. His spectacles are adequate, but poring over manuscripts late into the night by candlelight clearly does not help.

Of more pressing concern is his perennial problem of abdominal pain and poor digestion. Diarrhoea is a malady he has lived with all his life. It flares up, then subsides, then flares up again. In the spring and summer of 1825 he is in almost permanent pain and discomfort. 'I'm not feeling well at all,' he writes in a note to Schindler. 'I've had terrible diarrhoea today. I'm taking medicine for my poor ruined stomach.' The doctor has put him on a strict diet: nothing to eat during the day except barley in warm milk, no alcohol, coffee or spices. Along with stomach pains and diarrhoea, he is frequently hot and flushed, suggesting a fever. He complains of heartburn and occasional nosebleeds.

The illness of April 1825 is worse than anything hitherto. So ill is he that he is convinced he will not recover. His doctor confirms this worst fear. Death awaits him. Miraculously he does recover, and that good fortune – against all the odds – is what inspires him to compose the *Heiliger Dankgesang*. Inevitably, though, in the optimism that recovery brings, he begins to ignore his doctor's advice and return to his bad habits. Soon all the old problems with his health come back. Despair over the inevitable, despair over Karl. This is what informs the deep melancholy of the *Cavatina*.

The only hope of salvation, as he sees it, is to reinforce his efforts to bring Karl into line, to make a Beethoven of him. He instructs Karl to come down to Baden to visit him every Sunday. He orders a young musician by the name of Karl Holz not just to keep an eye on Karl in the big city, but actually to trail him, stay close, report back on his activities – is he drinking too much, is he playing too much billiards, is he visiting the city's red-light districts? Most important, is he defying strict orders and secretly visiting that immoral woman, his mother?

As might be expected, the two Karls form something of a friendship. Nephew Karl suspected his uncle was spying on him, and now it is confirmed. Karl is not happy at the polytechnic institute and his studies are not going well. He simply has no interest in the subject, just as he did not at university. He wants to join the military; he wants to become a soldier. That is what he wishes to do with his life, and he finally confronts his uncle and puts it firmly and clearly to him. Tensions rise, tempers flare, Karl grabs his uncle by the chest, Beethoven grabs him back. Just as violence is about to ensue, Karl Holz rushes in and separates uncle and nephew.

The following day Beethoven is overcome with remorse, sending a note to Karl stating that 'all is forgiven and forgotten'. But Karl has had enough. More than a decade – his entire teenage years – of being controlled and manipulated by his uncle, of having his relationship with his own mother destroyed by an absurd and irrational family feud, have come to a head. Karl buys two pistols and gunpowder and climbs into the Rauhenstein ruins in the Helenental, the Valley of St Helen.

⁂

Baden retains the elegance of two centuries ago, which it acquired when Emperor Franz chose it to be his summer residence in 1796. I first visited it with Bonnie in 1994 when I was researching the *Last Master* trilogy. We took a bus from the Ringstrasse opposite the opera house for the brief ride down to Baden.

It was the height of summer, a scorchingly hot day, and as we stepped down from the bus I was hit by an almost overwhelmingly powerful smell of sulphur. You could almost reach out and squeeze drops from the thick air. The town, I decided immediately, was appropriately named. In the small main square a huge and intricate memorial to the Great Plague stood, echoing its near twin in the wide Graben in Vienna. Around it were many small tables and chairs, fully occupied by locals well used to the sulphurous smell and enjoying a morning coffee. The hum and buzz of conversation, the chink of china cup against saucer, echoed in the heavy air.

Thirty years later Nula and I stepped out into a very different Baden. It was early December, the air now ice cold. The plague monument had an eerie look, the morbid skulls seeming to register pain at being made to suffer the freezing temperatures. The lively buzz of summer was replaced by a cold, heavy stillness.

We walked the short distance to the Rathausgasse, and the house on the corner where Beethoven worked on, and completed, the Ninth Symphony. Here was a buzz of a different kind. Tourists from all over the world, phones on sticks, taking selfies outside the house. I cannot recall exactly how it was thirty years ago, but I remember the ground floor stocking a few tacky souvenirs, one or two people inside. Now it was packed with a vast array of Beethoveniana (if there can be such a word) – everything from scholarly books to socks.

A steady stream of people climbed the narrow staircase to the first floor where Beethoven rented rooms. The larger of them, where he worked, is cordoned off; those legendary shutters, on which he scratched notes when he'd run out of manuscript paper, still in place. It is easy to understand his landlord's annoyance, subsequently charging Beethoven for the damage.

In the Helenental to the west of the town, a walk up the thickly wooded hill, signed *Beethovenweg*, leads to the Rauhenstein ruins. They have lost none of their menace in the intervening two centuries since Karl, in despair, climbed into them.

44

K arl's suicide attempt took place on Sunday, 6 August 1826. He was one
month short of his twentieth birthday. Beethoven was fifty-five years of
age, famous throughout Europe, recognised instantly on every street and in
every café in Vienna. He was also in the final full year of his life, only seven
months away from death. He was in no state, mentally or physically, to deal
with the fallout. Although Beethoven was well known for his eccentricities,
a doctor at the hospital where Karl was being treated for his head wound
took one look at the dishevelled, disorientated individual wandering the
corridors and ordered him to leave immediately, refusing to believe he was
who he said he was.

Karl remained in hospital for nearly seven weeks, receiving religious
instruction as the law prescribed for attempted suicide. Beethoven's younger
brother Johann wrote to him, urging him to get away from Vienna once
Karl was discharged, and come to stay with him and his wife at their country estate, Schloss Wasserhof, in Gneixendorf near Krems, about forty miles
north-west of Vienna on the north bank of the Danube. It was the last
thing Beethoven intended to do. Stay with the brother he despised, who
was married to his housekeeper against Beethoven's explicit instructions?
Ridiculous idea. Beethoven sent a caustic note back: 'I will not come. Your
brother??????!!!! Ludwig.'[1]

But he changed his mind. Karl had an ugly visible scar on his temple where the bullet had torn open the skin. Beethoven's friend Steffen
von Breuning had used his influence at the War Ministry to gain a place for
Karl in the 8th Infantry Regiment, based in Iglau in Bohemia, but it was
necessary first for Karl to attend an interview with the commanding offi-
cer, Lieutenant Field-Marshal Baron Joseph von Stutterheim. Steffen was

adamant that Karl could not attend the interview with such a visible scar. He should go away for two or maybe three months to allow the scar to heal, and his hair to grow sufficiently long to hide it.[2]

Karl left hospital on 25 September; three days later he and his uncle left Vienna to go to stay with Johann and Therese in Gneixendorf. By all accounts Johann went out of his way to please his brother. He gave him a small, self-contained apartment of three rooms on the first floor of the south-west side of the house, and a dedicated servant by the name of Michael. Things between them, though, were tense from the start. Johann did not help matters by asking his brother to make a small contribution to running costs, which he considered reasonable given that the original invitation for two weeks' stay looked like being extended to two months. A housekeeper made up Beethoven's bed each morning and swept the floor, but when Beethoven's banging on the table, arms waving, singing under his breath – in the act of composition – caused her to burst out laughing, he sacked her on the spot. From now on, only Michael would be allowed into his room.

Beethoven's failing health was evident. His stomach had swollen to such a degree that he wore a belt around it to restrain it. His ankles and his feet were swollen to the extent that he was in constant pain. That did not inhibit him from taking his habitual walks in the countryside, striding across fields, wildly gesticulating and singing. On one occasion, oblivious to what he was doing, he caused a small herd of oxen to stampede, to the fury of the farmer. On another, he accompanied his brother to a client's house to deliver medication. The husband was out, and the wife served Johann a glass of wine while Beethoven crouched sullenly by the boiler. Later, explaining to her husband that Johann van Beethoven had called with his servant, the husband questioned her further, established who the 'servant' was, and berated his wife for ignoring the greatest musician of the day.

Far from any sort of reconciliation, it was not long before Beethoven refused to sit at the dining table with the family, ordering Michael to bring meals to his room. Things could not go on like this. On the night of 2 December, the two brothers had a blistering row, arguing over Karl's inheritance. Beethoven insisted Johann make a new Will, cutting out his wife and her illegitimate daughter, and leaving everything to Karl. You have to feel for Johann. First his brother refuses to allow him to marry the woman of his choice; now he is demanding Johann rewrite his Will![3]

Beethoven ordered Johann to get his carriage and a servant to transport him and Karl back to Vienna. Johann pointed out the folly of this. It was gone midnight on a freezing cold December night and – probably more out of concern for their welfare than revenge – Johann refused to make the covered carriage available. Beethoven and Karl would have to travel in a rickety open-top milk cart. Beethoven was adamant. They were leaving, no matter what. And so, at some point soon after midnight on Saturday, 2 December 1826, Beethoven and Karl left Gneixendorf in an open-top milk cart.

Extraordinarily (or not, given that this is Beethoven), while in the Wasserhof Beethoven worked on the last complete piece of music he would ever compose – a replacement final movement for the String Quartet in B flat, Op. 130, to take the place of the mighty *Grosse Fuge* – and it is surprisingly joyful.

∞

So where were Beethoven and Karl heading when they left Gneixendorf sometime after midnight in an open-top milk cart? Vienna, obviously. The story is well known. A freezing two-day journey, staying overnight in an under-heated rural inn. The storm windows of Beethoven's room were broken, and so unable to prevent the ice-cold air blowing in. Beethoven arrived back in Vienna mortally ill, with pneumonia to add to his already disease-ravaged body.

But is this what really happened? New research casts doubt on the oft-told story.[4] In the first place, is it really likely that a 'rickety open-top milk cart' would, in any circumstances, make a two-day journey in icy conditions along rough roads to the capital city, with human beings as opposed to milk churns as passengers? Secondly, there was an alternative, convenient and cheap way of travelling from Krems, down the hill from Gneixendorf and on the banks of the Danube, to Vienna, and that was along the Danube by freight barge. It was not comfortable or luxurious. The English conductor and organist Sir George Smart had made a similar journey, from Linz to Vienna via Krems the year before, describing the barge as a Noah's Ark of animals with around a dozen or so of the 'dirty kind of men, women, dogs, birds of all sorts and live crabs, besides other strange creatures'. But it did cost him only two gulden. The barge stopped for the night at Krems, where Smart stayed in an inn where he would never forget the 'bad supper, or the heat and odour of the room which was crowded with passengers'. But at least he secured a single room and a tolerable bed.

Smart was on his way to Vienna, where he met Beethoven, who wrote a canon for him. Smart had conducted the first performance of the Ninth Symphony in London earlier in the year and no doubt informed Beethoven of how it had been received. Apparently the words of the final movement, from Schiller's poem 'An die Freude', were sung in Italian! He might even have regaled him about the discomfort of his journey down the Danube, planting the idea of a cheap mode of travel in Beethoven's mind.

It seems more likely, therefore, that Beethoven and Karl, rather than making the two-day journey from Gneixendorf to Vienna in a milk cart, made the two-hour journey down the hill from the Wasserhof to Krems. It was in Krems that Beethoven stayed in the under-heated room of an inn with broken storm windows, probably the same inn that Smart had stayed in, but without the heat and odour, this being December while Smart had travelled in September of the year before.

Beethoven and Karl left the Wasserhof at one or two o'clock on Saturday morning. The barge was scheduled to leave Krems at 4 a.m. on Sunday morning. Beethoven thus spent a restless night in ice-cold conditions, leaving just before 4 a.m. to catch the barge. By the time he arrived back in Vienna he was suffering from 'fever-chill, a dry hacking cough accompanied by violent thirst, and cutting pains in his sides'. Karl relates how, on arriving at the apartment in the *Schwarzspanierhaus*, he had to help his uncle up the stairs, then carry him in a fireman's lift and lay him on the bed that, almost three months later, would become his deathbed.

❧

The village of Gneixendorf is today more proud of its association with Beethoven than it is of being the site of Stalag XVII-B, the largest prisoner-of-war camp in Austria during the Second World War. It stands high above the town of Krems and its monastery, looking down towards the Danube, vineyards spread on the hills below.

On an Easter Saturday in 1996, Bonnie and I hired a car and drove along the Danube to Krems, then up into the picture-postcard-perfect Austrian village of Gneixendorf. No satnav or digital maps in those days. We drove through the village on the main street, straining – and failing – to see any sign with the name Beethoven on it. Finally, I concluded all traces of the Wasserhof must have gone, and slowed down, preparing to turn round and head back to Vienna.

'There!' said Bonnie. 'Look.' A small sign, eminently missable, said *Beethovenhaus* with an arrow. The house stood on the outskirts of the village, grand and beautiful, dominating the vineyards that surrounded it. A tall, forbidding perimeter wall ran round the house. It was clearly a private residence, with no sign or notice referring to its famous past occupant. We decided to go in, aware that what we were doing was close to trespassing.

We rang the bell. A woman answered the door. I apologised for our unannounced arrival, and enquired if this was the house owned by Johann van Beethoven where his brother and nephew had come to stay. 'Yes,' she said, smiling. 'Would you like to see his rooms?'

She took us up to the second floor and the self-contained apartment that Johann had made available to his brother. It consisted, then and now, of an entrance hall, four rooms, and a piano room. All the furniture, she explained, was original or of the period. The small stove in the corner of the bedroom was the actual stove that Beethoven himself had filled with wood. I gasped at the knowledge that I was looking at something that Beethoven had touched. The walls of the sitting room were decorated with murals of the Rhine that Johann had commissioned to remind him of his childhood and at which Beethoven had no doubt gazed nostalgically as he worked on the replacement final movement of the Op. 130 String Quartet.

After the Second World War, the lady explained, Soviet soldiers were billeted in the house, and used to build a small fire on the floor of Beethoven's sitting room. She showed us scratches on the window frames where they used to drag the matches down to light them. By some miracle they had not defaced the murals, still as vibrant and fresh today as they were two centuries ago.

We found it extraordinary that such an important site was not a museum, financed by the government. Times have changed. The family that owned the house in the 1990s, producers and bottlers of local wine, have gone. It is now owned by a Viennese architect who has carried out a complete renovation. The Beethoven apartment is now officially part of the cultural heritage of Austria, with several rooms furnished as a private museum. Tours can be arranged by appointment. Chamber concerts are held in the Wasserhof, there is a Beethoven festival, and a commemorative plaque set into a wall in the garden.

45

Beethoven scholarship does not stand still. New research is being carried out all the time. When I began this book in October 2022 I believed, as I had done for forty years, that sixteen-year-old Beethoven went to Vienna to meet Mozart but had to return after less than three weeks because of his mother's terminal illness, the evidence being that he twice checked into the same Munich hotel only a few weeks apart. I now know that both stays in the hotel were made on the way back to Bonn, with a detour to Regensburg, and that actually he was in Vienna for around four months. I also thought that after that stay with his brother in Gneixendorf in the final full year of his life he made the two-day journey back to Vienna in an open-top milk cart. It now seems far more likely he travelled by barge, with the milk cart a small prelude to that journey.

Do details like these matter? Do we really need to know how long he was in Vienna as a boy of sixteen? Why should we worry over what means of transport he used to return from Gneixendorf to Vienna? I can answer these questions best by relating them to my own experience. For more than thirty years I worked as a television journalist, first as writer, then reporter, and finally newscaster. The skill required of a television journalist is to compress a big, multi-faceted news story to a manageable, easily comprehended length, while still conveying the essential facts. TV journalists always talk in terms of story length. It might run for two minutes, two-and-a-half minutes, three minutes or more. Anything over four minutes was always referred to, in my day, as a Ben-Hur.

The time constraints of TV news tended to be belittled by newspaper reporters. In 1979 I flew back with Ayatollah Khomeini from exile in a Paris suburb to a triumphant return to Tehran, covering the Iran revolution that followed, the first modern Islamic revolution. My camera crew and I spent the whole of day one on the streets of Tehran. It was dangerous. The revolutionaries were fighting the Shah's Imperial Guard, the elite soldiers whose job it was to protect him. But the Shah had gone into exile. Which way would the Imperial Guard turn? Would they remain loyal to the departed Shah, or support the revolutionaries? It hung in the balance. Bullets and explosions were all around us. I did a piece to camera on top of an American Chieftain tank that the revolutionaries had 'liberated' from the Guard's headquarters.

At the end of the day's filming, mercifully unscathed, we took a taxi to the main television station to process our film, edit it and satellite it to London for ITN's *News at Ten*, where my report was scheduled to be the lead story. In pre-video days this was time-consuming and difficult. We finally put together a three-and-a-half-minute piece, I voiced it, a technician threaded it into the telecine machine, and tried to satellite it to London. Tried and tried and tried. 'We've got the picture OK,' said a voice on the phone at the London end. 'But not your commentary. You'll have to feed your voice down a phone line.' This created even more problems. The deadline for *News at Ten* was fast approaching. We rushed back to the hotel, urging our driver to go faster, faster, praying we wouldn't be hit by bullets or shells, and that wrecked vehicles would not be blocking the road. At the hotel I went to the room set aside for the international press corps. Fleet Street's finest were in there, typing away, telex machines clattering. I apologised, asked if they could give me just a few minutes' silence. On the fourth or fifth attempt I got an outside line, dialled up ITN in London, the switchboard put me straight through to the sound department and, trying to remain as measured as I could, albeit out of breath, hot and frazzled, read my script, which would then be married to the film. Allowing for natural sound on the film, along with the piece to camera, I had written a script maybe two to two-and-a-half minutes long. 'Got it! Well done, John,' said the voice at the London end. I put the phone down, leaned back, closed my eyes and offered up a small prayer of thanks to the god of TV news.

'Is that it?' said the *Daily Express* correspondent on the other side of the room. 'A few sentences and you're done? Blimey, I should have your job. My newsdesk wants two thousand words.'

How things had changed just seven years later, when I was covering the Philippines revolution, which saw off the dictator Ferdinand Marcos and his wife Imelda, she of the two thousand pairs of shoes. By now we were on video; film was a thing of the past. The night the Marcoses fled in a naval helicopter provided by the US, and the young revolutionaries invaded the presidential palace, I led *News at Ten* with a report that was eight minutes long. Two Ben-Hurs! Video cameras meant no more developing of film, or feeding into an old-fashioned telecine machine at the local TV station. Now we converted a hotel room into an editing suite, put a small satellite dish up on the roof of the hotel, and satellited our coverage direct to London.

If you will permit a small boast, I won the Royal Television Society's TV Journalist of the Year for my coverage of the Philippines revolution. The citation noted my 'ability to bring clarity to a confused situation'. I quote that to make my point that a TV journalist needs to compress a story to its essential facts, to be able to see the wood for the trees, and that is something I did over the course of more than three decades. When I turned my attention to Beethoven, by contrast, I wanted to do the complete opposite. No more seeing the wood for the trees, I wanted to see each individual tree. No more skimming the surface, no more distilling to the essential facts. I wanted to know everything there was to know about this man whose music meant so much to me, every little detail. I wanted to be able to tell you what he did on any particular day of his life, what he had for breakfast, what music he wrote or performed, the people he saw. Every smallest detail.

That is why it matters to me how long he was in Vienna during 1787, or how he returned to Vienna in December 1826. These details matter, because each one, however seemingly trivial, brings me closer to the man himself and helps me to understand him just that little bit more fully.

All of which is to say that I both was and was not prepared for the biggest news about Beethoven to emerge for more than twenty years to be revealed just as I was writing this book. I heard about it three months before it was announced to the world, and I will readily admit to initial scepticism. Not any longer. Putting it into the context of everything I have said above, it is breathtakingly exciting.

This book began on a baking hot July day in 2022, in the garden of the cottage in Heiligenstadt where Beethoven wrote his Will, as I regaled Nula with the tale of how he came to write those fateful words, and she urged me to write a new, more personal, story about him. Just a week or two later, by total coincidence, I received an email from the American Beethoven Center at San Jose State University in California, announcing a Beethoven tour of Vienna in December to be led by the Center's founding director, William Meredith. When I suggested we sign up for it, on the basis that however much I already knew, I was bound to learn something I didn't know, Nula enthusiastically agreed.

Learn something new? Little did I know! I had met Will many years earlier at the Beethoven Center in San Jose, and we had regularly corresponded on matters pertaining to Beethoven. On our second night in Vienna, Nula and I had dinner with him. He told us, over a fine bottle of Grüner Veltliner, that there would be a big announcement sometime early in the new year concerning Beethoven.

'Big?' I queried.

'Really big,' he replied. 'Enormous.'

Swearing us to secrecy, he said a team of scientists at the University of Cambridge and the Max Planck Institute in Leipzig, led by Tristan Begg, had carried out a sequencing of Beethoven's genome, and that the results were astounding. They showed he had suffered from hepatitis B since 1821, six years before his death, and had a predisposition to liver disease. These factors, combined with his heavy drinking – probably around three-quarters to a whole bottle of wine a day – exacerbated the cirrhosis of the liver that was one of the two diseases that killed him, the other being kidney failure.

There was something else, something utterly intriguing. The international team of researchers acquired DNA from five people with the Beethoven family name living in Belgium who believed they were related to the composer, but the results showed they did not match Beethoven's Y chromosome. The team concluded that this was likely to be the result of at least one 'extra-pair paternity event'. To put that in layman's terms: at some point in the seven generations before Beethoven was born, at least one woman in the Beethoven line gave birth to an illegitimate child.

Will speculated that, in theory, that woman could have been Beethoven's own mother, and that Beethoven himself might therefore be that child. More probably, he continued, the genetic break in the lineage occurred with Beethoven's paternal grandmother, Maria Josepha Poll. Little is known about her, apart from the fact that she may have had roots in Moorish eastern Spain, along with the recent discovery of her baptismal certificate, that she became an alcoholic in later life and was put into an institution in Cologne where she died.

Equally mysterious is the fact that there is no birth certificate, or record of baptism, of her son Johann, Beethoven's father. We do not know the date or place of his birth, nor details of his eventual burial. We do know he became an alcoholic, like his mother, in the decade after Beethoven's birth. If Johann had been conceived outside the marriage, might this not go a long way to explaining the difficult relationship between Ludwig van Beethoven, the Kapellmeister, and his (possibly) stepson Johann? It would also help explain the older man's utter opposition to Johann's marriage and antagonism towards Maria Magdalena. The Beethoven name was being passed on to another generation with no Beethoven blood!

Look at the only portrait we have of one of Beethoven's younger brothers, Nikolaus Johann. His facial features bear not the slightest resemblance, in any way, to Beethoven. Perhaps he was legitimate and Beethoven was not, or perhaps it was the other way round.

Warming to his theme, Will then said it was also possible that Beethoven's other brother Carl was not the father of Karl, the nephew who would cause his uncle so many problems in the years ahead. Did a suspicion that Karl might not be his brother's son lead Beethoven to oppose Carl's marriage so vehemently, or fuel his visceral hatred of Carl's wife Johanna?

There is no question that Beethoven had a fondness for Spain, which would make sense if his grandmother had Spanish blood, as has been reported. His dark skin earned him the schoolboy nickname *Der Spagnol* ('The Spaniard'), which became something of a badge of honour in later life. At one stage he put Karl into a school in Vienna founded by a Spaniard,

Cayetano Anastasio del Río. For the plot of his only opera, he chose a story set in Seville, and he was overjoyed when news reached Vienna in June 1813 of the victory of the allies over the French Army at the Battle of Vitoria in northern Spain, composing his *Battle Symphony*, or *Wellington's Victory*, in celebration.

The Cambridge team's report generated worldwide publicity when it was published in March 2023. In the first twenty-four hours after its release, there were nearly two thousand items in news media across the globe. The *New York Times* carried the story on its front page. Newspapers in Europe treated it as a major news story, particularly – for obvious reasons – in Germany and Belgium.

'Beethoven wasn't a Beethoven at all,' read the headline in the *Frankfurter Allgemeine Zeitung*. For sheer pithiness, and a touch of humour, the prize goes to the Hamburg weekly *Die Zeit*, which announced in huge bold type LUDWIG VAN MÜLLER. Belgian media were faced with the potential loss of a Flemish hero. The Dutch-language broadcaster VRT asked, 'Is Beethoven not really of Flemish descent? DNA analysis turns the composer's family tree upside down.' The French-language version of the same report was in no doubt: 'Beethoven's origins are not Flemish at all!'[1]

Beethoven might not have been of Flemish descent. If so, that would mean his beloved grandfather was not his grandfather; it is at least possible his mother might not have been his biological mother, and even more likely his father was not his biological father. It seems far-fetched. I am in no doubt though that one day – next year or next century – we will know. Science continues to advance and Beethoven research continues to advance with it.

So how were the scientists able to sequence Beethoven's genome? By analysing authenticated locks of his hair. The last time this happened was more than twenty years ago when analysis from the Hiller lock of hair revealed that Beethoven was suffering from lead poisoning at the time of his death.[2] As I said before, this was an interesting, though not particularly remarkable, finding. Kitchen utensils in Beethoven's time were mostly made of lead, paint was lead-based and the waters of the Danube were heavily polluted. It is likely anybody living in Vienna in the early nineteenth century would have high levels of lead in their blood. But the latest findings established that the Hiller lock of hair actually belonged to a woman! The findings based on that lock, which generated worldwide publicity at the time, we now know cannot be applied to Beethoven and must therefore be discounted.

Something else can be discounted too – the most bizarre rumour ever to have surfaced regarding Beethoven's paternity, and one that circulated widely during his lifetime. It was said that he was the illegitimate son of the King of Prussia, first identified as Friedrich Wilhelm II and then later as his uncle, none other than Frederick the Great. Beethoven was well aware of these rumours, as were his friends and colleagues. Frequently they beseeched him to rebut them as totally preposterous, not least because they cast a slur on his mother. Always he refused. In a letter to Wegeler in December 1826, only three months before he died, he wrote:

> You say that I have been mentioned somewhere as being the natural son of the late King of Prussia. Well, the same thing was said to me a long time ago. But I have adopted the principle of neither writing anything about myself nor replying to anything that has been written about me.[3]

According to the Cambridge report, there are two illegitimate patrilineal descendants of the grandson of Friedrich-Wilhelm II, but it has now been established that their Y chromosome does not match Beethoven's. I suspect that Beethoven would be rather disappointed that modern science has proved he is not of royal Hohenzollern blood.[4]

On another matter we might see results soon. In July 2023 an American businessman and collector, Paul Kaufmann, donated what he believes are fragments of Beethoven's skull to the museum of the Medical University of Vienna. The small pieces of bone were brought by his family to the US when they fled the Nazis. Austrian media trumpeted the return of Beethoven's skull fragments to his home city. A small group of California-based osteologists are not so sure. They believe the fragments do not match the shape of Beethoven's skull. Kaufmann has allowed the Max Planck Institute to test the fragments' DNA. We await the results.[5]

So far the one question that the latest tests come no closer to answering is: what caused Beethoven's deafness? Beethoven himself expressed the hope that after his death the cause of his deafness would be explained to the world. If those souvenir hunters who snipped locks of hair from his head on his deathbed to keep as mementoes had only known what scientists would be able to glean from those locks two centuries later, who knows what further discoveries might become possible two centuries from now? One day the world will know the answer to the greatest medical mystery in the history of music.[6]

⌘

On 7 May 2024, the 200th anniversary of the first performance of Beethoven's Choral Symphony, the *New York Times* carried a report on the results of new testing on two authenticated locks of Beethoven's hair. The results confirmed that Beethoven did indeed have serious lead poisoning at the time of his death, which will have exacerbated his kidney disease.

Wine in Austria is believed to have contained lower alcohol content in Beethoven's time than it does today, but it was common practice to add lead acetate to sweeten it. There is plenty of evidence wine could be pretty unpalatable, whether treated or not.

Around 5 February 1820, Beethoven's friend Franz Oliva wrote to Beethoven: 'The wine from Seelig is as bad as the last stuff. It burns in the chest and in the stomach.' Three years later Beethoven's secretary Anton Schindler wrote to him: 'Don't drink any of this wine, because it is scandalously adulterated. I wanted to tell you the other day that it made the whole roof of my mouth full of blisters.'

Even a single glass of such wine would have worsened his kidney disease. Given he drank up to a bottle of wine a day, it is hardly surprising Beethoven's health was affected.

As an ITN reporter, I was sent to Vienna in 1985 to cover the Austrian wine scandal of that year. Wine producers were found to be adding diethylene glycol – car antifreeze – to wine in order to sweeten and fortify it. *Plus ça change …*

———

46

Everything I have talked about in preceding chapters matters, because everything connected with Beethoven – speculatively or definitively – matters. But ultimately nothing matters as much as the music. Beethoven's music is his autobiography. When he wants to communicate something, he goes to the keyboard.

I mentioned early on that one of my own favourite compositions is Piano Sonata No. 31, Op. 110. (I am in exalted musical company, as I shall explain in a moment.) No. 31 is the middle of the three that were to be the final piano sonatas he would write. Although much liked – frequent nods of approval when I declare my love of it – it has always been somewhat over-shadowed by the sonata that followed it, No. 32, Op. 111, which breaks the rules in so many ways – only two movements, key changes, bar lines ignored, even two pages of music that is pure boogie-woogie[1] – that it is regarded as more important than its predecessor.

Op. 110 can be described quite easily in musicological terms. Three movements, the first marked by Beethoven to be played very expressively in a singing style. It is a lovely upbeat opening in the key of A flat major, Beethoven's favourite key for expressing calm and contentment, the four flats of the key imparting a softness to the tone. Things change, though, after a brief and rather disturbing fast movement. The final movement opens with a quiet, almost eerie, passage, leading to a section Beethoven marks '*arioso dolente*' and a theme above which he writes *klagender gesang* ('doleful song'). This leads, after repeats, to a gigantic inverted double fugue that brings the sonata to a tempestuous end.

Beethoven's life is in his music, and perhaps more so in the piano sonatas as a whole than in any other form, simply because the piano is his voice.

Beethoven composed Op. 110 in 1821 at the age of fifty. His deafness was total and his health in terminal decline. Listening to the *klagender gesang* knowing that, it becomes one of the most melancholy themes Beethoven ever wrote for the piano. When it is repeated, Beethoven ends it, then sounds a chord, which he repeats no fewer than nine times, marked *crescendo*, to lead into the huge fugue. To me, this is Beethoven telling us about his deafness. The *klagender gesang* is his lament over his deafness, the nine chords representing his determination to overcome the affliction, not to allow it to prevent him from creating his art, the sole purpose for which he was put on this earth. The fugue that follows, as it grows in intensity and passion, is proof that he has overcome his deafness. The ending builds and builds, each individual bar marked *sf* then *ff*, and the final run beginning right at the top end of the keyboard, descending to the very bottom, and then right up to the top again, ending in a final chord in both hands spanning five octaves. It is triumphant and a triumph. It is Beethoven telling us of his achievement, and the implicit message I draw from it is: 'If I can triumph over the worst fate that can befall a musician, then you too can defeat whatever challenges you may face.'

In contrast to the final movement of the Ninth Symphony, where Schiller's words are used by Beethoven as a cry to all humanity to come together as brothers, in Piano Sonata No. 31 his message is deeply personal, to each one of us and to countless future generations.

A vivid example of this came only days after I had written the above. Menahem Pressler, renowned pianist and founding member of the Beaux Arts Trio, died on 6 May 2023 at the age of ninety-nine. His obituary in the *Times* newspaper two days later recounted how, in 1940, after escaping from Nazi Germany, as a teenager in Palestine he was haunted by the horror of what he had witnessed, together with the loss of his grandparents, aunts and uncles, the destruction of his way of life, and his family's desperate flight to freedom. The obituary relates how Pressler said it was in playing Beethoven's Piano Sonata No. 31 that he found the will to live:

> It has idealism, it has hedonism, it has regret, it has something that builds like a fugue. And at the very end, something that is very rare

in Beethoven's last sonatas – it is triumphant. It says, 'Yes, my life is worth living.'[2]

Beethoven's music is life-saving, not just to musicians who have a deep understanding of it, but also to those from any and all walks of life. To hear it is to encounter solace in despair and to inspire purpose when life feels very dark. After one of my earliest talks on Beethoven, soon after my Beethoven trilogy *The Last Master* was published in the late 1990s, an elderly gentleman, waiting at the end of the queue while I was signing books, leaned forward and said quietly, 'Beethoven saved my life. Twice.' He walked away without elaborating. I do not know to this day how Beethoven saved his life, but I can quite believe that he did.

Soon afterwards I received a letter from a man in his mid-forties, telling me that when he was a teenager, his brother, a soldier, was killed in Northern Ireland. Six months later his mother died. 'Only Beethoven's music got me through,' he wrote.

More recently, in December 2022 in Vienna, Nula and I made the acquaintance of a musicologist and opera specialist with a particular love of Beethoven. For a time she had been married to an authority on Beethoven's music, but the marriage had ended in acrimony. On the day we met, she told us how she had 'reclaimed Vienna and Beethoven' for herself with a symbolic act intended 'to pave the way for fresh layers of memories'. Intrigued, we asked if she would tell us more. Her husband had once given her a precious silk scarf, she said. Returning to Beethoven's original grave in the village of Währing, now the Schubertpark in Vienna – once a place of pilgrimage for her and her then husband – she first draped the scarf over the wrought-iron railing, took a photograph to preserve the memory, then dug a shallow hole to the left of the grave, buried the scarf, and walked away. She stopped at a Kaffeehaus with a sense of lightness and freedom. It was her hope, she told us, that someone would one day find the scarf and allow it to enjoy another life.

Further testimony to the profound effect of Beethoven's music came in April 2023, while I was in the process of writing this book. After I had given a Beethoven talk at Strode Theatre in Street, Somerset, an elderly lady said to me, 'When my husband was terminally ill in hospital I played him

Beethoven's last three piano sonatas. Afterwards he said to me, "Now I am healed."' Contradiction? Not at all. He was talking of his spirit.

My wife Nula, to whom this book is dedicated, turned to the *Choral Fantasia* and *Emperor* Piano Concerto for comfort and strength when she was at her lowest coping with her husband's dementia. For me, as Bonnie descended into dementia, it was the *Eroica*, the *Hammerklavier*, Piano Sonata No. 31, the Late Quartets. Beethoven. Only Beethoven.

Beethoven's music, and the courage, fortitude and self-belief it inspires, is his timeless gift to humanity.

47

When I first finished writing this book, in February 2024, this chapter did not exist. But my Beethoven journey truly is a journey without end. As I was finishing off the final edits, I received an email. It was from a name I did not recognise, inviting Nula and me to stay at the family seat outside Vienna, Schloss Breiteneich ('Castle Broadoak'). That name I most certainly did recognise, and the very familiar name that goes with it. It brought memories cascading back. How could I possibly have imagined that a story that began around twenty-five years ago would, totally unexpectedly, re-enter my life at the exact moment I was bringing this book to completion?

Sometime in the late 1990s, with my trilogy *The Last Master* just published, I was invited to give a Beethoven talk at the Hurlingham private members' club in west London. It was only the second or third time I was asked to stand up and talk about Beethoven.

One of the stories I told, which subsequently became a staple of the many talks that followed over the years, was how Beethoven's Piano Sonata No. 14, which he dedicated to his pupil Giulietta Guicciardi, came to be known as the *Moonlight* Sonata. After the talk, as I was signing books, a lady came up and introduced herself. 'I was interested in the story you told about the *Moonlight* Sonata and Giulietta Guicciardi,' she said. I looked up at a tall, elderly, strikingly handsome woman, head held at a slightly elevated angle as if to accentuate that she was talking down to me. In her refined voice, I detected just the slightest trace of a foreign accent.

'Did you know,' she continued, 'that after Giulietta turned down Beethoven's proposal of marriage, she married a composer by the name of Count Gallenberg?'

'Actually, yes, I did,' I replied perhaps just a touch testily. I was tired, after talking for more than an hour.

'Did you know that they left Vienna and went to live in Italy?'

'Yes, I did.' I really had done my homework, after all. I had written a trilogy, three books on Beethoven. I felt almost as if there was nothing anybody could tell me.

'But did you know,' now looking down at me and smiling conspiratorially, 'that Gallenberg was impotent?'

'No, I did not,' I said, suddenly very interested indeed.

'Yes, Gallenberg was impotent, and because he was impotent he allowed Giulietta to take a lover, by the name of Count von Schulenburg. With Schulenburg she had five children, a son and four daughters. I am the great granddaughter of their son, and so I am directly descended from Giulietta, the woman to whom Beethoven dedicated the *Moonlight* Sonata.'

I felt my chest constrict and my breathing quicken. Could this be true? Could I really be speaking to a direct descendant of the woman to whom Beethoven proposed marriage and to whom he dedicated the *Moonlight*?

We chatted on. She told me her name was Pia Chelwood. She had been the wife of the Conservative MP Sir Tufton Beamish. On his retirement he had been elevated to the House of Lords as Baron Chelwood. Sadly, he died in 1989. Lady Chelwood's family name was von Roretz. She was Maria Pia von Roretz, a member of a noble Austrian dynasty whose family seat was a castle in the town of Horn, around forty-five miles north-west of Vienna.

We exchanged phone numbers and addresses, and it was not long before Pia invited Bonnie and me down to her house in Blackboys, East Sussex,[1] where she lived with her husband until his death. Pia was a Friend of Glyndebourne, and over the ensuing years we were her guests for performances of *Fidelio*, *Tristan und Isolde* and more.

In her home Pia had a white marble bust of Giulietta Guicciardi, her great-great-grandmother, done from life. The nose had been damaged, 'hit by my son with his tennis racket when he was small'. Each time we stayed with her, while feeding her miniature Shetland ponies, she told us about Schloss Breiteneich. 'We hold musical events there, especially Beethoven of course. Why don't you come and stay? You can do your Beethoven talk, John.' Several times we made plans, but for some reason – we were both working full-time, holidays were spent trying to renovate a tumbledown French farmhouse – it never happened.

Pia lived to a great age, dying in 2019 aged ninety-six. In every Beethoven talk I have given over the intervening years, and in every Beethoven book I have written, I have recounted the story of Giulietta, the *Moonlight* and Pia Chelwood.

But not in this book, until now. And what occasioned its reappearance? The email that dropped out of the blue into my inbox at exactly the right moment. The name I did not recognise was Dr Christian Lippert. He informed me that his wife was the great-great-great-granddaughter of Giulietta Guicciardi and the niece of Pia Chelwood. He and his wife had heard so much about me from Pia, and they wanted to invite me and Nula to stay at Schloss Breiteneich.

'Remember when I said in Bonn that I thought Ludwig was looking after you?' said Nula. 'I think he's working overtime.'

❧

On 27 June 2024 Nula and I arrived at Vienna airport to stay at Schloss Breiteneich with Christian and his wife Gea. The invitation had come out of nowhere and at precisely the right moment. It would complete a story that had begun a quarter of a century before. It would, I felt sure, increase my knowledge of Beethoven's world.

Little did I know! 'We have arranged a lunch here at the castle,' Christian told us. 'I have invited some people, friends of ours, I think you would be interested to meet. There will be a member of the Waldstein family, a member of the Lichnowsky family, also I have invited Princess Metternich. These are all important names in the Beethoven story, yes? You will be interested to meet them?'

Not for the first time in the writing of this book, something entirely unexpected and utterly serendipitous had occurred. Names that I have lived with for forty years, names I feel almost that I know personally – Count Waldstein, Beethoven's 'first, and most important, Maecenas'; the kind, generous, long-suffering Prince Lichnowsky who was ultimately rejected and humiliated by Beethoven. And Metternich. A name that Beethoven knew well, under whose rod of iron as Austrian Chancellor he and his fellow musicians were obliged to live. All coming to Schloss Breiteneich to meet me!

I had assumed these friendships were down to the Beethoven connection, but I was mistaken. They were all personal friends of Christian and Gea. 'You have to understand,' Christian told me, 'the high aristocratic class in Vienna is actually quite small. We all know each other.' The Beethoven connection was coincidental, another unbelievable stroke of good fortune.

Long-standing friends they may be, but as they arrived at the castle, traditional Austrian formalities were followed. In turn Christian took each lady's hand and held it briefly to his lips, head bowed. Men were in suits and ties on a swelteringly hot summer's day.

I was about to find out how true Christian's words about Viennese aristocracy were. Sitting next to me at lunch was a delightful, voluble lady. Her name, she told me, was Aglaë, a Greek name and one of the Three Graces. 'How lovely,' I said, silently wishing I was sitting next to one of those familiar Beethoven names. Her husband, who was sitting next to Nula, was the former Austrian ambassador to Ireland. I could see they were chatting animatedly, probably about Nula's home city of Dublin.

'My husband is also, like you, a Beethoven specialist.' Ah, so that's why they're here, I thought. I decided to come to the point.

'There are some people here who belong to families who knew and supported Beethoven,' I said. 'I believe a Waldstein is here.'

'Yes that's me,' she said.

I gasped. 'And Lichnowsky,' I added.

'That's me too,' she said, smiling from ear to ear. 'I am also a Thun.'

I nearly choked on my food. Thun! I searched rapidly for the brain cell that I knew held the information I needed. Remember I wrote in an earlier chapter about the aristocratic lady, known to be slightly eccentric, who had prostrated herself before Beethoven begging him to play the piano?[2] That was Countess Wilhelmina Thun. 'Yes I have blood of all three families – Waldstein, Lichnowsky, Thun – in me.'

'I want to take a photograph after the lunch,' I gabbled. 'Please will you permit it?'

'As long as you do not ask me to kneel down!' she said, exploding with laughter. 'By the way, the lady on your other side is a Waldstein also. Yvonne Waldstein. So I am related to her too. From two centuries ago!' She was enjoying every moment, while I hurriedly made notes on a piece of paper, determined to remember every part of these complex and complicated relationships.

That brain cell was now delivering. I remembered that Countess Thun was Prince Lichnowsky's mother-in-law. Aglaë confirmed that, and further told me that Lichnowsky's daughter married a Thun, and later the Waldstein and Thun families intermarried. Yvonne Waldstein on my left informed me that the family name was originally Wallerstein, but in the Middle Ages the family lived in Italy, the Italians could not pronounce the name, and so it was changed to Waldstein. 'Waldstein. Wood Stone. More Austrian,' she said smiling.

At one point I spoke across the table to Princess Metternich. I said it was sad that after fleeing the 1848 revolution in Vienna, Prince Metternich and his wife took exile in England, where they ended their days.

'Ah no,' she said. 'They had a flat in Eaton Square in London, but they returned to Vienna when things calmed down, and they were much respected here once again.'

The photograph I took after the lunch, on the balcony of Schloss Breiteneich, is unique. So many names well known to Beethoven gathered together. Shaking with excitement, I could barely hold the camera still.

❧

So now to our hosts, who have a unique connection to Beethoven and who came so fortuitously and unexpectedly into my life. Christian and Gea Lippert[3] live in Schloss Breiteneich, which stands outside the town of Horn in Lower Austria, about an hour and a half's drive north-west of Vienna in the Waldviertel (Forest Area), and only a short distance north of Gneixendorf, where Nikolaus Johann van Beethoven lived and where his elder brother and nephew came to stay in the autumn of 1826. Gea spent her childhood in the castle, in time inheriting it. The castle dates back to the twelfth century; the von Roretz family have inhabited it for two hundred years. For many years it has been the couple's permanent home. Now both in their eighties, they will celebrate their sixtieth wedding anniversary in 2025.

Gea is the niece of Pia Chelwood and therefore the great-great-great-granddaughter of Giulietta Guicciardi, the woman to whom Beethoven dedicated the *Moonlight* Sonata and who turned down his proposal of marriage. Gea and Christian have now told me the whole story.

Giulietta, after turning down Beethoven's proposal of marriage, went on to marry a musician and composer of ballet music by the name of Count Gallenberg. (I knew that.) They left Vienna and went to live in Italy. (I knew that too.) Gallenberg was impotent. I did not know that! Now I should pause for just a moment to look more closely at the revelation. How do we know he was impotent? What is the source? Where is the evidence? The short answer is there is no evidence. It is hearsay, family legend, passed down through the generations. Though family legend, I believe, is often more accurate than formal history.

Pia Chelwood had told me all those years ago that Gallenberg had sanctioned Giulietta's love affair with Count von Schulenburg. 'It wasn't quite as simple as that,' Christian told me. 'Gallenberg was not happy about it. In fact he was rather jealous of Schulenburg, which is understandable.' That throws an interesting light on the situation. It suggests that it was Giulietta herself who instigated it. I put this to Christian. He nodded. 'She was a strong lady, apparently,' he said with a wry smile.[4]

With Schulenburg, Giulietta had five children. Clearly it was much more than a fleeting romance. The eldest child was adopted by Gallenberg, who gave him the aristocratic surname of von Roretz, which had been his mother's maiden name and which had died out with her. It is possible he believed the boy was his own son, Christian told me. In 1947 one of the descendants passed a bust of Giulietta to Pia Chelwood, née von Roretz. This was the bust Pia had proudly shown me in her Sussex home all those years ago. Pia died in 2019 at the age of ninety-six. Her wish that the bust should be returned to Schloss Breiteneich after her death was fulfilled.

Today the bust stands on a piano in the castle library, a framed photograph of Pia alongside it. I confess that when I saw it again, twenty-five years on and this time without Pia herself standing proudly beside it, tears pricked my eyes. 'Come with me,' said Gea. 'I will show you something.'

We crossed the interior courtyard of the castle. She pushed open a heavy wooden door and a small room with wooden benches opened before us. Dark, save for a few spots of light, there was an air of coolness and calm. My eyes adjusted. Those benches were small pews. We were in a chapel. On a wall opposite the door a rectangle of low glowing light shone through a panel of deeply hued stained glass.

'Pia's ashes are there,' said Gea, 'behind the stained glass.' There was that pricking at the back of my eyes again.

Christian showed us the order of service for Pia's memorial, which had been held at the castle. Pia had herself chosen the music. There was Mozart, Schubert, Fauré, and Pia's own setting of the Lord's Prayer. The very first piece she chose was the *Moonlight* Sonata.

Christian asked me to choose a piece of music. Moments later the defiant, uplifting, life-affirming opening chords of the *Eroica* Symphony echoed through beautiful, majestic Schloss Breiteneich.

References

3

1. 'Johannes der Läufer, lauf nur, du wirst doch einmal an dein End laufe.' Susan Cooper, 'Des Bonner Bäckermeisters Gottfried Fischer Aufzeichnungen über Beethovens Jugend', translated into English as 'The Bonn Master-Baker Gottfried Fischer's Reminiscences of Beethoven's Youth', with editorial commentary and notes, *The Beethoven Journal*, vol. 35 (2022), article 3, p. 15.
2. Today Malines in Belgium.
3. Ibid., p. 19.

6

1. Cooper, 'The Bonn Master-Baker', p. 37. Translation amended. Gottfried Fischer's memoir, written with his elder sister Cäcilie, is an invaluable source of information on Beethoven's childhood years, and is extensively referenced in these Bonn chapters.
2. Franz Wegeler, who will feature again in these pages.
3. Franz Wegeler and Ferdinand Ries, *Remembering Beethoven* (André Deutsch, 1988), p. 13.

7

1. The same Siegfried who would go on to star in Richard Wagner's epic opera cycle *Der Ring des Nibelungen*.
2. O. G. Sonneck (ed.), *Beethoven: Impressions by His Contemporaries* (Dover Publications, New York, 1967), p. 9. Translation amended.

8

1. Only the solo piano part survives of this concerto, sometimes referred to as 'Piano Concerto No. 0'.
2. 'Die Holländer, das sind pfennigks Fückser, die lieben das Geld zu sehr.' Cooper, 'The Bonn Master-Baker', p. 69.
3. Ibid., p. 48.
4. Ibid., p. 49.

10

1. Cooper, 'The Bonn Master-Baker', p. 30. Translations amended.
2. Ibid., p. 38. Translation amended.
3. Ibid., p. 71. Translation amended.
4. Ibid., p. 38. Translation amended.

11

1. Elliot Forbes (ed.), *Thayer's Life of Beethoven* (Princeton University Press, 1967), p. 79, p. 66.
2. Ibid.
3. Check the recording of the complete Beethoven Piano Sonatas in your collection. The likelihood (bordering on certainty) is that there are 32, beginning with the set of three that make up Op. 2. Professor Barry Cooper of Manchester University, Britain's leading Beethoven scholar, has argued convincingly that the three Kurfürsten (Princely) Sonatas, to which Beethoven did not accord opus numbers, should be included, so that the complete set numbers 35.

13

1. His account, 'Beethovens erste Reise nach Wien 1786/87', is published in Norbert Schlossmacher (ed.), *Beethoven, Die Bonner Jahre* (Böhlau, Bonn, 2020), pp. 435–59.
2. *Dieser Jüngling wird noch viel in der Welt von sich reden machen.*
3. *ein feines aber zerhacktes Spiel.*

14

1. Quoted in Cooper, 'The Bonn Master-Baker', p. 77, n. 129.
2. *El País* newspaper, May 30, 2018.
3. Theo Molberg, 'Beethovens Grossmutter wurde in Châtelet geboren', *Die Laterne Bonner Familienkunde*, 48/2 (2021), pp. 247–55. I am grateful to Professor Barry Cooper for alerting me to this information.

15

1. Mozart similarly allowed Count Walsegg to claim authorship of the *Requiem*.

16

1. Waiter?
2. Quoted in John Suchet, *Beethoven: The Man Revealed* (Elliott & Thompson, 2012), p. 59.

17

1. Emphasis (underlining) in the original.

19

1. Both quotations from Johann Pezzl's 'Sketch of Vienna' (1786–90), quoted in H. C. Robbins Landon, *Mozart and Vienna* (Thames and Hudson, 1991), pp. 65 and 137.
2. Named after the nineteenth-century Schrammel brothers, who popularised Viennese folk music.
3. Nearly thirty years later, in January 1820, Beethoven's assistant Franz Oliva wrote in a conversation book that police were raiding bookshops and confiscating banned books. Austria had become a police state.

20

1. The allegorical fountain represents Providence and the four tributaries of the Danube.
2. On the site of the fiercest fighting, there is today one of the largest and most beautiful parks in Vienna, the Türkenschranz (Turkish Trench) Park. When the land was excavated in the 1880s, many remnants and artefacts from the battle were recovered.
3. It is easy to dismiss the legend, but there is today a Kolschitzkygasse just outside the Ringstrasse. On the corner wall, high up out of reach, is a statue of Kolschitzky, dressed in Turkish clothes – fez on his head, baggy trousers, upturned shoes – balancing on one hand a tray with coffee cups, and holding in the other a coffee pot from which he is in the act of pouring. Not out of reach, though, for a petty thief. For some years past, the tray, with its cups and saucers, has been missing.
4. The theatre was recently closed for two years for complete restoration.

23

1. My translation.

24

1. The story of the founding of the Ira F. Brilliant Center for Beethoven Studies is told in Russell Martin, *Beethoven's Hair* (Bloomsbury, 2000), pp. 6 and 154–63. Further information comes from private conversations with William Meredith, founding director of the Center from 1985 to 2016.

26

1. Quote from Beethoven's pupil and devotee Carl Czerny in Sonneck (ed.), *Beethoven: Impressions by His Contemporaries*, op. cit., p. 31.

2. Ibid.
3. Letter from Ferdinand Ries to Nikolaus Simrock, taken from *Letters to Beethoven*, vol. 1, translated and edited by Theodore Albrecht (University of Nebraska Press, 1996), p. 119.

27

1. Wegeler and Ries, *Remembering Beethoven*, op. cit., p. 69.
2. Pip Eastop, one of Britain's finest horn players and a virtuoso of the natural (valveless) horn, has told me that playing the natural horn is akin to a bloodsport. 'Imagine trying to get a tune out of a coiled-up garden hose,' he said, 'and you'll know how difficult it is.'
3. Ibid. p. 68.

28

1. Wegeler and Ries, *Remembering Beethoven*, op. cit., pp. 89–90.

29

1. Forbes (ed.), *Thayer's Life of Beethoven*, op. cit. p. 375.
2. John McCarthy, Brian Keenan and Terry Waite would soon be kidnapped in Beirut and held hostage for several years.
3. You think I exaggerate? This book was finished and on its way to the printers when I was sent a new recording of the Triple Concerto, issued on Decca Classics on 31 May 2024. The three soloists are young stars of British classical music: Nicola Benedetti (violin), Benjamin Grosvenor (piano) and Sheku Kanneh-Mason (cello). The opening solo on cello is a yearning and longing of an intensity I have never heard on any other recording (and I have many). A *crescendo* builds to a top note that you expect to come in *fortissimo*, but Beethoven suddenly pulls it back and you gasp at the surprise. However, this is no empty longing. Violin and piano join, and the yearning is fulfilled.

30

1. Today Olomouc in the Czech Republic.

31

1. Gerhard von Breuning, *Memories of Beethoven: From the House of the Black-Robed Spaniards*, edited by Maynard Solomon (Cambridge University Press, 1992), p. 19.
2. Formerly a monastery, now converted into an apartment complex.
3. Ibid., p. 35.

32

1. Sieghard Brandenburg, *Haydn, Mozart, and Beethoven: Studies in the Music of the Classical Period* (Oxford University Press, 1998), p. 243.
2. A reference to the villainess in Mozart's *The Magic Flute*.
3. Beethoven's emphasis (underlining).
4. Emily Anderson (ed.), *The Letters of Beethoven* (The Macmillan Press Ltd, 1961), vol. 2, Letter 611, pp. 561–2.
5. Ibid., p. 562.
6. Elliot M. Abramson, 'Beethoven and the Law: The Case of the Nephew', *Florida State University Law Review*, 1990, p. 124.
7. Quoted in Martin Cooper, *Beethoven, The Last Decade, 1817–1827* (Oxford University Press, 1985), p. 25.
8. Ibid., p. 28.

33

1. Abramson, 'Beethoven and the Law', op. cit., p. 141.
2. Ibid.

34

1. From Ernest Newman, *The Unconscious Beethoven* (Littlehampton Book Services, 1968). Quoted in Abramson, 'Beethoven and the Law', op. cit., p. 131.
2. Ibid., p. 124.
3. The 1994 film *Immortal Beloved* went so far as to identify Johanna as the woman Beethoven has a secret affair with, addressing her in a letter as *meine unsterbliche Geliebte* ('my immortal beloved').

35

1. Quoted in Barry Cooper, *Beethoven* (Oxford University Press, 2000), p. 261.
2. *Hammerklavier* simply means 'hammer-keyboard', reflecting Beethoven's instruction that the sonata is to be played on the fortepiano, the predecessor of the modern piano, and not on the more delicate, and more prevalent, harpsichord.
3. The delivery had not been entirely straightforward. Viennese authorities billed Beethoven for custom duties. He refused to pay, claiming the piano was a gift and he was therefore not liable. He won the argument. More seriously there was some damage to the piano, which Viennese piano builders were reluctant to repair, being unfamiliar with the English construction. Finally essential repairs were made. I am grateful to William Meredith, founding director of the Ira F. Brilliant Center for Beethoven Studies, for this information, relayed to me in private conversation. The Broadwood piano was subsequently owned by Franz Liszt, who presented it to the Hungarian National Museum in Budapest, where it stands, fully restored, today.

4. As noted in Barry Cooper, *The Creation of Beethoven's 35 Piano Sonatas* (Routledge, 2017), p. 167.
5. Quoted in Theodore Libbey, *The NPR Guide to Building a Classical CD Collection* (New York: Workman Publishing, 1999), p. 379.
6. Paul Bekker, *Beethoven*, translated and adapted by Mildred Mary Bozman (J. M. Dent & Sons, 1925), p. 134.
7. Ibid., pp. 171–2.

36

1. *Musical Times*, founded in 1844, is still published quarterly, the oldest such journal in the UK.

37

1. The opening of the *Moonlight* Sonata is invariably taken at a very slow pace, almost funereal, as the pianist attempts to convey the moodiness of a moonlit night. This is entirely inappropriate for two reasons. First, Beethoven's marking is *Adagio sostenuto – attaca*. This means 'steadily', with the added *sostenuto* implying a sense of underlying energy driving the piece forward. *Attaca* is self-explanatory. Second, Beethoven had no thoughts of a moonlit night when he composed the sonata. The title he gave it, and under which it was published, was *Sonata quasi una Fantasia*. The comparison to moonlight was made by a music critic some years after Beethoven's death.

38

1. The original negative life mask has not survived. Of the few first positives, one is housed at the Beethoven-Haus in Bonn, clearly showing skin blemishes and the ravages of smallpox. The original bust created by Klein is alongside the collection of ancient musical instruments in the Kunsthistorisches Museum, Vienna. A reproduction welcomes you as you step inside the birthplace in Bonn.

39

1. Quoted in Sonneck (ed.), *Beethoven: Impressions*, op. cit., pp. 20–21, with updated wording.
2. Ibid., pp. 38–9, with updated translations from the original quoted in 'Die gute Kocherey', (Beethoven-Haus, Bonn, 1988), pp. 5–6.
3. Ibid., p. 42.
4. 'die bohrenden Nachforschungen in der Nase', from Dr Theodor von Frimmel, 'Beethoven als Gasthausbesucher in Wien', *Neues Beethoven Jahrbuch* 1 (1924).
5. See Theodore Albrecht (ed. and trans.), *Beethoven's Conversation Books*, vol. 1 (The Boydell Press, 2018), pp. xxvi–xxvii.

References

40

1. I am very pleased to call Jonathan Del Mar a friend, having first made his acquaintance more than thirty years ago, our lives brought together by Beethoven. To spend time in Jonathan's company is to come as close as it is possible to come to understanding and appreciating Beethoven's original intentions.
2. Sonneck, (ed.), *Beethoven: Impressions*, op. cit., pp. 98 and 40.
3. For a fuller account of the turbulent run-up to the premiere of the Ninth Symphony, and the performance itself, see Suchet, *Beethoven: The Man Revealed*, op. cit., pp. 197–202.

41

1. Nula and I went to see Chris Barber and his band at Cadogan Hall in London in 2016, when he was eighty-six years of age. Afterwards I met him and told him he was my trombone hero. Nula took a picture of us together, which I cherish. Chris Barber died in March 2021 aged ninety.
2. Through the school's old boy network I was able to make contact with my fellow pupil Michael Pares and thank him, more than sixty years later, for lending me his trombone and igniting a lifelong passion.
3. A decade or so after I left Uppingham, an official school punk rock band was formed. I like to think I blazed the trail.

42

1. In his memoir of the Lindsays, cellist Bernard Gregor-Smith writes, 'We had spent more time on rehearsing and trying to understand Beethoven than any other composer: he was a god to us.' See Bernard Gregor-Smith, *A Quintessential Quartet: The Story of the Lindsay String Quartet* (Mirador, 2019), p. 7.
2. Fourteenth in order of composition, thirteenth in order of opus numbers.

43

1. Composed before Op. 130 but published later, hence the higher opus number.

44

1. In earlier correspondence between the two brothers, Johann wrote to Beethoven after buying the estate and signed the letter 'From your brother Johann, landowner'. Beethoven signed his reply 'From your brother Ludwig, brain owner'.
2. Karl would leave to join the regiment on 2 January of the following year. In a complete volte-face, putting aside all his opposition to a military career for Karl, Beethoven wrote to Baron Stutterheim thanking him profusely for his great kindness in giving Karl a place in his regiment, and dedicated his String Quartet in C sharp minor, Op. 131,

which many musicologists regard as his greatest (it was Beethoven's personal favourite) to him. Thus the name of Stutterheim lives on in musical history.

3. Ironically, Therese died a little under two years after Beethoven. Johann rewrote his Will, leaving his entire estate to Karl. Beethoven achieved his wish posthumously.

4. The following account is based on Theodore Albrecht, 'Beethoven and Smart's Donaufahrt: The Composer's Return to Vienna from Gneixendorf', *The Beethoven Newsletter of The American Beethoven Society*, winter 2023, pp. 14–20. (Donaufahrt = Danube journey.)

45

1. John D. Wilson, 'Beethoven in European News', *The Beethoven Newsletter*, winter 2024, pp. 27–8.
2. Named for Ferdinand Hiller, who cut the lock from Beethoven's head the day after his death.
3. Anderson (ed.), *The Letters of Beethoven*, op. cit. pp. 1321–22.
4. I am grateful to both Will Meredith and Tristan Begg for reading this chapter in draft, both correcting and amplifying what I had written. Further information has been gleaned from private correspondence with both, for which I owe an enormous debt of thanks.
5. Wilson, 'Beethoven in European News', pp. 27–8, and *New York Post*, 22 July 2023.
6. The full report by the Cambridge University team can be read here: T. J. A. Begg *et al.*, 'Genomic analyses of hair from Ludwig van Beethoven', *Current Biology* (2023). DOI: 10.1016/j.cub.2023.02.041.

46

1. In the words of the great pianist Mitsuko Uchida.
2. From the obituary in *The Times*, 8 May 2023.

47

1. Named for the local lads who would emerge from the wood after burning charcoal.
2. See ch 39, p. 195
3. Gea, pronounced Gaya, was christened Andrea but as a child she could only say Gea. It stuck.
4. Thayer, in his biography of Beethoven, describes Giulietta as 'having a good share of personal attractions, and is known to have been a fine looking woman even in advanced years.' Forbes (ed.), *Thayer's Life of Beethoven*, op. cit. p. 289.

Acknowledgements

It seemed, at times, as if there was a lucky star shining down on this book. In Bonn there were the two strokes of luck that prevented me from misidentifying the church where Beethoven was baptised, and the site of the house in the Rheingasse that was flooded out. Having written the early chapters, I then learned of the ground-breaking results of the genome testing that were about to be released; thank you Will Meredith for entrusting me with this. With perfect timing I found out about the recent research that made me re-examine the teenaged Beethoven's visit to Vienna and Mozart. An edition of *The Beethoven Newsletter* dropped through my letterbox as I was about to depict that grim journey he made back to Vienna in the final months of his life, causing me to re-examine detail I had known for decades. Most remarkably of all, in the process of writing the final chapter I received an entirely unexpected email from the husband of the great-great-great-granddaughter of Giulietta Guicciardi, inviting Nula and me to stay at the family seat outside Vienna, Schloss Breiteneich.

When Nula told me to write this book, I responded with 'Nice idea, it might even fill twenty pages.' 'Write it anyway and see where it takes you,' she said.

I decided first to discuss it with Olivia Bays, Director at Elliott & Thompson, who has edited every one of my composer biographies. She responded with enthusiasm, which I was not expecting.

'But I don't want to write about myself,' I said.

'Why not? How many times have you been asked why you have this passion for Beethoven, what started it, what are your favourite pieces, what is it about him?' The truthful answer is, more times than I can remember. Hundreds of times, maybe thousands; after every talk I've given, as well as in emails to me at Classic FM by the electronic sackful.

So I started writing – and the book took on a life of its own. Personal stories I have told for years, but which have never appeared in any of my previous books. Writing about Beethoven as if he was in the room forced me to confront some difficult facts. Try as I might to skirt round it, if I was going to be brutally honest I had to confess I did not find him a likeable man. I was dubious about revealing this.

Olivia encouraged me. 'This is your story as much as his. I want to know what you think of him as a man, and how that has affected you.' I am grateful for that, Olivia.

The cover of a book is important. When I opened the email attachment of the first draft of a cover design, I gave a slight gasp. I felt embarrassed that my image sat alongside Beethoven's, and equally prominently. I showed it to Nula with a sceptical shake of the head. 'It's perfect, illustrates exactly what the book is about,' she said, echoing Olivia's accompanying email. I was outnumbered. So thank you to designer Luke Bird for getting it right first time.

The end result of this book far exceeds my expectations, and for that I am grateful to Jill Burrows, Marie Doherty, Sarah Steele, Pippa Crane and Marianne Thorndahl at Elliott & Thompson for their work in turning it from a computer file into a book; to Gail Halley for organising an audiobook version; Louisa Pritchard for dealing with foreign rights; to Damaris Laker and Amy Greaves for handling publicity and marketing; and to Anna Stelter, Mathew Watterson and the Simon & Schuster sales team.

First and last, my thanks go to my wife Nula, who first suggested I write it in the garden of the cottage in Heiligenstadt. After saying I should make it more personal than my earlier books, she added 'After all, this will be your last Beethoven book.' She may be right.

Index

Index

Neuester
PLAN
der Haupt- und Residenzstadt
WIEN
mit allen von Seiner Majestät allerhöchst genehmigten
VERSCHÖNERUNGEN
mit dem Glacis und Eingang in die Vorstädte,
mit höchster Bewilligung Sr. Kais. Hoheit des
GENERAL-GENIE-DIRECTORS.
Nach dem Original Plan
herausgegeben
von
ARTARIA und COMP. in WIEN
1827.
Eigenthum der Verleger.